For my mother, Norah May Robson

Love in Good Time

a memoir

CLAIRE ROBSON

Michigan State University Press • *East Lansing*

Michigan State University Press
East Lansing, Michigan 48823-5245

Printed and bound in the United States of America.

09 08 07 06 05 04 03   1 2 3 4 5 6 7 8 9 10

LIBRARY OF CONGRESS CATALOGING-IN-PUBLICATION DATA
Robson, Claire, 1949–
Love in good time / by Claire Robson.
p. cm.
ISBN 0-87013-694-1 (pbk. : alk. paper)
1. Robson, Claire, 1949- 2. Authors, English—20th century—Biography.
3. Lesbians—Great Britain—Biography. I. Title.
PR6068.O195Z47 2003
828'.609—dc21
2003009749

Cover design by Heather Truelove Aiston
Book design by Sharp Des!gns, Lansing, MI

The epilogue to this book first appeared in a different form in *The Underwood Review 2, no. 1*
(Hanover Press, Inc., 1999, ed. Linda Claire Yuhas and Faith Vicinanza).

This is not a work of fiction, though in the interests of clarity and narrative flow I have
invented some scenes, included composite characters, and telescoped the chronology. I have in
most instances altered the names of persons outside my family. Apart from this, I have tried
to stick with the truth as I perceive it.

Visit Michigan State University Press on the World Wide Web at: *www.msupress.msu.edu*

Acknowledgements

SINCE THIS IS A FIRST BOOK, I WANT TO THANK ALMOST EVERYONE I know, since it has taken almost everyone I know to support me through the long process of completing this memoir.

Firstly, thanks to several groups of women who are my extended family: my Lesbian Couples Group (Joy Butler, Becca King, Cheryl Harrell, Tilda Hunting, Jo Ann Share, Rochelle Weichman, Robin Yerkes), my Boston Critique Group (Toni Amato, Julie Barnes, Marian Connor, Jaclyn Friedman, Andrea Horlick, Ann Killough, Laura Nooney, Dawn Paul, Lisa Vaas), my New Hampshire writing group, Women of Words (Carli Carrara, Kate Donahue, Kathryn Drexel, Jenny Highland, Ellen Richards, Patsy Sargent, Nyla Lyman), my women's community choir, Womansong (particularly director Tere Kipp), my open and affirming church (Plymouth Congregational) and finally all the regulars at my Boston reading series New Voices, who've heard extracts from the book in its various stages.

Other individuals have given great support and encouragement. They include Kathryn Deputat, Wallace Hardin, Ruth Houseman, Gen Howe, Carolyn Jenks, Joyce Kravets, Meg Petersen, Deborah Repplier, Mary Rotella, Art Shirk, and Heidi Wormser, who shares my taste in all things literary. Thanks to Ellen Kaplan, my therapist, who helped me understand my mother. Thanks to Linda Marshall for help with research, to Doreen Williams for advice on English grammar usage, to Cindy Clark and Nancy Walsh for helping me out in the microtext department at Boston Public Library, and to Alice Staples and Susan Nowell for help in the library at Plymouth State College. Writers Susan Hubbard, Kathryn Kilgore, Linda Peavy, Ursula Smith, and Faith Vicinanza have shared their publishing know-how and been generous in their time, love, and support. Thanks to Edmund White, whose encouragement was timely and invaluable. Thanks to Liz Jones, whose sheer bloody-minded persistence in pursuing agents and publishers provided a crucial model just when I needed one. Thanks to Julie Barnes, Carli Carrara, Mary Crowley, and Becca King for input on the manuscript. Thanks to Raphael Kadushin at the University of Wisconsin Press and to his reviewers (well most of them) who helped me to strengthen the manuscript. Thanks to everyone at Michigan State University Press for their care and attention to the production of this book, especially Kristine Blakeslee, who nursed it through production, and my editor, Martha Bates. She's a great editor—sharp, honest and funny—and she cares about writers.

Special thanks to the following: Jaclyn Friedman has been my most trusted reader, my best writing buddy, and a hugely loyal friend to this book (and to me) throughout its journey. Joy Butler, my partner, has maintained an unshakeable faith in my work and has held my hand on the roller coaster for fifteen years. Norah Robson, my mother, loved me unconditionally and passed on to me her gift of the gab.

Prologue

Dear Granny Hodgson,

I remember the Spring medicine. It was your recipe, Mam said, and we could drink as much as we liked, whenever we liked. The usual rules and restrictions did not apply. She'd brew it up in your big white china jug, with slices of lemon and bicarbonate of soda to cleanse our blood after the gloomy north of England winter—a time when everyone got spots and caught colds. She'd set the jug on the sunny part of the kitchen counter and when my brother and I came in hot and thirsty from playing, she'd pour us big glasses. We'd gulp it down standing, while she watched, satisfied, as if she could see our seething blood settle before her very eyes.

She followed all your advice this way—blind and unswerving, like it was from God Himself.

I have only one memory of you. You brought me something wrapped in shiny paper, and even at the time, I knew that it was important. My mother fussed and flapped around you, but you ignored her. You sat square in your chair like a big granite rock, watching me rip down to the gift. I know now that you were dying.

"What do you say?" my mother kept asking, as I stared at the blue tin drum, adorned with red stripes and golden lions. There were two wooden sticks to play it with. "Say, thank you, Granny Hodgson. Say thank you."

I toddled over to you, the drum clutched carefully in my arms. You wrapped my fingers around the sticks and took my hands in yours and lifted them and dropped them to show me what to do. It was the most wondrous thing—a joyful noise, and I could make it!

I chuckled and banged, and you laughed and clapped your hands together slowly. My mother put hers over her ears. "Put it away for later!"

But you smiled and nodded, like something had been accomplished. "Let her be, Norah," you said. I banged on the drum and I was happy.

Love from,
Claire

Part One

Vows of Silence, 1960–1967

The Weardale Clarion

Sunshine and Roses

From Buckingham Palace to Westminster Abbey, 250,000 people watched and cheered as Princess Margaret of Windsor and Anthony Armstrong Jones entered "that honorable estate, instituted of God Himself." The Princess was a vision in white silk organza, bearing a bouquet of pink orchids and lilies of the valley. A tiara of diamonds surrounded her hair, which she wore in a majestic chignon. Escorted by eight tiny bridesmaids, all in silks and bows, she looked every inch a Princess and a bride. Queen Elizabeth, who remained as still as a statue through most of the ceremony, wore a turquoise-blue dress, and the Prince of Wales wore Highland full dress in Royal Stuart tartan.

The Princess hesitated slightly over the words "for better or worse," but otherwise the ceremony was conducted with faultless precision. This evening, when the Royal Yacht *Britannia* dropped down the misty Thames carrying the happy couple to their honeymoon in the sun-splashed Caribbean, she steamed to the faint sound of cheers borne from the shore.

1.

THOUGH SHE WAS PROUD OF MY DAD FOR LANDING A HEADSHIP SO young, my mother looked down her nose at Glenburn, the village to which he was assigned, and never really forgave him for stranding us all there. Given that this was back in the days when ambitious young teachers were posted off like soldiers at the whim of Durham County Council, my mother's crossness might seem unfair, but then being unreasonable was as natural to her as breathing, and in any case, she couldn't shake the idea that if she had been born a man she would have done better at it than my father, especially in the matter of assertiveness and particularly where the needs of his wife and children were at stake. She failed to understand that a man who had fought to save us all from Hitler was incapable of making a fuss about bad service in a restaurant. When she could, she counteracted Dad's softheartedness by judicious nagging, and tried to ginger him up with pep talks before important negotiations.

Glenburn was more hamlet than village. Its Post Office was no bigger than a tuppenny stamp and my mother affected to sniff at the Village Shop whenever she went inside, in the days when she was still able. There was but one bus a day to Sutton—itself no great shakes as a place to shop. Mam longed for a Binns or a Debenhams, where she could have looked at the fashions all afternoon then swanned up in the lift to the restaurant. She'd have ordered cream cakes and a heavy silver pot of tea. She'd have acted snooty to the waitress and made her refill the teapot twice with hot water. For a few minutes, at least, my mother could have pretended that she belonged, in her new sheepskin jacket that she had scrimped and saved two years for, and her pheasant foot brooch my dad had bought her for Christmas (but only, she confided to me later, after she dropped enough hints to sink the *Queen Mary*).

Just as Glenburn never compared to Houghton, nor Sutton to Sunderland, so Pond House couldn't hold a candle to the bungalow my mother had left behind as tearfully as Eve did Eden. Even though we'd lived here for a year now, she still missed Cranbrook. Cranbrook had been a modern house, with a glass lean-to out back that my mother trained us to call "the conservatory." Its walls sat square and its cupboard doors closed and all our neighbors were teachers too.

Pond House had started life a hundred or so years before as dairy for the farm next door. Its walls were three-foot granite, stubborn enough to survive life on the windy plateau that was Glenburn, perched high above Weardale in the scrubby Pennines. The building had been roughly converted for the use of the last dairymaid—made redundant by the advent of the milking machine. Annie Briggs was a classic Glenburn eccentric who kept a pig in the shed, slapped up an annual layer of wallpaper with flour and water, and fed the ducks who clambered out of the pond across the road, marched up the front path, through her open front door and into her kitchen every morning. The day she overreached herself and fell off a ladder halfway through hanging layer twenty-five (a nice floral) was the day my dad came up house hunting.

My dad took it as a sign. Not that God wanted poor Annie to die on a cold stone floor just so that we would have somewhere to live. My father's God was gentle and kindly disposed, not much given to grand drama. That kind of thing was necessary in the olden days, I was given to understand, when God had to work some showy miracles to get the Israelites out of Egypt and such. Through a long and troubled historical process, which I learned about at school, mankind had progressed to the point where it found true expression in the white British middle class family. This prototype had been tested against the evil Hitler who wanted to take over the world but had been prevented from doing so by people like my dad who had more common sense and fought in the big war. Now that people like my dad had restored normality, we could all relax—even God—and contemplate an orderly world in which everything happened for the best and the trick was to enjoy or endure it. Thus, the timing of Annie's fall was merely fortunate, as was the location of her house, since it was just across the road from the school.

My mother wasn't convinced that God had a decent grip on things (look at the Russians!), nor did she entirely trust His motives. To her, Pond House seemed the instrument of darker forces, hell-bent to ridicule and destroy her. From behind the brand-new embossed anaglyptic wallpaper and the Dulux off-white eggshell finish leaked the stink of pagan origins—the dirty old maid and her moldy flour. They reminded her of all the things she had hoped to leave behind when she left the Scotch Woolshop and married my father: a mother in service and a house with an outdoor privy in a back-to-back terrace. Whenever we put something down at Pond House, my mother tripped over and cursed it ten seconds later. Soil wriggled out of the front garden onto her newly swept path. Spiders crawled into her mixing bowl to die. Arthritis spread through her thickening joints. The banished ducks plotted their attack.

Dad was proud of his renovations, but my mother said that that was only because he never did any cooking. The kitchen was too small. The only work surface was a drop-down flap whose hinges my mother knew would give way under the weight of her rolling pin one baking day. No matter how hard we tried to step only on the black floor tiles if our feet were wet, the white ones in the chessboard of a floor showed the crinkles of our footprints. It looked nice when it was clean, she said, which was for five seconds once a week. She sprained her aching wrists trying to wrestle her heavy old saucepans into the tiny cupboard next to the sink. The coke burning stove leaked puffs of acrid smoke that stained the ceiling and teased the fridge into rumbling life every ten seconds, rattling its load of pill bottles and running up the electric bill.

"I suppose you want to rush off over to Heather Braithwaite's," my mother said without turning from the sink, as I perched the last of the dried dinner plates carefully on the rack above the stove.

She must have noticed that I had changed out of my school clothes into my shorts with the snake buckle belt and my brother's castoff penknife hanging from a loop. She turned and eyed up the plate rack with a sniff, wiping the back of her hand across her brow. "That yellow bowl goes with the pans, so I'll put it away later. No, don't put it on the windowsill. If I've told you once, I've told you a thousand times, it'll mark the paint."

I set the bowl on one of the kitchen chairs, rubbed the blades of the knives till they shone and put them all the same way up in the cutlery tray.

My mother tipped the dirty water out of the washing-up bowl and started her lengthy wiping down ritual, which began with the dishcloth and ended with the driest of the used tea towels.

"I don't know how you can stand the smell of that kitchen of Martha's," she said, chasing Fairy Liquid suds down the plughole. "What with all those dirty cats and dogs and her B.O." She made a face. "I've never smelt the likes of it. The car stinks for days after your dad takes her to church."

The hushed voice of BBC commentators drifted through from the living room, where Dad and Matthew were drinking their tea and watching the endless prelude to Princess Margaret's wedding to Anthony Armstrong Jones. I prayed that the royal car would drive up soon, because my mother loved nothing better than a good wedding. She'd settle down with a quarter of aniseed bull's-eyes, and I could leave her to her devices. I wouldn't have to speak ill of Martha Braithwaite, who was one of my favorite people, nor would I have to offend my mother, who had rheumatoid arthritis and worked her fingers to the bone taking care of us, her ungrateful family.

She took hold of the dishcloth to squeeze the water out, and I could tell from her theatrical wincing, her deliberate ineffectiveness, that she was going to start in on me. I hardened my heart, as if she had bound me to a chair and was about to interrogate me, like the Gestapo. I had seen in films how the men in black uniforms walked slowly around their victims and begged them to just give them what they wanted, their voices soft with fake kindness. It would be easy to give her it, just to let drop how Martha's orangeade was the cheap kind made up from powder, say, or that I had once seen mouse droppings in the kitchen. The truth was that my mother's cleanliness made us all miserable. Nothing was ever done right unless she did it herself. She said so twenty times a day.

She watched my face as if she could read my mind, her face tight with disapproval.

"If she got herself out of that chair once in a while she might lose some of that fat. Here's me struggling around on my feet all day working my fingers to the bone, and her ensconced in that kitchen like a queen—a perfectly healthy woman who never lifts a finger from one day's end to the next. I wish I *could* walk to church and see all the spring flowers and take communion. I can't even get from our pew to the communion rail."

I hung the tea towel on the radiator to dry, with the picture of York Minster outside and right way up. She squeezed her rings back on over her swollen knuckles.

"Does Martha ever ask after me?"

"Yes," I said. "She always asks how you are." It was true.

"Just take that tea towel and clean those finger marks off the fridge will you? I don't know why on earth your father bought something that shows the dirt like that."

I couldn't see any marks, but I polished away dutifully.

"So does she ask how bad my pains are then?"

I answered obliquely. "Heather's Uncle Tyler had rheumatism. Martha says he suffered agony."

"Nobody knows what it's like," she said. "Nobody understands. It's spread into my elbow now. It's like something's inside there gnawing at it. It never stops. Here," she said, holding out her arm. "See if you can feel it."

My heart sank as I touched her. "It feels hot," I guessed. Actually, it felt like the Sunday chicken did when I rubbed it with butter, the dead skin sliding over the knobbed bones.

She took my fingers and pressed them hard. "That's it," she said. "It's right in there. Can you feel that?"

I nodded numbly. It felt like an arm with lumps in it. It felt like there'd been an oil leak and everything was grinding on itself.

"Just rub it, pet, will you, just for a minute." She stood transfixed as I kneaded the joint, trying to keep the misery out of my face. This felt worse than torture, but I couldn't say why. It didn't take long. It didn't hurt. It was easy to give her this pleasure. Afterwards I could run out and play. She couldn't do that ever again because she was housebound and there was no cure known to Man. The gold injections and the cortisone hadn't worked. She would end up in a wheelchair.

"Oh, that's heaven, pet. You've no idea," she said, her face all softened up now, so that she looked like she was going to cry. "Nobody knows what it's like," she said, glancing though to the living room to check on my dad. "I was telling Dr. Murray last week. 'My family are sick of hearing me going on about it, Doctor Murray,' I told him. 'Paul's sick of me always complaining.'"

I carried on rubbing. I couldn't stop until she had had enough, because my code of honor dictated that, as it dictated that I could never hesitate when she asked me to run and fetch her something, but must run and fetch it at once, as if I were eager to do so. When she pulled her arm away she was smiling.

"Don't you want to watch Princess Margaret's wedding? See all the beautiful dresses? It's an historic event, you know. Don't you want to watch it with me?"

I shook my head, terrified that she'd keep me in.

"Oh well," she said finally. "Tell Martha Mrs. Robson was asking after her. Make sure you're back before dark."

Conscious of the living room window trained on my back, I walked down our front path trying to look as if I were in no great hurry to escape. I snicked the latch of our front gate firmly behind me, as the ducks swiveled their bobbing heads at the noise. Their pond lay on the other side of the unnamed road that lay humbly before our house, as if aware that it was too small and quiet to warrant a white line down its middle. The village clung to each side of it like a rope, and was in effect a long line of buildings, interrupted only by the ancient communal village green, which left houses like ours with a view of the mowed grass, the little granite two-room school, the duck pond, the massive Parliament oak and George and Martha's rutted driveway, which I now ascended. I imagined gunfire breaking out from our living room window, and how I would hurl myself into the nearest shell crater when it did, because good soldiers were always alert to danger. I wished for the thousandth time that I could join a women's army somewhere and show what I was made of. Heather and I had practiced warfare endlessly, dodging arrows from Indians, short circuiting Daleks, throwing hand grenades at Germans, leaping from behind doors and aiming police revolvers at New York lowlife. My mother sighed and said I was a tomboy. She hoped I'd grow out of it when I went to Wallingford Grammar and became a teenager and mixed with a better class of girls. I too hoped to find better outlets. I was getting tired of games.

The blind old dog barked at me, so I slowed down at the top of the driveway and gave her a wide berth.

"It's all right, Bessie," I heard Heather call. "It's a friend."

She was sitting on the creaky old gate next to the cow byre. A square, solid block of a grimy, freckled nine year old she was, astride the top rail, baling twine reins collected loosely in one hand. Her little palomino approached at a leisurely walk, and Heather made the sound of its clop-ping hooves with her mouth, riding the gate gently from side to side, then kicking with her heels to make it dance a little, showing me her paces. I put my foot on a rung and mounted Midnight, my jet-black stal-lion. He shied a little and I leaned down to pat his glossy neck. Heather's face was deadly serious. She got to start the game, even though she was two years younger, because she had the front end of the gate, which had a little post sticking up, almost like a head.

"Well, howdy there, Billy Boy," she said, relegating me to cowhand.

"Howdy boss."

She squinted her eyes and scanned the herd as our horses swayed across the prairie, and I clicked my tongue at a steady walk. "I want you to keep your eyes skinned tonight, Billy Boy. These old steers seem kinda restless."

"Sure do seem restless, boss."

"Hope them ole injuns ain't about to strike, Billy Boy. When them ole lonesome coyotes gets to howlin' it sure does make a man afraid that those ole injuns is ahiding in tham thar bushes."

"Say, boss! Did you-all see something kinda moving in tham doggone bushes? I coulda sworn I see somethin' like feathers, kinda moving sneaky like."

"Waal, I'll be dad busted, Billy Boy. Them's Injuns! Let's ride pard-ner!!"

Here followed wild galloping on the gate, much aiming of forefingers, the death of large numbers of Indians (achieved by leaning perilously over the gate to avoid arrows).

"Bang! Take that you red varmint!!"

"Pchow! Pchow! C'mon Billy Boy, let's round'm up. WATCH OUT BEHIND YOU!!! Zonk! I got'm for ya Billy. He was about to knife you from behind!"

"Bang! Bang! Waal how about that, boss? There was TWO behind you."

One of the unspoken rules of our play was that we could never confer in 'ordinary' language about the direction of the plot. Half the fun lay in trying to wrest it to selfish ends and hog the glory. After a suitable period of genocide, one of us would engineer an heroic death—in this case, Heather.

"Aargh! He got me!" she yelled, clutching an arrow that protruded from her chest. She toppled from the saddle in a stylish blend of drama and cautious avoidance of nettles. The rules dictated that I, as healthy pardner, should hold the head of my dying comrade and listen to her final words, delivered with difficulty in very prolonged, but bravely endured, agony.

Although we always stoically accepted the lesser role of "healthy buddy" when it was thrust upon us, we naturally vied for the more glamorous part, engineering early deaths in various ingenious ways.

"What say I check out that narrow gorge over there?"

"Let me try and talk to their chief."

"I'll go out and distract them. You go round the back way, get the horses and fetch a posse."

"O.K. pardner . . . aargh . . . it's an ambush. He got me!"

"Lemme see. You're lucky. He only got you in the arm."

"They're using poisoned arrows, pardner. . . . Guess it's time to . . . to say goodbye . . ."

As the poison moved slowly through her system, Heather sent several tender messages to her sweetheart back in Tennessee, to her mother and her dog. I promised to go to Tennessee and find her sweetheart and marry her myself so that she would have someone to take care of her and the children. We both shed a tear or two at my generosity, and the sadness of it all. After that we were thirsty, so we hopped our way across the muddy forecourt of the byre, pitted and tracked by cow hooves and tractors, and entered the house by the side door, negotiating a cluttered foregathering of shucked-off wellies, dented metal buckets, bags of cow cake, and bits of baling twine. The stove was lit, as it always was, even in summer. Martha's placid voice drifted up from the depths of her armchair, without any of the flurry and alarm that an unexpected knock on my parents' door would have generated. "Well hello, pet," said Martha. "I thought I heard you coming up the driveway a while ago."

As my eyes adjusted to the smoky gloom, illuminated only by the blue flicker of the telly, I made out her vast bulk, first the ghostly white of her pinny, then her massive thighs, materializing slowly at first, then so precisely that I could see where her pop socks bit deep into them. On a little table next to her lay a plastic bag of Wonderbread and a plate in which three chips lay curled in a pool of tomato ketchup. A couple of bluebottles circled them and Martha waved at them ponderously with a copy of *The Farmer's Weekly*.

"Push them dogs off, pet, and sit down for a minute. I'm waiting for the wedding. Poor Margaret! The queen's making her suffer for being in love with a commoner you know. Eeh Claire, you shouldn't ever interfere with true love. No good will come of a loveless marriage you know."

On the TV screen, the camera was panning the assembled crowd in Westminster Abbey, as they rustled genteelly, aware of the cameras. Martha turned to Heather, who was staring absentmindedly at the scene. "Heather, look after your guest, pet. Get her a glass of that orange squash and a biscuit. There's some chocolate digestives in the Balmoral Castle tin."

Mam had enjoined me to rinse any utensil personally before drinking at Martha's, and to refuse all food, but I didn't really see how I could in this situation, so I squeezed onto the sofa between Tess—the young dog—and two orange cats. Heather went off to get the juice, while Martha contemplated me quietly from a pair of shrewd black eyes buried in the flesh of her face.

"And has your Matthew got his exam results yet then Claire?"

"Yes," I said. "He did really well. He got an A for Technical Drawing."

"Eeeh, Claire. You've some brains in your family! There's your brother coming up for his O levels, studying all that technical information and then you off to the grammar school as well after the holidays. But then your father's such an intelligent man and a perfect gentleman with it. Just look at how he jumps out of that car of his every Sunday and goes running round to the other side to open the door for me! George laughs and calls me the Queen of Sheba, but I wish he had some of your father's manners. And I wish our Heather had some of your brains, but I'll tell you this, pet—our Heather has a good, kind heart. There's not a drop of malice in her. She never has a bad word to say about anybody, and she thinks the world of you, and she'll always remember you were friends."

"We'll still *be* friends," I said, alarmed at this turn in the conversation. "I'll still come and play."

"Well, maybe," she said, "and you'll always be welcome, but you may find you have different interests. Things change, and change they must, and that's part of life, and how the Good Lord planned things. Just remember not to get snooty. It's like Vicar Smith was saying last week, Claire, it's not always the rich man that walks into the Gates of Heaven, nor the proud and the clever man neither, which is just as well." She stopped and broke into a wheezy laugh, which seemed more painful than anything, necessitating the squeezing shut of her eyes, and the clutching of each elbow in either hand. "If there was an eleven-plus exam or a means test none of us Braithwaites'd be getting handed a harp any time soon."

As Heather came in with the biscuits, Martha was wiping her eyes with a corner of her pinny. "Now then, Claire," she said, "How's your poor Mam?"

"Her pains are bad at the moment. Oh, by the way, she said to send you her best regards and she hopes you're keeping well."

Martha nodded her massive head slowly. "Well, tell her I was asking after her. It's a shame she doesn't come to church any more. I haven't seen her in weeks."

"It's her knee. She can't kneel for communion."

"She could stand at the altar rail. Vicar Smith wouldn't mind."

"She says it would be disrespectful to God if she didn't kneel."

Martha considered this for a moment, cocking her head to one side. "Well, that doesn't sound quite right, pet. Wouldn't God rather see her standing up than not see her at all?"

There was no escaping the logic of this question, which I had already put to my mother with disastrous consequences. I tried to steer a course between truth and loyalty.

"I think she doesn't want to draw attention to herself. She'd be all stuck out there on her own."

Martha struggled upright in her chair, her moist face alive with happy revelation. "Eeh, Claire. Here's a suggestion, then! I could stand up with her. That way she'd not be on her own."

I bent and stroked Tess to avoid looking at Martha's broad, happy face. Telling the truth seemed to get more and more difficult.

"I'll suggest it to her when I get in," I said, knowing that I wouldn't.

Martha smiled and settled back into her battered old armchair. The *Farmer's Weekly* slid from her lap onto the floor. "Maybe not," she said. "She'd maybe not want me standing up there next to her like a great cart horse." A chuckle started in her stomach, and worked its laborious way through her body to wobble her jowls. "We'd look like Laurel and Hardy. Maybe we could do a skit at the W.I. social." She shook her head slowly till the chuckle subsided, then looked at me significantly. "Your mother's a proud woman," she said. "It's not easy being dependent all the time, nor in pain, nor being an object of pity. She must feel badly, very badly. God works in mysterious ways, pet, but he always knows what he's doing."

Heather handed me a glass of orange pop and two jaffa cakes, then lifted one of the cats up so that she could sit down next to me and plunk it on my lap.

"Here, Jasmine," she said. "You can keep Claire company for a while." She looked at me, her face excited, "She's got kittens in the barn. We can look at them when you've finished your pop."

Martha clasped her hands together suddenly and her eyes went wide. "Eeh, Heather," she said. "Did you tell her what happened yesterday?"

Heather's eyes filled with tears. "Oh, Mam. Not that," she protested. "Don't tell her about that. I don't want to think about it." Martha waved a heavy arm at her in a brushing motion and sailed on.

"It was one of Jasmine's kittens," she said. "It was last out and so tiny you could fit it an egg cup and Heather and I were feeding it with a little eyedropper. She was shivering cold so I just set her in the stove here to warm her through, Claire. You know pet, like George does the new lambs when they're ailing. Well. I only had the oven on low, and I popped it in just for ten minutes or so, I thought, on a little blanket, but then our Heather shut the door and I forgot it."

Heather turned to me, horror spread across her guileless, freckled face.

Her eyes filled up. "It was awful," she said. "I won't forget it in a million years. Its skin was all crackly, like brown paper. Its hair came out in clumps." The tears spilled out from her eyes and ran down her face, and she wiped them away with the back of her hand.

"She's sensitive our Heather, aren't you pet?" said Martha. "She takes after her dad that way. Eeh, it was terrible though, Claire. I screamed that loud when I saw it, Gwen rushed round from next door, thinking I'd been murdered by those gypsies camped down at the beck."

"Maybe it would have died anyway," I said, trying to be nice.

"Aye," said Martha, "probably it would. But what a terrible way to go, Claire. I felt just like one of them Hitler Nazis." She sighed, and then giggled. "Eeeh, Claire. You'd better not tell your mam, pet. She'll think Glenburn folk are all feckless. She'll think she's landed up with a bunch of loonies."

2.

I GOT HOME JUST AT THE RIGHT TIME, AFTER PRINCESS MARGARET HAD been married off, and in time for *Doctor Who*. As I hurried down the front path in the dusk, I could hear the electronic wailing of the theme tune and see the flicker of its psychedelic visuals against the curtains. Dad was out for the count with his chin on his chest in his cottage suite armchair. Kondra, our boxer, lay slumped at his feet. Matthew was glued to the screen. My mother, who affected to find the whole business of interplanetary time travel silly, sat a little more upright in her chair as the credits rolled, and unwrapped another bull's-eye. It looked like I could keep quiet about the whole kitten business.

Doctor Who transported a succession of chirpy young women around the universe. His spaceship, the *Tardis,* an ordinary and unprepossessing telephone box on the outside, seemed to have a fatal knack for luring harebrained flibbertigibbets into its magical interior. They began well enough, cheeky and independent, dressed in the latest mod clothes and refusing to be overawed by the amazing technology of the *Tardis*. This latter, it would seem, was powered by a single large piston which emitted a loud clanging noise and briefly reduced the TV screen to a psychedelic kaleidoscope. Doctor Who's girls were unafraid when the piston ran out of control, as it always did, and the clock (which showed the current date of arrival) ran crazily through the millennia.

My mother passed me the bag of the sweets, as we watched the eccentric doctor tinker at the piston with an improbably large screwdriver, only to be thrown backwards by a big bang. The girl of the moment, a long-legged blonde clad in hot pants and snatched only minutes before from a London disco, did not seem worried by the doctor's collapse, the imminence of disaster, or the loss of her loved ones. Instead, she munched an apple and gazed with interest out of a porthole.

After the usual crash landing on an unknown planet, the girl was so anxious to explore that the doctor had to stop her from rushing straight

out of the door. "Wait till I have checked the oxygen levels and the tem-
perature," he cried plaintively, as she wrestled with the large wheel on the
door (fortunately for her, it was too heavy for her scrawny arms). As soon
as the doctor let her out, off she trotted, hopeful and excited, as if en route
to a Harrod's sale. By this time, I'd been seduced into caring about her.
Maybe she wouldn't turn out to be hopelessly silly. Maybe she'd last more
than one episode. Maybe she'd prove to be a heroine.

"Don't wander off," I yelled. "You'll just get captured." Even my
mother cried out—"Stay near the *Tardis,* you silly girl"—but no—deaf
to all warnings, off she went, plucking flowers and twirling them around
girlishly, though I could have told her not to touch *anything.* She
hummed loudly and crashed through the undergrowth, as if she *wanted*
to get caught, I thought, despairingly. With my superior knowledge of
the *Tardis*'s history, I knew something of the terrible fates out there on
unknown planets—the living zombies, the plants that turned human
flesh into cotton wool that poked out through one's buttonholes, the
glum and sullen mud people whose arms fell off if they dried out. Worst
of all were the dreaded Daleks, large robotic saltcellars on wheels, each
possessed of one eyeball thrust forward in a permanent Nazi salute by a
single mechanical arm. When the Daleks were angry or suspicious,
which was pretty much all the time, little tweezer-shaped things came
out of their eyeballs and emitted sizzling death rays. Heather and I had
thought of a way to deal with Daleks, and we practiced it incessantly.
One of us would jab around with an arm and utter threats in the grat-
ing mechanic voices and somewhat formal English the Daleks favored:
"Warning! Warning! A human prisoner has evaded capture!
Exterminate! Exterminate!" The other would sneak up behind and throw
a hanky over the Dalek's eyeball. It was their Achilles heel, we had
decided, the curse of a one-armed Cyclops. With no second arm avail-
able to remove the hanky, the Dalek would blunder around wildly, bleat-
ing horribly, till it knocked itself over and could be dispatched, or left
to starve to death.

I was cunning and I'd thought these things through. If I'd been there,
I could have helped the doctor, even if I was not as decorative; I felt it
in my bones. I would outwit the Daleks. I would become the doctor's

right-hand companion, maybe learn to oil the piston so we did not have so many crashes. But no, instead he had this stupid girlish girl who didn't even run when faced with a mud person, or throw a stone, or grab a stick, but instead put one useless hand to each side of her face and screamed. Every week, the credits rolled, to my disgust and the sound of helpless squeals. "Doctor! Help me! Doctor! Where are you?"

By this time I was reading voraciously, much to my mother's consternation. If I wasn't out killing villains, I was happiest tucked up in an armchair with a book, across from my father, who picked alternately at the crossword, and, in an absent-minded sort of way, his top lip. Unfortunately, as soon as I sat down, my mother always seemed to want me in the kitchen, since she saw my reading as a lamentable vice.

During these periods in purgatory, I passed the time by watching our kitchen clock. It was electric, though the thick coat of paint it received every year to match the kitchen walls made it seem somehow organic. As its long golden second hand swept around the dial, it twitched nervously every so often and its mechanism whispered faintly, as if it were breathing. As my mother made gingersnaps or boiled beetroots, I practiced passing the time, closing my eyes as the second hand passed the hour. Counting slowly under my breath, I peeked every now and again to check my progress. Once attuned to the clock, I aimed to pass a whole minute without looking, enjoying a small triumph if I timed it just right.

I became more and more ambitious, and was eventually able to count off several minutes at a time while performing satisfactorily as a kitchen companion. Every once in a while, I sneaked a look at the clock to stay in touch with progress, meanwhile dealing obligingly with spooning out cake mix and maintaining what I hoped to be an interested smile. Occasionally, my mother would catch me out, her senses sharpened by her suspicion that I would rather be reading. She would see that my eyes were glazed, or that my lips moved ever so slightly, or catch the quick glance at the second hand. Inflamed by a betrayal she didn't fully understand, but whose enormity she grasped, she would hand down the worst possible indictment in her vocabulary.

"You look just like your Auntie Phyllis," she would cry, "off in cloud cuckoo land. I don't know how I managed to have you. You're not from my side of the family. Sometimes I believe what my mother used to say about changelings. Maybe the fairies switched you at birth."

This theory made sense to me, too, though I never said that. I longed to be somewhere different, somewhere else, somewhere I could build things or chop them down, own a knife and lash things together with rope. I read *Robinson Crusoe* twice, and never understood why he left that island, where he had a box of real tools and his own hut, and a gun to shoot goats with so that he could make hats out of their skin. How much better to wear a goatskin tunic than the checked gingham dresses my mother insisted on for school, refusing to let me wear shorts and my favorite-colored shirt, the one with the button-down pockets. Living on a desert island would be a bit like living on the Braithwaites' farm, but without George, and yes, if I was really honest, without Heather, or at least with a different Heather, Heather transmogrified into someone more adventurous, sharper, less willing to please. Every night I dreamed about the nut-brown girls, whose lives were invisible and unknown to Man. They lived inside a huge oak tree in the forest, which they had hollowed out and converted into a series of smoothly chiseled rooms. Somehow their windows were like the glass in the line-up rooms in American cop shows, except instead of looking like a mirror, the opaque side looked like tree bark. Fey, they were, the nut-brown maidens, and magical, like wood nymphs but more robust, lean and lively, beautiful and competent, shrewd and strong. It came about that I could dream about them at will, simply by thinking of them before I fell asleep.

If I couldn't live on an island or in the forest, my next choice was a boarding school, like the ones I had read about in *Wilmington Towers, Cheryl of the Lower IV*, or *That Madcap Jessica*. I knew in my heart that I was chock-full of madcap potential. I would organize pranks and outings and be a demon on the hockey field. I would strum my ukulele by the campfire while my best friend Babs rested her fluffy blonde head on my knee, tired from our hike through the woods, even though I had carried her knapsack for her. My girlish heart would swell with pride and love, because that's how they said things in those books.

Perhaps Wallingford Grammar School would be a bit like Wilmington Towers. I had passed the eleven-plus, like Matthew, while poor Heather had to stay on at the two-room village schoolhouse where my dad was the headmaster. In a couple of years, she'd head off to the Secondary Modern School in a drab green skirt and a blouse with an open neck and learn typing and shorthand. I would wear a shirt and tie and take hard things like Algebra and Chemistry. My new navy blazer sported a crisp school badge and an inside pocket with a zip. A close rival for my affection was the military style beret, with a smaller badge of the same design. I had a navy-blue duffle coat with real horn toggles and leather round the cuffs. Stitched into the collars of all these splendid military items were impressive white tapes that read "Claire E. Robson" in gothic script.

I had a new Parker fountain pen and a set of colored pencils, a sharpener and a protractor, a compass, a ruler, and a plastic tartan pencil case to keep them in—so academic, so esoteric! At last I would understand why Babs hated Trigonometry. I gazed at the lines and numbers on the protractor, and wondered what they meant. Would I understand them? Would the other pupils have already studied them? I had a brand-new leather satchel, with an adjustable shoulder strap, and a special slot with a piece of cardboard that said, "NAME. ADDRESS." How grown up! How pungent, as I pressed its gleaming, chestnut splendor to my face! All this money spent, with scarcely a grumble, on me! My mother must have saved up for ages.

She was almost as excited as I was, it would seem. After *Doctor Who,* she persuaded me into yet another "try on." She showed me how to pull some of the new tunic up above the belt tie until I grew into it. We experimented with the beret in various positions on my head. Since I was the first girl in the village to have passed the exam, we had no models. I preferred a military sideways slouch, which my mother decided was acceptable if I had my kiss curls nicely sculpted with her spit and comb. She also initiated me into the use of my first suspender belt, purchased to hold up the thick black stockings prescribed for the autumn term.

As she showed me how to loop the tops of the stockings into the clips that dangled from its lacy belt, she became confidential. "You're a young lady now," she said. "You know your dad was as proud as punch when you passed that eleven-plus exam—the first Glenburn girl ever to go to the grammar school! Mavis Brant-Jefferson's daughter had to go to private school. Your dad said she would never have made it to Wallingford. Of course you're not a Glenburn girl in the real sense. You were educated at Houghton."

She stepped back and examined me. "You're still very skinny," she said with a sigh, straightening the front of my tunic, where my breasts would be if I had them. "That's from your dad's side. Your Auntie Phyllis has nothing to speak of, either, but you're young yet. You'll fill out."

She pushed herself up from the chair heavily, with a stifled exclamation of pain, and rubbed her knee automatically. "Well, pet, I can't wait to see you walk down the village in your uniform. When you wear it, make sure you do the buttons up, not like those secondary modern girls with their blouses half undone and everything flying in the wind. Thank the Lord you don't have to wear that uniform. Whoever chose bottle green I'll never know."

When my first day at Wallingford finally rolled around, there were only three of us Glenburn kids waiting at the bus stop: Matthew, his friend David Tallentyre, and myself. As I hitched the strap of my new satchel onto my shoulder, Heather came running up to see me off. She skidded to a halt and looked at me solemnly. "You look different," she said. "More grown up. It'll be three years till I take my eleven-plus. I probably won't pass. I'll have to go to the secondary modern."

"Don't worry," I told her. "I'll be like a spy. I'll find out how it all works and tell you everything. I'll help you with the exam."

"My mam sent you this." She handed me a paper bag as the Durham County Council taxi pulled up and stopped. "I hope it's nice there, and I hope you make friends with someone. Mebbe you can come over tonight and tell me all about it."

"I will," I said. "I'll come right after tea." I scrambled in front with the driver, as my brother and his friend appropriated the back seat and began a technical conversation about fishing. After the taxi disgorged us, I trailed disconsolately in their wake, trotting to keep up. My brother paused as he reached the sign saying Wallingford Grammar School.

"There you are, Our Kid," he said, not unkindly, but as one who sets down an onerous burden. "That's your playground."

I looked helplessly at the heavy metal gates, which stood ajar, and at the stone arch above them, on which was inscribed a single, uncompromising word: GIRLS.

"What?" I said. "Through there?" Where were the happy faces of the girls who would share my class, the stern but kind countenance of my form mistress?

"Yes," he said, "that's where the girls go. Welcome to Auschwitz. I hope you enjoy it. See you back here at four o'clock."

I walked through the gate into a vast expanse of asphalt, covered in strange white and yellow lines. Although I looked around anxiously for a teacher, a sign, a door—anything that would give me a clue about the next step—all that I could see were girls, big girls, hundreds of them. They jostled and jabbered and swaggered, played unfathomable games, walked arm in arm, ran, yelled, and pushed. I found myself staring at four of them, trying to work out how they were different from girls in Glenburn, and why I couldn't imagine them at Wilmington Towers. Their tunics didn't cover their knees like my tunic did, but stopped halfway down their thighs. Their cardigans came down over their bottoms. Despite my mother's predictions, their ties were half undone, and so were their buttons. One of them was chewing gum. Transfixed by her beehive hairdo, I stared too long and she caught my eye.

"Seen enough, have yer?"

"Pardon?"

"Ooh, par*don!*" she said, affecting a French accent. "La di fucking da! I *said,* 'Seen enough have yer!' Whatcha staring at? Seen enough?"

I reassured her of my good intentions. "I wasn't being rude. I was just wondering where I should go next."

The group dissolved in hysterical giggles.

"Listen to how it talks! Gobble gobble gobble. It sounds like a Martian!"

"Look at its uniform! That tunic'll last till she's popped her clogs! Its mummy must have knit that cardigan with size one needles!"

"Hey everybody! Here's a first year Martian that needs telling where to go! Ask Valerie, love. Valerie'll tell yer where to go."

A huge girl with a purple love bite on her neck stepped up to me. "Where's all yer friends?"

I hadn't realized till then that everybody else would have friends except the girl from Glenburn. "I haven't got any. I'm the only girl from Glenburn."

"Come here," she said, glancing sideways at her friends. "*We'll* take care of you, won't we?" and they all collapsed into hideous laughter. Valerie snatched the bag from my hands, the one Heather had given me, and ripped it open. "Ooh!" she yelled. "The village kid's mummy's given it some chocolate biccies!" She took the wrapper off one and threw the rest to her friends.

"Hey," I said. "They're mine! Give those back!" As she took a step towards me, a bell rang, loud and clanging, and my tormentors scattered. *The* Tardis, I thought distractedly. *The doctor has come to rescue me.* Being attacked by the mud people would be better than this.

Mysteriously, the mass of wriggling, gesticulating, shouting girls had formed itself into row upon orderly row of attentive pupils, facing towards the front, where a short woman, the first teacher I had seen thus far, stood stiffly to attention in an empty expanse of tarmac. A brass bell hung loosely from her right hand.

Eager to please after the morning's disasters, I joined a line of girls I thought looked about my size. The teacher's chin came up, and her mouth tightened. At that slight signal, even the slight rippling whisper ceased. She gazed around her, as if waiting to pluck divine inspiration from the air. When she spoke, it was in a clear, precise voice that carried without effort.

"Lead on from class five. First years remain in line."

As if at the flick of a switch, lines of motionless girls galvanized, marching with serious expressions, like the inhabitants of Planet Zombie where no one ever died. I didn't know what to do next. What if my line began to move? Could I step out of it and ask enlightenment from the godlike being? Should I march off with them? What if I ended up in the wrong place and had to extricate myself? Both possibilities seemed inconceivable. I turned to look at the person behind me.

"Is this a first year line?" I asked.

Her eyes widened, but she gazed rigidly ahead and didn't answer.

"Is this the right line for first years?" I persisted.

Her eyes flickered towards mine, and rolled in some sort of attempt at communication, it seemed to be a pained appeal, even a warning—

"Come out here." It was the quiet, commanding voice. I turned to see the teacher gazing in our direction. "Come out here."

I turned to look behind me, as did the girls in front. Who did she want? I'd hate to be in *her* shoes, whoever she was! I realized that the girls behind me were not turning round, but staring at me in horror, as if I had been transmogrified, as if cotton wool was sprouting from beneath my clothing. I looked quickly at the teacher again.

"Yes," she said. "You. Come out here."

It seemed an impossible task, to walk out in front of all those eyes, across that empty black stretch of asphalt, but I felt my legs begin the long journey.

"Were you talking?"

"Yes Miss. I was trying to—"

I was eager to explain, certain that once she heard me out, things would get better. Teachers were on my side.

She emitted a thin sigh, as if leaking years of bitterness and disappointment. "Now that you're a student at the grammar school, I suggest you try to develop some manners, however difficult that task might be. My name is Mrs. Stagg. That's what you should call me."

"Yes Mrs. Stagg."

"This is your first day at a new school, and you have managed to get into trouble almost immediately. I can't imagine that your parents will be pleased to hear that their daughter talked to her friend five minutes after being told not to." She stared at me brightly, and I opened my mouth to explain. "No I don't want any arguments or excuses young lady. The purpose of the eleven-plus examination is to sort the sheep out from the goats. Did you know that?"

I knew what sheep and goats were, but had had no idea how they could possibly be involved in a scholastic examination. "No, Mrs. Stagg. I didn't."

"Well you're going to learn. I'll be watching you very carefully from now on. You can stand here and watch how the rest of the first years manage to behave themselves as they walk in. Then we'll find out where you're meant to be. What school are you from?"

"Glenburn, Mrs. Stagg. My dad's headmaster there."

She smiled for the first time, but none of the humor made it into her eyes. "Oh, he's headmaster at Glenburn is he? Plenty of goats in Glenburn, I imagine."

I thought hard. Heather kept goats. So did the Featherstones, and I thought maybe Arthur Miller had two. "Yes, about seven I think."

Three hundred assembled girls allowed themselves to ripple with mirth as Mrs. Stagg's smile widened. "Not too many sheep though."

I didn't know what to say. I thought of all the sheep that wandered George Braithwaite's farm alone. There must be a couple of hundred. What did she mean? It must be a trick question. I decided to keep silent.

. . .

"So how was your first day?" asked my mother as she carried out the soup.

The chair next to mine had remained empty in every single lesson. No one had spoken to me at dinnertime. I was like someone infected by an alien virus. "Oh," I said, "fine."

"Did anyone say you looked nice in your uniform?"

"No."

She looked disappointed. "What? Nobody? Did none of the other girls say anything about your hand-knitted cardigan?"

I was a goat in sheep's clothing. The fairies had switched me at birth. I should have been sent to boarding school.

"We were really busy, getting our books and everything."

She was not mollified. "Did any of the teachers say they knew who Mr. Robson, your dad, was? Did you tell them he was headmaster at Glenburn?"

"Well, yes, I did. I told Mrs. Stagg, one of the teachers."

She brightened up. "What did she say? Did she say she knew him? Did she sound impressed?"

I had asked my dad about sheep and goats, casually, over tea, and finally worked out what she had been getting at. She thought everyone from Glenburn was stupid, and I had confirmed her suspicion. "Oh yes, about seven goats, Mrs. Stagg." No wonder she had smiled.

My mother was still waiting for me to say something. "Did she ask if your mother came from Glenburn, too? Did she ask where we lived?"

"Actually," I said, "she asked who'd chosen my tunic."

"Did she? Did she now! And what did you say?"

"I said we'd gone to Binns in Sunderland, and that you'd picked it out because you liked the quality."

"Did she ask how much it was? You didn't tell her it was on the sale rack did you Claire?"

"Of course I didn't. She said it was excellent quality. I'd forgotten all about the conversation till now. She said I looked really nice in my uniform."

"There," said my mother, in satisfaction, "what did I tell you?"

I stayed home that night and watched *Coronation Street*. I was tired, and somehow I didn't fancy playing with Heather.

3.

WE KNEW MY MOTHER WAS FEELING BAD WHEN SHE DRAGGED THE vacuum cleaner out of its lair in the understairs cupboard and banged and whanged and thumped it around the house. In a full-scale state, she locked the shivering dog out on the lawn, swilled water around the kitchen floor and stacked chairs upside down till everything looked strange and uncomfortable. She enlisted us all in a mindfulness of decay that would have done a medieval mystic proud. Upon entering the house, we were not to step on the hall carpet, but to make a small leap, so as not to wear it down in one place. We were not to lean on the armrests of our chairs, nor leave a single item of clothing visible in our rooms overnight. Whenever carrying something that might spill, we were to sing the National Anthem in our heads. It would make us remember to walk slowly, and with a measured pace.

I'd hear my mother's tearful voice in the kitchen. "Something's got to go. We need to cut back. There's our Matthew to get fitted out for college soon, and our Claire needs new school shoes. I can't last out till the end of the month."

I began to dread mealtimes and ate with my eyes fixed on her face, waiting for that internal, questing look she'd get. The periods she spent doubled over became longer and more frequent. Often she would go and lie on her bed after meals, and that was better, because I couldn't see her, but it was worse too.

She threw coals in the oven and cakes on the fire. She didn't hear what I said to her, and her words came out funny. "I keep getting my merds wuddled," she would say, and Matthew and I would giggle, tentatively. Only when she chuckled too, in a helpless sort of way, would we roar with laughter, run and find my father. "Guess what Mam said! Guess the latest!" We fetched out all the best examples and laughed till we wept.

"It's just as well I give you something to laugh at," she'd say plaintively.

"Eeh Paul, those cakes were absolutely ruined. I don't know what you find so funny," and off we'd all go again in helpless waves, my father's face turned red by mirth.

Other times, she flew into terrifying rages. I spent my time pretending to be normal and cheerful, lest her eyes narrow and her claws sprout. Hoping to avoid attacks on my bookish nature, eager to please, I'd leap up to clear away the supper things before we had finished eating. As we washed the dishes, I maintained a stream of cheerful banter of the sort I knew my mother enjoyed.

"We made sausage rolls today in D.S. I quite enjoyed it." (This was a lie. I loathed the subject and our teacher, Miss Perry, detested me and made me sit at her desk with her to keep me out of trouble.)

"I should hope you did, because that sausage meat I had to buy cost me one and six a pound. For goodness sake, watch what you're doing. That hot teapot's going to mark the Formica."

"It's not hot, Mam, it's the one we used earlier on—"

"Can't we do anything in this house without a major argument? It's about time they taught you a bit of real housecraft at that school. You need to be learning about how to manage a house and a budget for when you get married. Not that you ever show any interest in practicalities, with your nose always stuck in a book. You'll ruin your eyesight and then it'll be glasses, which are the worst thing in the world for a girl your age, never mind the expense."

Things came to a head one Tuesday evening, when she left the table after supper. Some time later we heard her plaintive, distant cry. As I scurried about, fetching her nightie from the wardrobe, a glass of water with a piece of ice from the kitchen, Matthew sat on the linen basket looking scared, and my father on the end of the bed, looking helpless. It was a strangely close occasion.

"Should I call the doctor, Norah?" my dad kept asking, and in my mind I begged him just to do it without asking her, so we would have someone who knew what to do—a leader.

"No Paul. You know he hates coming out to Glenburn along that awful road."

"I think we should just ring him to ask his advice."

"No, let me try some of that medicine he gave me last week first. It might settle my stomach."

I ran downstairs to get it, and poured it carefully into the spoon without spilling a drop, but it didn't help. She was gray with pain, and I saw that the sheets were soaked with sweat. She kept asking me to open the window. "It's open," I told her, looking fearfully at my dad. "Mam, I already opened the window for you."

"Hang my clothes up," she said. "My best suit. In the wardrobe. Open the window." And rolled over to the side of the bed and said no more as my dad finally ran down the stairs to phone for an ambulance.

The ulcer she had been nursing for months had burst, he told us, when he got back from the hospital. A kind of poison had been eating at her stomach.

"Did she nearly die?" our Matthew asked. He was much more forthright than I was. Dad told him things because he was older than I was, and he was the boy. He nodded now, and I felt my insides flutter. "Dr. Murray said it was touch and go," he told Matthew. "Another fifteen minutes he said, and it could have made all the difference. He gave me hell for not calling him any earlier."

One wonders how Dr. Murray felt about prescribing aspirin for her pains and milk of magnesia for her stomach all those months.

4.

THE WORLD, WHICH HAD UNTIL NOW BEEN ORGANIC, IF CONFUSING, became separated into Geography and Mathematics, History and Biology, and more. Each subject filled its own exercise book with meaningless notes that I copied slavishly from the blackboard in my optimistic cursive. I drew pictures of amoeba, waving their tentacles, floating around like space blobs from *Doctor Who*. What were they? I occasionally wondered. Where did they live? Did they catch things with those tiny tentacles and swallow them whole? Seemingly, as long as we drew them neatly in tests and put the labels in the right place, we did not need to know. Garibaldi sailed from Genoa in seven leaky vessels. Why were they leaky? Where was he going?

Life was confusing and brutal. We learned a name for it—survival of the fittest. Heather was no help. She didn't understand a thing I explained to her, and in the end I stopped trying. I visited the farm less and less frequently. I had homework to do, and in any case, I started noticing things—things I had never seen before. Heather's nose ran and her face was dirty. She would never survive at Wallingford. It was hard enough for me to survive, without Heather clinging to my shirttails.

I arrived early for classes and settled myself in a seat about four rows back, close enough to be under the protection of the teachers, but not so close as to attract their attention. Sometimes another girl sat next to me, the least favored member of a threesome, perhaps, using me for protective camouflage (another name we learned), to hide her own isolation. Then I would be friendly, but not so friendly as to seem desperate. Sometimes it was someone even less popular than I—Betsy Eliot with the thick pink glasses, perhaps, or the girl who came three weeks after the term started and still wore a green uniform instead of navy blue. I didn't talk to these outcasts in case I became tainted, lost the acceptance I had scraped together by walking down corridors at the edges of a group, skipping and hopping with the effort to keep up, to seem part of the conversation without treading on anyone's heels.

Towards the end of that first term, I finally kidnapped a girl I didn't like and stole her friend. They had had a fight and Sandra—the one I didn't like—plumped down, pouting, next to me. I played her like a fish, offered her bait she couldn't resist, let her complain about Eleanor, how unkind she had been, what a snob she was. "Don't talk to her," I told her. "She doesn't deserve it. You can sit with me for a while," I told her magnanimously, "till she comes around." After three days of this, I moved in on Eleanor. First I sat with her at lunchtime, played hard to get, cut her off when she complained about Sandra. "I can't be two-faced," I told her virtuously. "It wouldn't be fair. I wasn't involved in all that."

Eleanor made the switch one Biology class, paused beside my desk, and rested her hand on the back of the chair. I glanced at her, casually, as if surprised. "Oh," I said. "You can sit there, if you want." When Sandra took the empty seat behind us, I turned around. "It's time you two made up," I told her. "We can all be friends. You can get a stool next to us when we do the practical." She looked at me venomously, but from that moment on, she was third wheel.

After my mother's brush with death, I began counting seconds at night. I lay in my room and listened to the tick of the grandfather clock on the landing, across from the amaryllis, which gathered dust behind the net curtain and never flowered.

Seconds marched towards me in a long line, and then over me to become the past. I would try to grab one as it came by, but always it would stamp along, disappearing in a trail of new seconds, like the manic buckets and brooms in *Fantasia.* To focus on one of the seconds was to miss the rest.

"There's another one gone," I whispered, but in the time it took to say even that, another three had slipped by, never to be experienced. It was impossible to really get hold of a second, to keep it there and look at it, even now, when it was all I thought about. If I slept, seconds would fly past in their hundreds, in their thousands. *These* seconds—the ones I could concentrate upon in my waking moments—these, at least, I would monitor. I was determined to experience this section of time as clearly as

I could. I counted each second under my breath, giving each due weight and credit, until eventually I was pinned down by seconds, trampled by time, unable to speak or even think for fear of interrupting, of missing something.

I felt the weight of my body on the bed, the weight of my bed's four feet on the floor, the beams of the house pressing onto the earth, clamped there by gravity, as we whirled through space, spinning at impossible speeds through eternity, which I knew it was impossible for me or the kitchen clock or even the grandfather clock to monitor. My own father's father had made that clock, and now he was dead, the flesh melting from his bones in a Shildon graveyard.

It was a fact that I was going to die. I did not know when, or how, but I knew I would be terribly frightened, and it would hurt. My death was a definite event, carried towards me on the wings of one of those seconds, and each second that sped by me brought death nearer. Maybe I would step under a bus; maybe I would catch pneumonia; maybe I would be trapped in a burning house and have nowhere to run to. Whatever precautions I took wouldn't count. I was definitely going to die. Everybody did.

Three days after my mother was admitted to hospital for the third time, my father handed me eight pound notes, and told me that she was going to be in there for a while this time, so here was the month's house-keeping. Thus, we all entered a new phase of our long and intimate relationship with illness, and I learned to manage the household, washing the floor, feeding the dog, and going shopping with my dad, who rambled obediently behind me in the aisles of Tesco's, never doubting my selection of food, nor complaining when his fried eggs leaked viscously onto his chips. He ate his stolid way through everything I served him and said at the end, "Very nice, pet, thank you," with exactly the same polite obedience as he used with my mother. "I could serve him a bowl of porridge," she would say to me sometimes, "and he'd say the exact same thing." I began to understand what she meant—he was unexacting, my dad, but unrewarding.

It never failed to astonish me that although my mother fought like a mad dog to avoid being admitted to hospital, she seemed serenely happy once she was there. I would approach the first visit in considerable trepidation, remembering how Matthew and I had listened the night before from the bottom of the stairs. My father's voice was a quiet reasonable mumble. We heard only my mother distinctly, moving between rage and pleading. "Don't call him Paul. Don't. Wait a minute. It's getting a bit better. Just wait. I don't want you to call him, because he'll take me to that awful place. I'm not going in there. No. I'm not going, Paul. I'll never get out once they get me in there."

Expecting to find her still defiant and miserable on our first visit, I was astonished to see her smiling and angelic, looking ten years younger and talking interestedly about her fellow inmates. Nurses and doctors paid her compliments which she repeated proudly as we clustered around the bed on the angular regulation chairs. Other patients poured their troubles into her sympathetic ear and spoke cheerily to us when we arrived with the Lucozade.

"She's a wonderful woman, Mr. Robson. She keeps us all going, you know. And laugh—I thought I was going to burst my stitches."

No sooner had we all grown accustomed to this paragon, than there was talk of a discharge date, and the three of us exchanged nervous glances. On our return home, over poached eggs on toast, I drew up a list of jobs. Methodically, I scrubbed, vacuumed, dusted and tidied. I washed the blankets, scrubbed the paths, and spring-cleaned the dog's basket. I trampled on my parents' king sized eiderdown in the bathtub. Even my father would help occasionally, flourishing a duster with more vigor than effect. Finally the house, gleaming and orderly, waited for its mistress.

We sat through the journey home in considerable anxiety, which Dad tried to dispel in various ineffectual ways.

"Now then, Norah, we've spent a lot of time on the house. We've even had Ida round to check it over, and she thought it was fine, so you can just have a cup of tea and rest when you get in, like Dr. Murray said you should."

"Ida? What on earth did you get Ida over for? I suppose my own sister thinks I'm crazy as well now. I don't know what you all take me for. All I want to do is to get home, and get away from that dreadful place."

Our suspicions allayed but not dispelled, we would assist her from the car and along the front path, from which vantage point her eyes scanned the frontage. "Matthew! What on earth have you done with your bedroom curtains? They look terrible like that."

Once we were inside, the situation deteriorated even further. After a brief tour, my mother soon found cause for an anguished tirade, launched mainly in my direction.

"I've only been in there for seven weeks and the place is like a pigsty . . .

"If I've told you once, I've told you a hundred times to turn the sofa cushions when you vacuum . . ."

"That plant at the top of the stairs hasn't been watered in all the time I've been away . . .

Soon the vacuum cleaner would come crashing out of the understairs cupboard like a Valkyrie. Mam rumbled it across the upstairs carpets, cannonading it off the sideboards. A forlorn little group, we listened to the thunder above, and the steady, imperturbable tick of the grand-father clock.

5.

IT WAS AT ABOUT THIS TIME THAT *THE SOUND OF MUSIC* CAME OUT, AND my mother started going to see it as often as she could persuade someone to join her—once with my brother and my dad and I, once with my Auntie Phyllis, once just with me, and twice with my Auntie Ida. (This was when my mother and Ida were still speaking—back before my Cousin Helen got pregnant and had to marry my Uncle Ben and my mother only found out about it from a friend she bumped into at Sutton Coop and so refused to go to the wedding.)

I liked Julie Andrews when she was Maria, the madcap nun. She didn't care about clothes and makeup and ran around the countryside in a plain gray habit that seemed to offer lots of leg room. When Maria was supposed to be scrubbing the church or grinding up herbs or something, she escaped outside like I used to with Heather, like a tomboy, acting wild and singing at the top of her voice. She was so in love with life that it sent her whooshing up to the very top of a mountain, where all the world was spread in promise at her feet and she flung open her arms to welcome it. Nobody ever told Julie Andrews to take smaller steps, like my dad did me when he said only boys walked like that. Nobody ever told her she couldn't climb trees. She didn't have to go to a school where everyone laughed at her sensible shoes and she had to knit stupid bobble hats in Home Economics.

Everybody loved Maria just the way she was. It was true that the Mother Superior sang a song about never being able to solve a problem like Maria because she was like a moonbeam who never listened to good advice, but I never suspected that the Mother Superior actually meant it. She was kind and benevolent. I thought that she understood that Maria was different, that she had a special mission.

I never fully understood what went wrong at that point. The kind Mother Superior suddenly bundled Maria off to a splendid mansion to be a servant to some obnoxious aristocrat. She looked sad and noble instead of happy and alive, and the special mission got sidetracked by a bunch of sniveling children (who should have been in school), and even worse, by the obnoxious aristocrat, played by Christopher Plummer. He strode around the mansion in a very haughty fashion with this baroness, who was an expert at clothes and makeup and thus acted very snooty with Julie Andrews who only wore a plain gown. Christopher Plummer had no special talents whatsoever, as far as I could see, apart from singing *Edelweiss* very slowly, and that was much later, after Julie Andrews had taught him how to love. I didn't mind that Christopher Plummer learned how to love—he was much nicer to his children after that. I just didn't see why Julie Andrews had to stay around after she'd taught him. I couldn't help thinking that it was the reverse of the usual story, in which the heroine is made pregnant by the obnoxious aristocrat and then is bundled off *away* from him to live with the nuns. Here, the nuns bundled the heroine off to the aristocrat in the first place, seemingly as some kind of antidote to natural exuberance.

I was certainly disappointed, but I didn't entirely give up on Julie Andrews and trusted her to do better things when they made it over the mountains to Switzerland. Someone that beautiful and energetic had to be more than just a housewife.

For my mother, the film became an icon and Julie Andrews a saint. She stocked up on licorice allsorts and Kleenex and gazed, enraptured, at the screen, crying copiously through the love scenes and chuckling at the antics of the smallest children. She even enjoyed the sickening *I'll depend on you* mush from the sixteen year olds, though it didn't surprise me that the blue-eyed boy turned out to be a nasty little fascist. All the boys I knew were cruel too.

Mam launched into the songs at the drop of a hat. She particularly liked *Edelweiss* and *My Favorite Things,* though later in life she switched to *Climb Every Mountain.* My brother and I were united in contempt for Christopher Plummer, and romantic love in general. Since Matthew had gone to teacher training college, he wore tweed sports jackets with leather elbow patches. He also had taken to smoking a pipe, emitting dictums along with clouds of blue smoke. Though I agreed with him that Christopher Plummer was a right prat, I defended Julie Andrews from his cynical jibes and joined my mother on the choruses as we washed up the dinner things. She decided that I would suit my hair cut short, too, which was in itself a victory for freedom.

My mother was always a sucker when it came to smooth professional men like Christopher Plummer. She just loved his laconic calm, though if she had been married to him she would no doubt have had conniptions at his easy assumption that it was possible to transport an entire tribe of children over the Alps without so much as a teapot. She thought the world of her doctor too, because he always treated her like a lady and took an interest in "how she was in herself" when he made house calls.

"And how are you today Mrs. Robson? Those pains of yours acting up?"

"Well, they are, Dr. Murray. I'm not too good to be honest, though it's not so much the pains. It's more that I seem to get all churned up in my stomach. I mean the arthritis pain is always there. I live with it, as you know, but when I get upset, it's like there's a mouse or a little animal inside chewing at my vitals, and a tight band around my chest as though someone's tied a rope around there, and they're squeezing as hard as they can."

The suave doctor paused for thought, struck, even through his natty sports jacket and debonair charm, by the biblical directness of her imagery.

"Dear, oh dear, Mrs. Robson. Is there a lot on your mind lately?"

"It's just one thing after another, Doctor. I can't seem to make ends meet. I miss my friends and my bungalow in Houghton. Our Matthew's bought this gun from someone at his college, and he and David Tallentyre roam the fields with it every weekend when he comes home. I lie awake every night, thinking of him being carried home on a stretcher. And then our Claire's going through a funny phase. It used to be that she couldn't care less about clothes, so at least I could dress her up nice, but now she insists on wearing shorts or dungarees everywhere like a farm laborer. She's sixteen years old and she hasn't the least interest in boys or fashion or any of the things girls normally care about. She lives in a world of her own, with her nose stuck in a book half the time.

"My sister Ida says I should be firmer with them, but Paul's no help. I've asked him and asked him to speak to our Matthew. After all, it's a father's job, but if I don't say anything, it never gets said. It's always me that's the villain."

She looked at Dr. Murray through her tears. "I'm that pent up, I feel my head's going to burst. Do you think I'm going mad, Dr. Murray? Should I take up smoking to calm my nerves?"

"No, Mrs. Robson. Probably not a good idea," said the doctor, a little out of his depth, and somewhat regretting his plunge into the morass of my mother's feelings. "I don't think you're going mad, not for a second, though you certainly seem to worry a great deal."

"My mother always said I was a terrible worrier," said my mother proudly. "I worry about all sorts of things. Like the Gestapo."

The doctor blinked. "The Gestapo?"

"Well I've been having these dreams you know. They come to the house in the middle of the night dressed in those black uniforms and sometimes they try to take our Matthew and Claire away. They threaten such terrible things you know—rape and pulling our fingernails out with pliers. Paul tries to stand up to them, but their leader normally just shoots him and laughs."

The doctor took a surreptitious glance at his watch as my mother began to cry.

"He never really listens to me. He just puts on that irritated expression of his, or leaves the room. It's anything for a quiet life with him and don't rock the boat. Sometimes I just feel like walking out. Eeh, Dr. Murray," she said through her tears, "you'll think I'm just one of those erotic housewives."

Doctor Murray suggested that my mother persist in her efforts to talk to my father. "Mustn't bottle it all up inside Mrs. Robson—worst thing you can do—but try and take things one at a time. Don't give him the whole lot at once, and stay calm. Maybe get out of the house a little more if you can. How about that sister of yours in Etherley? Visit her, why not? Drink coffee, chat about clothes, talk through the problems—woman to woman sort of thing. You can't drive? Well, Good Lord, Mrs. Robson. It's the twentieth century. Get that husband of yours to teach you—doctor's orders."

Since it was difficult to organize lessons without me, once Mam had begun to "master the basics," Dad taught her *en famille*. As my mother jerked and bounced us along the quiet roads to Barnard Castle on Saturday mornings, Matthew and I perched nervously in the back seat and my father sat beside her, wincing at each clash of gears. Although she did seem able to steer and use the gears and pedals, my mother was dogged by a tendency to panic. At these moments, she forgot what she had learnt, confusing pedals, knobs and levers, none of which had played a large part in her life before. It was this simple confusion that brought her bid for freedom and independence to an abrupt end.

As she negotiated a left-hand turn at a junction, the interplay of clutch and accelerator became too absorbing, and she failed to notice the fact that she was over-steering, directing the car towards one of Lord Barnard's large white houses. When she finally looked up, satisfied that the car was safely in motion and had finished with kangaroo leaps for the moment, she was horrified to see the building looming above us.

Initially, my father controlled his panic.

"Brake, Norah," he said, in his schoolmaster voice.

My mother pressed the accelerator pedal firmly. Matthew and I sat rigidly in the back seat, watching the house grow larger.

"BRAKE!" my father yelled, all composure gone. As we mounted the pavement, he reached over and seized the wheel.

I suppose everything must have crystallized for my mother. She had pressed the pedal when he told her to and now he was shouting at her and pulling at the wheel. Couldn't he see that that was a dangerous thing to do? For once she was going to do it her way.

For what seemed like an eternity, my parents wrestled for control of the car, which slewed and pitched. I prayed silently that logic and reason would win and blessed my dad's superior strength as he wrestled the car around and away from the building. My mother, pressing pedals now at random, finally stalled the engine, and for a few minutes we all sat in silence.

"Why were you steering us into the building?" my mother said in a shocked voice. "You could of had us all killed."

"Norah," said my father, in barely controlled fear and anger, "*You* were steering us towards it. Why wouldn't you brake when I asked?"

"I did brake. I pushed the brake."

"It was the accelerator," he said. "You must have got confused."

She slumped over the wheel.

"I can't grip that steering wheel properly with my hand . . . and my bad leg makes it hard for me to press that brake pedal. You'd better drive us home. Maybe I'll try again when my pains aren't so bad."

The next day, I heard raised voices from the kitchen, and shortly afterwards my mother clumped upstairs, packed a suitcase and walked out of the front door, ignoring my father's protests.

"Don't be ridiculous, Norah! Where can you go?"

Sadly, he had a point. The Sutton bus trundled up the village once a day at noon, and the sun had long since set. My mother couldn't drive.

She set out on foot, closing the front door firmly behind her.

After waiting five or ten minutes for her return, my father set out in pursuit . . . in the car. He caught her up two hundred yards down the road, and curb-crawled the car beside her, before winding down his window to whisper entreaties at her stubborn form.

"Norah, for God's sake get in. What's everybody going to think?"

"Norah, there's nowhere to go. Let me take you home and I'll phone Ida.

"Come on Norah, get in the car. This is silly. Our Claire's in floods of tears."

All the while, my mother limped along, trying to look dignified, like Joan Crawford perhaps, with a seized-up knee, and a wobbly ankle. The suitcase was increasingly difficult to grip.

They returned home in the car ten minutes later, and we watched *Double Your Money* in silence.

Eventually the story passed into family legend: "The Day Mam Ran Away from Home." My mother laughed happily along as we recounted the tale.

6.

SLUMPED IN THE BACK SEAT OF THE MINI COUNTRYMAN, I GLUMLY regarded Kondra's yellow haunches. The dog's forepaws straddled the hand brake, and her head was held resolutely between the shoulders of my parents, who sat in front. Though Matthew was home for the weekend, he was off fishing. Although my father rarely exceeded forty miles an hour, the dog's claws scrabbled briefly for position as the Mini Countryman rounded the occasional corner. Panic invaded her bulging eyes at these moments, but she kept them fixed sternly ahead through the windscreen. Every movement of her head shook the copious strings of drool that dangled perpetually from her mouth, endangering my parents' Saturday afternoon shopping outfits.

My mother wore her ladies' sheepskin jacket. Caught in a gilt scarf ring and tucked into the neck was the chrysanthemum headscarf Auntie Ida had given her for Christmas. A crocodile skin handbag sat squarely on her lap. My dad wore his matching man's sheepskin jacket, with cavalry twill trousers and a jaunty Tyrolean hat with a feather subdued in its band. Their ensembles were completed by a brand new yellow dusting cloth—the kind my mother used to polish her silver fruit bowl—which they each wore draped across one shoulder.

The drive across the moors was the best part of these mindless excursions, I reflected, as I rubbed a hole in the condensation on the windowpane and peered out at their dark, featureless expanse. I liked the moors in all their seasons, from the short flowering of their purple heather, through the sodden, chilly autumn, and on into the savage winter. I liked them because they were untamed and uncaring. There had been forests here, Miss Watson told us once in Geography, until they cut all the trees down to build ships for the Napoleonic Wars. Now that they were shorn, the moors wore their ugliness with a certain sullen pride, like me.

What did I care if my mother sat me in a chair in the kitchen and tortured my rebellious hair with a home perm until it gave in, and sat tamely on my head like an alien helmet? She had asked me, too casually, if I didn't fancy being a hairdresser or a beautician when I'd got my A levels, instead of spending more time studying. What was the point of university, she said, when I'd just get married? A good hairdresser could earn money anywhere. It was always something for a woman to go back to when she'd had her children.

I wanted nothing to do with beauty. The moors were not beautiful and neither was I, nor did I ever want to be. Beauty was as stupid as a woman in high heels trying to escape a murderer in the movies. Beauty was for someone else—the girls who pretended to talk to me at the school party, laughing artificially, with their eyes on the boys at the other side of the room. Beauty danced to a complicated tune called fashion, and I couldn't keep step. If I tried to do anything with my hair, for example, my hands moved purposefully in the wrong direction as I watched them in the mirror. As if a secret inner self was sabotaging the whole process, my backward hands unwound hair from rollers and sent hairpins slowly upwards, towards the sky.

I looked awful in female attire; skirts and dresses dangled from my skinny frame like sacks; frills only served to emphasize my scowling visage, my gawky neck, my flat chest.

Beauty was stupid. Only last winter, a couple had died of cold on the moors, stranded in a sudden snowstorm on the way to their own engagement dinner at the Blanchland Arms. The woman wore a flimsy evening dress. When they found them, she had been wrapped in the man's rented dinner jacket, while he was in his shirtsleeves. They would never get their pictures in the *Weardale Clarion's* wedding section now—that catalogue of stocky grooms in suits and waistcoats, those perfectly bouffant brides.

My parents had done all that—that wedding thing. Their picture was propped up on the television, and now here they were, driving *en famille*, adorned with yellow dusters, to the market town of Barnard Castle. They would stop at predetermined locations to buy the same food they always bought, and then we would all drive home via Tatsworth and buy ice creams from the van on the village green. My dad would have a choc-ice, my mam would have a ninety-nine in a cone and I would have a strawberry mivvi. Mam would construct a mini cone for the drooling dog from the last of her ninety-nine, then we'd all head home for kippers, white bread, tea and meringues. After the dishes—TV and bed. Sunday was church, roast beef and a nap in the armchairs, followed by TV and bed.

No wonder we watched TV. It was a window into a bigger world—a world where things happened. We could see how other people lived, like Emma Peel in *The Avengers*. Emma Peel was married, but she didn't have a husband, a situation that seemed eminently satisfactory to me, though a little baffling. Her sidekick, Steed, always called her Mrs. Peel, but on the occasions that he visited her, it was clear that she lived alone. How I loved that London flat of Emma's, scrutinized every detail, tried to peer around the corners to look into her bedroom, wanted somewhere just like that when I finally escaped from home. Tiny, it was, clearly big enough for only one, and yet so modern, so elegant. Set every here and there was one exquisite piece of art. No clutter of horse brasses and family pictures for Emma, and no ironing or dusting or washing up either. When Steed arrived, she might be listening to classical music, or practicing her fencing, or reading some esoteric book. She'd drop everything in a second to join in the adventure, no last minute trips to the bathroom or checking in her handbag—Emma traveled light. She was skinny, like me, but instead of shrouding herself in fussy folds and lockets, she wore a skintight black leather suit, flaunting her angularity and muscle, her stork-like legs, her skinny waist.

Emma Peel would never consider dying in a car on the Pennine Moors—she would simply refuse the entire proposition with a wry curl of her lip, the stubborn lift of her chin. Emma laughed at danger.

Say a hulking villain should enter the restaurant where Mrs. Peel and Steed are dining—she raises a quizzical eyebrow at Steed as if to ask him, "You or I?" Always the gentleman, Steed gestures her to precede him, and then relaxes as she squares up to the thug. He even sips champagne, assured of her success.

The hairy villain approaches Mrs. Peel. He wears a brown leather bomber jacket and a foreign beard. His trousers are too short. His lumbering steps towards her speak of overconfidence. "She is a mere woman," we hear him think, as clearly as if he's said it. He grabs at her with a meaty hand. Emma launches into a balletic display, and even my mother claps her hands together as those long legs swoop in a graceful arc, a foot smacks under his hairy chin. The hairy villain—Vladimir, let's call him—looks baffled. His face appeals for help, for explanation from the Universe. "What is going on?" we hear him think. "How has the natural ascendancy of strong men over helpless women been so suddenly reversed?"

Mrs. Peel has considerately left him time for a breather, and passes the time in play. She holds the back of a chair as if it is a bar, and she a dancer warming up. She folds one hand primly at her waist and points her toes. She does not even look at the dastardly Vladimir, who whips a knife from his pocket and bares his teeth. *No one kicks Vladimir under the chin and lives,* we hear him think. It is time to get serious. Woman or no Woman, she is going to die. This time he is more circumspect in his approach. Emma too—she flicks back a strand of hair and circles her hands as she moves around him in a low crouch. He slashes with the knife, once, twice, aiming at her face (the rotter), but on the third attempt, she has his wrist. Vladimir sails through the air and lands with a crash right on Steed's plate. Steed, about to cut into his filet mignon, seems surprised to notice that it has been replaced by a Russian secret agent.

Emma saunters to the table, and places parsley on Vladimir's nose. His eyes turn to Steed in pathetic inquiry. "You are a man, like me," say the eyes of Vladimir, "so tell me this. How has a skinny, unarmed woman defeated Vladimir, pride of the KGB, son of Russia, currently intent on frying Europe with laser beams located on the planet Venus? How is it that I have blundered around a restaurant unable to swat this mere woman, a beautiful woman at that—damn it all, I would make her beg for mercy if I could." He snarls helplessly under his load of garnish, and Steed raises an ironic eyebrow as if to say, "I know it's hard, old man. I know just how you feel, but time's moved on and smart chaps must keep up with the times don't you know?"

"He looks nice," my mother said.

I snapped out of my reverie to see that we had pulled into the marketplace. My father was off on his first mission—kippers from Mr. Hanselman—and my mother was nodding with her chin towards a gangly youth who hovered on the steps of the National Westminster Bank. He looked nice enough, as boys went, but I didn't care to answer.

"I saw Heather Braithwaite walking down the village with a young man the other day. I wonder if they're courting?"

"Yes," I said, "they are. His name's Brian. I bumped into her the other night. She was trying to persuade me to come to the dances in the village hall."

"Well you should go," my mother told me. "She's right."

"Mam. I have to study. I need at least two Bs and a C to get into York University."

"You're always studying. Seventeen year olds are meant to have a bit of fun now and then. Meet the opposite sex. Our Matthew didn't have to work so hard."

"He's only at teacher training college, Mam. He just needed two passes. And I go to the youth club dances every so often."

"Don't any boys ever ask you out there?"

"Well, we dance with them sometimes," I said, as vaguely as possible.

I thought back to my last excursion to Crook. She'd die if she knew. Instead of going to the Youth Club, as promised, Eleanor and Louise and I had got pissed as farts at the Dog and Gun.

We smoked Embassy filters, one after another, crushing them out halfway in one of our ashtrays. In the other ashtray we piled our empty cheese-and-onion crisp packets. We faced the door so that we could watch out for Eleanor's Auntie Mary. She was Salvation Army, and we never knew when she might turn up with her collection box. Eleanor was sitting at the end of the table nearest the loo, so that she could slip in there if we saw Auntie Mary's frilled bonnet enter the crowded bar. This left me squashed in the middle of our two-person bench seat. I could feel the heat of Louise Robinson's leg as she spoke.

"Tony Anderson told me that if you drop cigarette ash in your drink you'll get drunk quicker."

Louise Robinson looked too well-bred to be in the Dog and Gun, which we frequented precisely because its sleazy reputation assured the absence of teachers or relatives, apart from zealous Auntie Mary. I had noticed that I liked to watch Louise Robinson laugh. Indeed I liked to watch her face in all its moods. It was like a hobby of mine, or some piece of research, to study her face. For one thing, I couldn't quite place what made her look well-bred. There was something about the paleness of her skin and its careless litter of freckles, and something about the way her lips were sharply cut, as if made for the pearl pink lipstick that she wore. She looked clean, like a princess would, even if she were forced to sit in a smoky saloon bar, leaning her elbows on that tiny piece of table that was unoccupied by overflowing ashtrays and the sticky rings left by our glasses of barley wine.

I marshaled my thoughts, which had taken to sailing around the room in slow circles.

"Tony Anderson's a wanker," I said, to make Louise laugh, but only Eleanor giggled, which didn't mean much, as she giggled pretty much non-stop when she got drunk. A gob of white ash dropped from her cigarette into her barley wine, and we watched it sink in silence, struck by the coincidence, until Eleanor laughed even harder. Smoke puffed out of her mouth as her shoulders shook.

"You need to practice your smoking, Eleanor," I said. "You're meant to inhale it, not just carry it around in your mouth. You look like Puff the Magic Dragon."

Louise finally gave a quiet little chuckle that wrinkled her face and lit up the blue in her eyes and set Eleanor off again, cackling and dabbing at her eyes with a hanky. "Is my mascara running?"

Louise looked at her critically. "Just a teeny bit," she said, though by now Eleanor looked like a giant panda.

"Well I think Tony Anderson's quite nice looking," said Eleanor.

"You think anything in trousers is nice looking," I said without reflection. "You even went out with Fletcher."

"At least I went out with someone," she said, a little sharply.

She had me there. Going out with somebody was better than going out with nobody.

"You've been out with boys though, haven't you?" said Louise.

"Of course I have," I said, reaching for my packet of Embassy. "Loads of times."

She tried to prop her head up on her fists to scrutinize me, and managed it at the second attempt. She gave me a full blue drunken stare.

"So, how far have you gone?"

I concentrated hard to keep the end of the cigarette in the flame of the Swan Vesta and to shake it out before it burned my fingers.

"That would be telling," I said, exhaling inscrutably.

Danny Sawyer had pulled me into an airing cupboard, but I had laughed in his face and escaped. Peter Smith had taken me for a walk down the river and put his tongue in my mouth.

"Have you done number three?" Louise asked.

I had done number three when Jonathan Taylorson pulled me into a bedroom at a party and grabbed my breasts.

I kept my face casual, but tried to inject a smirky underlay of guilt. "You're too young to hear this anyway."

She sat more upright on her stool.

"Have you gone number ten—all the way?"

Numbers one, two, and three had left me cold. I had no desire to progress even to number four, but I wasn't telling her that.

"Ask Eleanor," I said. "She went out with Derek Johnson for three months, and you know what *he's* like."

Eleanor looked suddenly serious and a little green. She picked up her handbag and clung on to it like a talisman. "I've got to go home," she said, frowning with the effort of articulation.

As she stood up, a shadow fell across our littered table. "Mind if we join you?"

"No," said Louise, as I said, "Yes."

Andy Mercer, the nicest looking boy in the sixth form, squeezed in next to Louise, and his friend hovered, looking round the bar for an empty chair. I could tell he was doing Andy a favor by picking up the extra girl.

"Actually," I said, "I was just leaving. Don't bother. Be my guest."

I took Eleanor's elbow and steered her out of the pub. The force of the cold night air sent us reeling, and I steered us in a controlled stagger around the back to the dustbins. Eleanor was crying by now.

"I did, Claire. You were right. I did go all the way. Derek fucking bastard Johnson. Never fucking bastard picks up the fucking bastard telephone."

She giggled again, her face slimy with tears. "*He's* the wanker," she said emphatically, "Bastard Derek fucking Johnson. Tony Anderson, now he's *nice.*" She clutched me arm. "Say it. Tony Anderson's *nice.*"

"He's very nice," I said soothingly, keeping hold of her arm as she threw up, careful to keep my shoes out of the way. "Tony Anderson's very nice."

· · ·

That Christmas, my mother bought me a pair of imitation leather pants, a black polo neck, and a leopard skin leotard, like the one Emma wore in the episode where a mystery death ray was killing astronomers when they looked through their telescopes. I wore the outfit at the Mecca ballroom on New Year's Eve. We put our handbags in a pile so nobody could nick them, and danced around them. At first I left the group to dance with boys when they asked me, and even stayed on for the slow ones, feeling their strange and wistful hands moving across my back as they guided me in circles through the crowded dance floor. Occasionally I would catch the eye of one of my friends as I looked around a shoulder, and we would wink at each other, or stick our tongues out, or roll our eyes in horror. Only Louise Robinson had moved beyond my gaze, resting her head on Andy Mercer's shoulder all evening with her eyes closed, enchanted. At midnight, the big silver ball was lowered from the ceiling, and the balloons set free from their nets. The DJ played *Telstar* full blast, one last time. I kicked my legs like Emma Peel, sent balloons flying, till I danced alone in my own space, lost in a million tiny points of light.

Part Two

Learning Curves, 1968–1969

The Radical

York University's Alternative Student Newspaper

July 30th, 1968

Authentic Love? Stop Pontificating!

So, in his latest encyclical, Pope Paul denies birth control to Catholics all over the world. He pontificates about the "wide and easy road" we're all taking towards a lowering of morality, and how we need to find "authentic love." Sure, Pope Paul! Why don't you tell that to the thousands dying of hunger in Biafra? Or the innocent women and children in Vietnam--you know, the ones who are being butchered by 486,000 U.S. troops? Tell it to the black activists rotting in Ian Smith's jails. There's a lowering of morality all right, Pope Paul, and The Radical says that your monolithic structure is part of the problem!

Even leading Catholics are appalled by this latest stupidity from the Vatican. Conservative M.P. Norman St. John Stevas spoke out on Panorama last might. For a full report and for information about how to get the pill free on campus, see page three. We say, stop pontificating! Make Love, Not War.

7.

MY FATHER COPED WITH PORTENTOUS JOURNEYS BY INTENSIVE RITUAL cleansing of the Mini Countryman. My mother had bought him a lamb's wool polishing mitt for Christmas—one of those pre-arranged ungifts mothers and fathers buy each other after years of marriage. As he deployed various bottles and rags out on the pavement at the front of the house, my mother and I watched him from the living room window, as if he were the feature at the Sutton Odeon Cinema. The show ended with a prolonged and athletic performance by the star of the show: the mitt itself.

"All that time he spent on a box for it!" my mother said with a chuckle. "He made all these different compartments for his dusters and tins of polish, and then he painted it with that eggshell blue we had left over from the bathroom cabinet. I tell you Claire, men are all just little boys at heart. My own mother used to say that, God bless her. 'They're just little boys, Norah,' she used to say, 'treat them like children,' and you know she was dead right. Our Ida says the same. You'll learn that for yourself when you get married. Eeeh, pet. I can't wait to see you on the arm of some handsome student. The boys at Wallingford just weren't up to your level. There wasn't anyone there of interest to you. I just hope you find someone as hardworking as your dad."

My mother's role, when it came to momentous events, was to oversee the thrifty purchase of necessary food and equipment. On this occasion, my final departure to York University, she had packed the picnic basket with egg and cress sandwiches, gingersnaps, and a flask of tea. We'd pondered at length about what I needed to take, since the powers that be had not provided an equipment list. A brand-new suitcase, made out of very substantial cardboard, sat in the boot of the mini. New bath towels took up most of the space inside. I hadn't brought many clothes, since I couldn't afford them, and in any case, didn't know how students dressed. At my mother's insistence, I had brought along the tweed suit I had worn for all my university interviews, and one of the quilted floral housecoats she kept for her stays in hospital.

My mother's other role on these occasions was that of a one-woman Greek chorus who revealed, through unprompted monologue, those feelings the protagonists were trying so desperately to internalize. She maintained a steady and unwelcome commentary all the way down the A68.

"Well, who would believe that you're off to university instead of our Matthew like we always thought. I wish you'd been a bit nearer home. I hope you make some friends early on, pet. It would be awful to be lonely your first time away from home. It's a shame no one else from Wallingford School could come. Don't you wish Eleanor was coming too?"

Eleanor had changed her mind about going to college, and in any case, hadn't got good grades. None of the girls in my year were going, apart from Sandra Haddock, who had done every piece of homework ever set and never gone to a single party. Louise Robinson, who was two years below me, was thinking of applying, but I wasn't sure if she'd follow through. I knew the signs by now. Her face had lost its shine. Her flesh had somehow coarsened.

"No," I replied tetchily. "There's no one I'd really want to carry on a friendship with." There had to be something better than too many barley wines at the Dog and Gun, or the dismal rows of gangly youths lining the walls of the youth club disco. I wanted to live in the glossy world of Art and Books—the one I'd glimpsed in the *Sunday Times Magazine* and Emma Peel's apartment.

"But at least you would have known someone, even if it was just to eat with on the first night. I wouldn't like to think of you eating all on your own. Maybe you'll eat with your roommate. I hope she arrives soon. Though maybe you might not like her. Eeh, wouldn't that be awful, if she was dead stuck-up or something and you couldn't stand her! It doesn't bear thinking about does it?"

I had been trying hard not to think about it for the last couple of months. What if everyone had boyfriends except me?

"Our Ida had someone like that when she went to London—that's what started her migraines. She used to clip her toenails in the living room, Ida said, and just leave the bits on the rug. You'd have to say something if she did that, pet. Polite, you know. Say your parents brought you up to clear up after yourself."

Growing ever more tense listening to this gloomy litany, I ground my teeth and stared out of the window at the hedgerows of Yorkshire, playing an old game. I lined up marks on the windows with passing cars or pedestrians and pressed the door handle to blow them up. "KABOOM!" I muttered under my breath, and imagined them exploding in flame— articulated lorries, mothers with babies in prams. "KABOOM!" As far as I was concerned, we couldn't get there soon enough. I was dying to be gone. If I had to listen to my mother's well-intentioned monologues for one more day, I'd go nuts. One more episode of *Coronation Street,* one more kipper on Saturday and I'd scream. I couldn't believe that the government was giving me a grant to read books and write about them. I would stay up all night and read and my mother couldn't stop me.

As we finally inspected my clean, white room with its smell of industrial polish, I was in a fever of anxiety to have my parents gone before anybody saw them. I felt that I would be marked for life by my father's fake cheeriness as he examined the Baby Belling cooker on the landing, and by my mother's random solicitude. I imagined her telling anyone she met that I was born with a cleft palate and hadn't dated many boys.

I watched my father peering at the spotlights on the ceiling track. He seemed suddenly small and out of place. He was trying to work out what sort of bulbs they used, and I could tell that he was dying to get up on a chair and take one out. It would have made him feel more at ease. I knew my mother's pains must be bad from sitting in the car so long and then climbing all those stairs. She was peeking through the Venetian blinds at the chilly autumn rain streaking the glass, and the wind ruffling the feathers of the ducks that swam on the largest artificial lake in England. She turned around as I looked at her, wiping away a couple of tears.

"Eeeh, Claire," she said. "I can't believe time's passed so quickly. Our Matthew's engaged and now you're off your own too. It'll be quiet as the grave at home Paul, won't it?"

My dad looked down from the light fixture guiltily. "It will," he said earnestly. "It'll seem very quiet."

"She's worked very hard to get here, hasn't she? We're proud of her," she prompted, and he nodded several times, looking solemn.

"But at least we can picture where you are now and know what it's like. I'm going to imagine you at this little desk doing your studying with this view of the lake and the ducks. When we look at the ducks at Pond House they'll remind us of you."

"She doesn't look like a duck," said my father, "at least not very much." I punched him on the arm, and he went off into moans of pain. "Norah! Norah!" he said. "A huge bruise, look. She hit her poor defenseless old father what's got white hair. I think it's broken. Call the doctor."

"Oh Paul!" she said. "You can't be serious for a minute can you? And I've got to put up with his joking on all the way back home. Come on, let's get those cups rinsed out and leave her to unpack. She probably can't wait to get us out of here."

8.

I LEARNED QUICKLY THAT FIRST TERM. FIRST I LEARNED HOW MUCH I didn't know. I didn't know how to play the guitar. I had never heard of Simon and Garfunkel or Joni Mitchell. I had never lived in a city before and could only find my way around the winding streets of York by walking towards the towering gothic spires of the Minster. I had a northern accent so thick you could cut it with a knife, while everyone else had southern accents, and said lunch instead of dinner. My underpants came up to my waist and I called them knickers. I had never shaved my armpits. Robert Kennedy was dead by the time I'd even heard of him. The war in Vietnam was not a good thing. Communists were not bad people. It might be better to throw things at policemen, like they were doing in France and America, than to ask them for help when you were in trouble.

Someone showed me a graph once, which represented humanity's learning curve. It shot up at the very end, after we invented the printing press, the television, and the computer. Apparently, Mankind had learned pretty much everything in a few hundred years. Now I was learning everything in a few weeks, moving from reluctant Christianity through atheism and Maoism and on to anarchy, from tweed suits and a Cathy McGowan fringe to bell-bottoms and long hair with a center parting. "Everything went" at university, except for blind conservatism—for that we reserved the deepest scorn. Nothing was sacred except freedom. I hid my mother's floral housecoat deep in my wardrobe. How had I ever thought to wear it?

Everyone else doing English had read more than I. I had assumed that you had to be dead to be a great writer, but here we were, studying people who'd lived after Chaucer, Shakespeare, Milton, Donne, and Hardy. Apparently, some great writers were still alive, and some of them were not even British! There were actually courses in American literature, and even a visiting American professor with a real American accent. Dr. Blum could have dropped in from Mount Olympus, as far as I was concerned. I imagined her spooning ideas, instead of cornflakes, into her mouth every morning, and turning them out as poetry later in the day. She was the cleverest person I had ever met, with her sad, wise face, like a Capuchin monkey, her drooping, weighted shoulders. I lived for those moments in tutorials when something I said illuminated her. Long into the night, I tapped out essays on my Olivetti portable, trying to capture the exact feeling, the clear phrase, the one that would earn me a perfect A, and a judicious compliment in Dr. Blum's crabbed, exotic script.

I dared not speak in her seminar, intimidated by skinny girls who "loved Lawrence" and drank endless cups of instant coffee, by intense young men with long hair who hated the war in Vietnam and carried well-thumbed copies of Baudelaire. Every day I shuffled into "An Introduction to Literature" and hid at the back behind my army surplus haversack. I felt like one of the trolls in the Hall of the Mountain King—squat and inarticulate, but waiting to dance.

Geoffrey, who was possessed of John Lennon glasses and extreme opinions, dominated these seminars. "The *only* way to understand Electra is to produce or act it," he would say, angrily. "I'm sorry, but if you've never been involved in a live performance, even at an amateur level, you're not qualified to comment on the play."

I couldn't always follow his logic, but was too scared to admit it, until one day my mother's genes got the better of me. "This line is about alienation," he was saying. "As Marx points out, all literature is ultimately about that."

Funny, I had thought it was about death! But surely . . . ? My mouth opened.

"Isn't this line about death?" I said, right out loud. Every eye turned upon me, and Dr. Blum sat forward in her chair a little.

"Now, Claire, what gives you that idea?"

Damn! My nose started to sweat as I read the line again. Sod it! Now I had to try to get to the bottom of it.

"Well, I don't know really, but look, when he says 'Thy root is ever in its grave,' that's death, isn't it? I mean it's obvious. Anyone can see that." Geoffrey opened his mouth, but Dr. Blum held up a hand as I blundered on. "What I don't really get and nobody's said anything about is this next bit—'only the seasoned timber lives, the pure and virtuous soul'—that's a bit of a contradiction. Well, it's a great big contradiction actually. I mean 'root,' 'branch,' what's the difference? It's the same tree, isn't it? I couldn't understand that when I read it the first time."

Professor Blum leaned forward. "Oh couldn't you now? So did you make any sense of it the second time, or is the poet just guilty of loose imagery?"

"Um, I don't know. Well actually, no, I don't think so. He's looking at the body as different from the soul. The soul is the seasoned wood. It won't decay, right? So it's not a contradiction, is it? It's more like he's getting these images to do something they can't. They sort of push us further than the words can go."

She broke open one of those smiles I'd walk a million miles for, leaned back in her chair and surveyed the group. "We could start with that," she told us, "as a working definition of metaphysical poetry." Everyone except Geoffrey scribbled in their notebooks.

After the seminar, I headed back to my room in Langwith, hoping that my roommate wouldn't be in. She was a leggy blonde who wore headscarves like Princess Anne. Her half of our room was occupied by neatly arranged cosmetics jars and expensive History books, while mine was a sea of unwashed clothes and coffee cups, punctuated by the odd overflowing ashtray. When we were home together, she perched among a pack of teddy bears on her well-made bed, doing something despicable, like painting her nails pink or eating salad. While she maintained a stream of bright chatter, I'd lie in chaos, drinking chocolate milk straight from the bottle, or eating canned soup and minute rice from the pan. I read a library copy of *Big Sur,* propped open by dirty underpants, and grunted now and again.

I was sick and tired of listening to her ramble on about her bloody boyfriend, as if having one was all that mattered. It was like living with my mother.

"I saw you dancing with that grad student again," she'd said last night, her face all coy and confiding. "He seems nice."

I imagined tiptoeing up behind her, one of her own pink head scarves wrapped around my fingers. I would flick it quickly over her head, like in the films and push my knee against her back. "You had so much to live for," says the judge. "Before I sentence you, I must ask, for the sake of her family, why you did it." Her mother, an older leggy blonde in a purple jump suit, sobs into a lacy hanky. "The color of her nail polish," I say. "I am made insane by that particular shade of pink."

"You're Claire, right?"

Buried in fantasies of violence, I had not noticed that someone was keeping pace with me, trotting a little to catch up as I strode along the covered walkway. I stopped.

"Yeah," I said.

"I'm Linda. I liked what you said in the seminar. I'm sick of listening to Geoffrey."

I sized her up. My mother had warned me about people who would try to latch onto me, and I was already in hiding from Pat next door, who had buck teeth and kept inviting me to Christian Union cheese and wine parties. Linda hadn't seemed like that though, when I'd seen her around. She was always talking to people, the more interesting types, I'd noticed, the non-conformists. With her mane of bright red hair, her pale, delicate features and her intense blue eyes she could have been striking, was striking, really, but there was some apology in her demeanor. She was gently spoken, tentative, and her smile lurked inside that Elizabethan hair, her blue eyes swam behind thick glasses. When she smiled, as she did now, she seemed unprotected—not shy exactly, but like she expected to be hurt.

"I live upstairs from you," she said. "I've seen you coming out of your room. You share with that girl who wears the headscarves."

"Princess Anne," I said. "I really need to move out next term. I was just plotting her murder."

"Oh," she said. "Well I'm looking for some more people"—like it was the most obvious thing in the world. "We're going to rent a house in the country, or thinking about it anyway. It's cheaper with a lot of people. What do you think?"

"Sure," I said. "Who else have you got?"

"You'll know some of them," she said. "Ros Pearmain. She's in Modern Drama. You do that, right?"

"Is that the little Ros or the big Ros?" I said.

"Look, why don't you come and have coffee? Everyone's probably up there."

In Linda's room, "everyone" was clustered around a Byronic youth who sat on one of the beds wringing a tortured melody from a steel string guitar and didn't look up as Linda and I came in. His hair was losing a grammar school short back-and-sides haircut. An older boy, a man really, was playing a galloping rhythm on the bongos. He sat cross-legged, in a fringed leather waistcoat, with his back perfectly straight and his eyes closed in rapture. He had long blond hair and a Viking face. He looked like a character from *Lord of the Rings,* a dwarf prince perhaps. A few women shook packets of dried peas or clinked teaspoons against their coffee mugs.

Linda filled the kettle and fished two mugs out of a pile of dirty dishes.

"The one drumming is Sue's boyfriend," she whispered. "He was studying to be an architect, but he dropped out, so his parents disowned him. He makes leather clothes now and sells them at concerts. He just got back from Glastonbury."

We took our coffee and sat down. I noticed a short woman in a peasant blouse take a drag from a large cigarette. She held the smoke in her lungs and passed the cigarette to the next person.

"Is that a joint?" I whispered to Linda. She nodded. "Isn't it addictive?" I asked.

She shook her head. "It's actually safer than alcohol," she said. "We made Sue read up on it in the library." She pointed at the woman in the peasant blouse. "She's doing Biology. My father's an alcoholic," she added, "so I'm pretty careful about that kind of thing. Don't ever touch opiates, though—you know, heroin. They say you can take it once and be addicted. You need to know where dope comes from too. This stuff's OK. Peter grew it in his back garden."

When it came my way, I inhaled like I saw everyone else do. For a while, nothing happened, then I became aware of the music as it wound around the room, like ropes of different colors, I thought, wrapping around each other to make patterns. *Wow,* I thought.

I opened my eyes, exhaled and looked at Linda.

"Wow," I said. It was all I could manage, but she seemed to understand. She nodded, her eyes wide with the effort of holding in the smoke. They were an amazing blue, and I thought of all the names we have for blue—"cornflower," "aquamarine," "violet," though that was more of a purple, and what was purple, I thought, just blue mixed with red, its opposite. Wow, that was pretty significant, that when you mixed opposites, you got something new. I had never thought of that before. There was a name for it, though. I nodded in time to the music for a while, then came up with the answer—"synthesis."

It was a revelation. I needed to share it with someone, so I nudged Linda again. She seemed like a really open person. She turned the blue gaze on me and I struggled to stay focused on my revelation.

"Synthesis is when you mix opposites together." I paused, so she could make the synaptic leap involved in this concept. "You get something totally new, a third thing. It's more than the sum of its two parts. Like purple is more than blue and red."

She nodded slowly. "Wow."

"Hegel," I said. "Never really understood him till now."

"Amazing."

I looked at all the different blues in the room. I found five on a Mexican blanket pinned to the wall. Normally, I would just walk by that blanket and never stop to look at it properly, to count colors. It was like slowing time down, that march of seconds when I was a kid, being able to pick them up and really look at them. Living in the moment like Kerouac did, listening to each wave and how it broke. I looked more closely. One of the blues was an eggshell blue, exactly like the box my dad kept his car cleaning kit in.

I nudged Linda again. She had taken her glasses off and her eyes were still huge.

"See that blanket?" I nodded at it and she nodded back, solemn, waiting for another gestalt.

"My father," I said, "made a box in his garden shed and painted it exactly that eggshell blue color. Exactly."

The joint came around again and we each took another drag. I was lost in the music till I felt a nudge from Linda.

"Did your mother keep her jewels in it?"

I was amazed. What on earth was she talking about?

"In the box," she said, "in the eggshell blue box." The blue eyes were fixed upon me, trusting, waiting for a romantic story, my father a magician and my mother a queen.

I started to laugh, and she giggled, just watching me. "What?" she kept saying, and I couldn't wait to tell her, because I knew it would make her laugh too, and I hadn't enjoyed watching someone laugh so much since Louise Robinson.

"What?" she said and shook my arm. I was laughing so hard by now that tears were running down my face. The music stumbled to an end and everyone looked around for the joke.

I took a deep breath. "Once upon a time," I announced, "my father made a box."

Peter, the dwarf prince, set aside his bongos and gave me a huge gap-toothed smile. "Groovy," he said, "story time."

"He sawed the wood just so, and he hammered the nails in one by one, holding the hammer just right, so that the weight of the hammer did the work."

"He sounds like my father," said Sue.

"He was just like your father," I said. "He was just like everybody's father. When he'd finished making the box, he looked on his shelf for some paint, and he found some lovely eggshell blue that was left over from painting the bathroom. 'That will be just right,' he said."

"Gloss," someone said. "They use gloss in bathrooms because of the steam."

Peter held up one finger. "Condensation, the curse of modern civilization."

"But what was the box for?" asked Linda.

I dropped my voice. "Inside my father's eggshell blue box are many compartments."

"Amen," Peter intoned.

"There is a place for everything, and everything is in its place—all that a man could possibly need for the proper maintenance of a Mini Countryman: the polish—"

"What about the spit?" Sue asked. "Fathers need spit *and* polish."

"The spit was there too, in a little blue bottle with a label that said 'spit.' Next to that was an old but clean section of a pair of my dad's cotton y-front underpants. This is the best kind of cloth to apply polish with because it doesn't scratch the paint work."

"He'd need chrome cleaner," the guitar player suggested, "for the bumpers."

"And wood polish," Linda said. "Mini Countrymen have those wooden strips on the back."

"Why *do* they have those?" a gangly youth asked and we all thought about this for quite a long while, but no one came up with a reason.

"What else was in the box?" said Linda.

"Well," I said, "in pride of place, smack in the middle of the box in its own special compartment was my mother's latest Christmas present to my father . . ."

Peter began a big lead up on the bongos, imitating a drum roll.

" . . . in its own special compartment, ladies and gentleman, my mother's Christmas present to my father, costing one pound sixteen from Halford's, made of real lamb's wool and in no sense imitation—a beautiful, white, fluffy cleaning mitt."

"Hail the mitt!" Peter cried.

"Do they kill the lamb to get the wool?" It was the gangly youth again, but we ignored him.

Peter leapt into the middle of the circle.

"Hail the mitt!" he intoned. "For it is fluffy and white!"

We bowed our arms to the ground. "Hail the mitt!"

"Hail the mitt! For it shall polish away your sins!"

"Hail the mitt!"

"Hail the mitt!"

"Hail the mitt!"

9.

I BEGAN TO SPEND ALL MY SPARE TIME IN LINDA'S ROOM AND LEFT Princess Anne to polish her nails undisturbed. I didn't care when her boyfriend broke up with her. When I walked in and found her crying, I just picked up the copy of Wilkie Collins I'd been looking for and walked out again. Linda and I went to an estate agent and found a big farmhouse in the country that we could rent next term. The land around it was used for intensive pig farming, and the rent was really low, perhaps because no one except students would want to live surrounded by three thousand pigs. As Peter said, students escaping from dorms were already used to it.

Life was good, except for one thing. I wanted to have sex, or at least I wanted to want to have sex, for a number of reasons.

It was not cool to be a virgin at nineteen. Even Princess Anne had had sex.

Sex was something I thought I should like—dangerous and forbidden.

Sex dangled unplucked from The Tree of My Knowledge.

Sex was a prominent theme in English Literature, and to have it would surely expand my understanding of the great writers.

Sue and Linda and Ros and I talked about sex over joints and cheap red wine. We sat on the floor and watched candle wax spill into arches and buttresses as we constructed our own moral code, for though we were iconoclasts, we were rigorously principled. We didn't want to get married like our parents, whose lives were disastrous. Sue's parents were divorced. Ros's father had left home when she was fourteen. Linda's father was a vicious alcoholic, she told us. One time he'd woken them all at midnight and thrown them out of the house in their pajamas. Her mother had tapped on the door and pleaded with him though the letterbox so that the neighbors wouldn't hear. As for my parents, well, by now I had analyzed their psyches so precisely that I could have straightened them out in a second, if they weren't so well defended.

They had been brainwashed by the Church and the television. My mother was an unwitting slave. Her illness was displaced rage. My father was a pawn in the system he perpetuated. Maybe there was hope for them; my father was intelligent, after all, but I wasn't going to be like them. Romantic Love was a trap and sex was the bait. There was no happily ever after. The bourgeoisie was controlled through the family unit. We should drop acid into the water supply. Sex was revolution.

I embarked upon a series of controlled sex experiments, reporting back to the caucus after every encounter.

SEX EXPERIMENT #1

Name: Andrew.

Major: Philosophy.

Personal details: Pale, intense, disillusioned.

Appearance: Leather jacket and seven black polo necks rotating through the laundry room.

Influences: Sartre, Gide.

My rationale: "He looks intelligent and sensitive."

Sexual practices: We lie on his single bed together discussing identity, the nature of being, the tyranny of choice. He is incapable of making the first move.

My exit line: "I need to find passion."

Closure: He gazes palely at me from lonely chairs at the far end of dance floors.

SEX EXPERIMENT #2

Name: Dave.

Major: Music.

Personal details: Graduate student, thus single room. Pipe collection. Likes hiking. Healthy. Boring.

Appearance: Stocky, bearded, hairy jacket, leather elbow patches.

Influences: Segovia and Julian Bream.

My rationale: "Maybe he's mature and uncomplicated."

Sexual practices: Day one. Open wine. Listen to first side of Segovia record. Finish bottle. Turn record over. Kiss.

Day two. Open wine. Listen to first side of Julian Bream record. Finish bottle. Turn record over. Kiss. Stroke breasts. Take off bra. Stroke breasts again.

Day three. Open wine. Back to Segovia. Finish bottle. Turn record over. Kiss. Stroke breasts. Take off bra. Stroke breasts again. Touch genital area over trousers.

Day four. Wine. Julian Bream. Kiss. Roll together on floor. Belt buckles tangle together. Stagger around room joined together at pelvis, attempting to get free. Bump into furniture and fall over.

Exit line: I erupt into raucous unromantic laughter.

Closure: He doesn't call.

SEX EXPERIMENT #3

Name: Unknown.

Major: Gate crashed one of our dances.

Personal details: Nice laugh.

Appearance: Skinny.

Influences: Unknown.

My rationale: "What the heck!"

Sexual practices: His fingers in my vagina in the car after the disco—at last—a distinct throb!

Exit line: "Oh, you already have a girlfriend."

Closure: none.

SEX EXPERIMENT #4

Name: Luke.

Major: Mathematics and Philosophy.

Personal details: Also a technical virgin, quirky, talkative, mercurial, musical.

Appearance: Tall, bearded, Byronic, exotic. Given to wearing capes and caftans.

Influences: Any new trend, pop psychology, a superficial understanding of philosophy, the *Kama Sutra*, the Kinsey report.

My rationale: "Since I'm not really turned on by anybody, I may as well just experiment with Luke, since we are both desperate to lose our virginity and do not believe in romantic love. He is an interesting person, and I will feel OK about being seen with him in public. He likes to be friends with women, and is the sociable type, so I can still hang around with Linda as much as I like. Also, if I'm frank, I'm getting a little desperate. I mean, I'd need to have a reason not to sleep with him and I can't think of one."

Sexual practices: Well researched. Methodical. Due attention to foreplay. Disappointing, but hey, deflowered.

Exit Line: Wait and see.

10.

I COULDN'T WAIT TO GO HOME AT THE END OF THAT FIRST TERM. I would be just like Julie Andrews visiting the Von Trapps—a ray of sunshine in a gloomy mansion. Christmas shopping had achieved new significance. It wasn't just about buying gifts for my family this year; it was about sharing my enlightenment. They had no clue. No one could have told them that anything was possible. I felt the inevitability of their illumination.

I bought a copy of Lyall Watson's *Supernature* for Dad. This would provide him with scientific reasons for the inexplicable, and thus encourage him to give up Christianity eventually. He had never mentioned God in my hearing, not once, so I wondered if he even believed in Him. It seemed likely that he had fallen into an unproductive habit of church attendance. That would be easy to unpick. I would let him read the book, then have a long chat with him about God.

I bought my brother a kite making kit, which I felt would appeal to his kinesthetic nature. He'd be skeptical, but he wouldn't be able to resist taking it out of the box on Christmas Day to see how it worked! Once hooked, he might discover that the thrill of wrestling with a dragon kite far outweighed the pleasure of slaughtering furry animals with a twelve bore shotgun.

My mother was a challenge, since she had no exploitable talents other than housework and cooking. It was Luke who finally hit on the answer. "Sad," he said, shaking his head as I told him how her creativity remained untapped apart from the Women's Institute Dyed Easter Egg competition, which she usually won. "That's terrible. Someone should teach her how to paint or something." I found the perfect gift in Boots—*Painting for Beginners: All You Need to Paint like the Great Masters.* I knew she'd laugh at it at first, but hoped I could cajole her into trying. After all, look at how far the Von Trapp family went from a simple "do-re-me"! My mother would probably be slow and awkward at first. She'd left school at fourteen and lacked confidence, but she'd get there. For the first time, I started to think of her as someone who'd missed out. How come my dad had all the education? How come we'd always teased her?

Despite these purchases, and others, such as cards and the customary soap and talc set for Auntie Phyllis (whose reform I was deferring till her birthday) I still had twenty pounds left out of my grant money.

It was at this solvent moment that I glanced into the window of a shop devoted to ethnic products and noticed the waistcoat, on sale for sixteen pounds. It was made out of sheepskin, with the fur on the inside and the undyed skin on the outside. The fur leaked out in tangled skeins to form decorative fringes at the armholes and down the entire front opening, which was innocent of fastenings. The muted yellowy-brown of the hide was decorated with embroidery in tough orange thread. The woman in the shop said that it was made in Afghanistan. It was perfect—daring and wild. My visit home would be a triumph—the unveiling of the new me. What's more, I was betting that my mother would like it.

Sure enough, she broke into broad smiles as she opened the front door and hugged me, and sat me down in the kitchen until she had extracted every morsel of information about my appearance. She liked my bright orange jeans, and the Indian beadwork belt I had picked up in the Oxfam Shop for one and six. She loved the waistcoat, and made me listen to her say "Afghanistan" till she could do so without stumbling. She was scathing, however, of my white cotton granddad shirt ("like old Bob Cowley down the village wears") and insisted that we climb the laborious stairs to her bedroom. Rummaging slowly through her wardrobe, she finally located a black polo neck that she had never worn (high necks gave her claustrophobia), and I tried it on. With a set of orange wooden beads that Ida had brought her back from London last summer, the whole ensemble was declared a success.

"You look just like Sonny and Cher. Wear it to church on Sunday. I bet Mavis Brant-Jefferson'll ask where you bought it. Afghoanistar is it called, Claire? Tell her you went there with the university. Her eldest's been to France with his boarding school and she's never stopped talking about it."

That night she cooked fresh sole from Mr. Hansleman's in Sutton. I had to admit that it was good to see real food again after my Campbell's soup and instant rice diet. I dipped chips into Heinz ketchup and popped them into my mouth, chattering busily in between bites.

"Two weeks ago we had a forty-eight hour fast for the Third World."

I glanced at my father, who was busy removing the bones and skin from his sole, but it was my mother who answered.

"Well, you don't look starved, at any rate. You've put on weight if anything. Now what about your hair pet? Are you going to book yourself in for a trim while you're here? How about a perm?"

"No. I'm letting it grow. Did you know Dad, that we spend about twenty times as much on defense as we do foreign aid?"

He looked up mildly, "No," he said. "I didn't know that."

I warmed to my theme. "Well, no one seems to know that, and if they did, and everyone took some notice about what the government was up to, things might be different. *You* don't think that's right, do you? I mean, God doesn't approve of war, does he?"

My father looked uncomfortable. "Well, you have to have proper defenses, Claire. As far as I can tell, these left-wingers want to get rid of the lot."

My brother, who was getting married next month and thus an authority on everything, looked up from his plate. "They'd get rid of everything if they could, even traditional sports like fox-hunting and pheasant shoots. Lunatic fringe."

"And what's so lunatic about that, Matthew? What's right about a whole lot of men with guns shooting defenseless birds and making a sport out of chasing one little animal to its death?"

Matthew pushed away his empty plate, drew out his pipe from its leather wallet and began to load it carefully with tobacco. He looked more and more like Dad these days, with his crinkly brown hair and his slate blue eyes, behind which moods passed like the weather. Right now, he looked amused. I felt my hackles rise. Arrogant bastard! He'd only been to teachers training college, and here he was thinking he could laugh at me! Killing was wrong! It was one of the few truths that were considered self-evident by the major philosophers!

"Two questions then, our Claire. Number one, have you ever seen a henhouse after a fox has been in there?"

"No, but that's not the point, the point is—"

"Hang on. I haven't asked you the other question yet. Do you know what would happen to the English pheasant if it wasn't hand reared on English country estates?"

"No I don't, but I'm sure you're going to tell me."

"Well, I know how you university students are keen to extend your knowledge is all. So point number one, the fox is a remorseless killer. It's one of the few animals that kills for fun and it can wipe out an entire flock of hens in an hour. Point number two, if pheasants weren't hand reared in England and protected by laws regulating hunting, they'd be extinct. I've got the figures upstairs if you want to see them. The trouble with all these left wing protest groups is that everything's based on emotion, and not fact."

Having carefully filled and tamped down his pipe, Matthew retired to his armchair to light it and watch the six o'clock news, while Mam and I cleared the table. As usual, she washed and I dried.

"Have you thought about what you're going to wear for the wedding?"

"No," I said, drearily. I didn't want to wear a skirt. I didn't want to wear a hat. I didn't want to wear little gloves in pastel colors. I didn't believe in romantic love. I didn't believe in marriage. I didn't want to drive 300 miles with my parents and stay in the Snow White Guesthouse and go to the wedding and to some hotel reception and make polite conversation and have everyone ask when I was going to get married, and was there a young man in my life yet?

"That little yellow milk jug doesn't go there. It goes in that kitchen cupboard on the second shelf next to the glasses our Ida brought me back from Spain. Have you seen anything more of that boy we met in your room?"

"Which boy?"

"That tall one with the great beard. He was wearing that blue nightie thing."

Sex experiment #4 had been putting up a lampshade for me when my parents came to pick me up at the end of term, and my mother had been hideously coy. He was wearing a blue Arab kaftan with white embroidery, and had employed his best public school manners. ("How do you do Mrs. Robson. Nice to meet you. Claire's told me so much about you.")

"What do his parents do?"

"Luke's? Oh. His mother doesn't work, except for meals-on-wheels and things. His father's well-off. They manufacture silk stuff—ties and things—and sell them. I think Marks and Spencers carry some of their stuff. Anyway, they're filthy rich, two cars and a big house and everything. Luke even has a car of his own."

"And have you met his parents yet?"

How could I begin to explain? Our eyes were opened to all the old lies and hypocrisy. His parents had nothing to do with it. Money had nothing to do with it. I took refuge in short-temperedness. "He's just a friend, Mam. There's no need to get interested. Anyway, I thought you didn't approve of men with long hair and beards."

"Well they all seem to have that these days, and he was very well-spoken."

It was with relief that I left in the family car to meet with my old school friends in Wallingford.

Nothing had changed at the Dog and Gun. My afghan waistcoat and I were greeted with restrained amusement by the women, and a more vocal form of it by the men.

"What're you drinking Claire? I see, a half for you. And what about your dog? What's he want?"

"Jesus Claire, you've got some funny hairy animal climbing up your back trying to nibble your neck. Let me give the bugger a swift karate chop."

"Where's the woad?"

"Did you kill that thing yourself?"

As ever, I pretended to join in the fun, and when one of the wits asked to try my waistcoat on, I handed it over without protest and found Eleanor at our old table, dying to bring me up to date. Sandra had dropped out of secretarial school and was working for the *Weardale Clarion*. Louise Robinson was engaged to a builder. Jean Anderson's sister, Moggie, was pregnant at fourteen. They had a new drama teacher at

Wallingford School who wore tights and let the sixth form call him by his first name, Richard. His nickname was Big Dickie.

Eleanor had dressed up for the occasion in a skirt and blazer. She'd acquired some gold jewelry and her makeup was more carefully applied. I suddenly thought that if I saw her on the street without recognizing her, I'd dismiss her as bourgeois and conformist. I remembered how we'd stolen the netball posts at the end of the fifth year and set them out on the stage, causing havoc at the final assembly.

"So what are you doing for work then?" I asked her, leaning towards her across the width of the puddled table.

"Mind your sweater in all that muck," she said, hitching her skirt out from under her so that it wouldn't crease. "That's a nice polo neck by the way."

"It's me mam's," I told her. "Answer the question, damn it."

She gave me a hard look. "Still a pushy little bugger then, are we?"

She nudged a cigarette half out of the packet and held it out towards me. I took it, even though I rolled my own these days.

"I'm a cashier at Barclay's Bank," she said.

"Oh," I said. "Great!" But hadn't I read something about Barclay's in *Peace News* recently?

Eleanor fished a shiny little lighter out of her handbag and ignited my Embassy filter. "It's alright," she said. "Actually, it's bloody boring, but it pays OK and at least there's some opportunities. They have this management-training program thingy. Don't know if I'll get into it though."

"Of course you will! Why the hell wouldn't you? That's great!" I said again automatically, still trying to remember that article I'd read. I had an awful feeling that Barclay's might be investing a stack of money in South Africa.

"Oh fuck off," Eleanor said, companiably, blowing smoke in my direction and downing the last of her gin and tonic.

"What?" I said, indignantly.

"You'd bloody hate it," she said. "It's mind numbing. Don't pretend with me, chuck. Don't come your polite university student mixing with the common people." She gave me an old-fashioned look.

"Well, all right," I said, reaching for her cigarettes and taking out another. "Why d'you do it if it's boring?"

She shrugged. "It's a job. It pays. There's not much around up here you know, Claire. There's forty percent unemployment. I need money, funnily enough. You know, all that necessary but boring stuff like rent, food, fags, gin and tonics."

"Speaking of which," I said. I downed the rest of my pint, and held up the empty glass invitingly. I'd never sell out to the system I vowed, as I headed for the bar. Never. You'd never catch me in a navy blue suit working for a racist corporation. I'd scrub floors first. But I wasn't going to tell her that.

"So what's university like then?" Eleanor asked me, when I brought our drinks back to the table.

"Well . . . it's great actually. It's incredible being away from home and independent. You know—not having your parents breathing down your neck."

"How do you get your washing done?"

"There's coin-in-the-slot machines in the basement of our hall of residence."

She put on a Queen Elizabeth accent. "Hall of residence! Hall of residence!"

I flushed, "That's just what they call them. They're only dorms. They're not posh."

"I bet all the students are posh though. I bet they talk posh—about music and all that. What d'you do all day? Read books and do homework like at school? I couldn't wait to get away from all that."

"Well yeah, we do have to work pretty hard. I read a lot, and I go to lectures and seminars and tutorials and write essays."

She sighed, and sipped her gin and tonic, raised her eyebrows at me from the glass. "You always were brainy, though Claire, weren't you? You actually liked all that stuff."

"I was no brainier than you, Eleanor, when you bothered. But anyway, it's not like school. We've got total freedom to do what we like, and we think for ourselves. Maybe we'll change some things about the world."

I was warming to my theme, about to break into the do-re-mi of Marxist theory and illuminate her.

She gave me a funny look, sad, and almost maternal. "And how's a bunch of students going to change the world exactly?"

"Well, for one thing, there's a lot of demonstrations in London that we can go to."

She stared at me as though I'd sprouted a second head. "Demonstrations! Jesus! You're never going to them! You're never walking along with one of them banners shouting all those slogans!"

"Why the hell not, Eleanor? If everyone got up and said what they thought, the government wouldn't get away with so much. Did you know we spend about twenty times as much on defense as we do on foreign aid?"

She stared at me for a couple of beats then cackled like a fishwife. "You sound like a communist! Hey everybody, Claire's come back a commie."

Len Dawson and Ian Fletcher wandered over from the bar to listen.

Eleanor was hamming it up by now. "Do you call each other 'brother' the whole time? Can I come to one? D'you want to come with me Ian?" She took hold of Ian's hand and he put his hand on her head affectionately, protectively, I noticed, turning his big grown-up man's face towards me, smiling his slow smile. I'd spent seven years in school with him, and we'd hardly ever spoken, I realized.

Eleanor was smiling up at him and, absurdly, I remembered how she and I had once stood with some other girls in an empty car park outside Durham University. There had been eight or nine of us that night, the girls without dates, all dressed up and nowhere to go. We'd come out of the pub at ten o'clock to try and wangle our way in to the student disco. Sometimes the boys on the door looked the other way and let you in if someone flirted with them. We huddled together, giggling, and everyone nudged everyone else towards the door ("You go, Sandra" "I'm not going, you go!"). Eleanor and I stood side-by-side, hands stuffed in the pockets of our mod leather jackets. I rolled my eyes at her and yawned, wanting to get back to the pub, wanting to tell mucky jokes and shriek with laughter. A girl called Moira, who had started the whole thing, was getting ready to approach the door, undoing a button on her blouse as her friends pushed her from behind. Ten minutes later she came back with a fat, bleary looking youth in a rugby shirt. A beer can dangled from the end of one meaty arm, and the other hung like a trophy across Moira's shoulders.

"This is Roger," said Moira. "He's captain of the rugby team."

He gave her a squeeze, and she slapped his hand. "Oy," she said. "Behave yourself."

"Any of you lovely girls under sixteen?" he asked. His eyes had the vague unfocused look of the deeply drunk. He might as well have been talking to the solitary Ford Fiesta parked ten feet away. No one spoke. "OK," he said. "Any of you got more than four O levels?" His skin was flushed and he had long blond eyelashes, like one of George's baby pigs. His fingers were like pork sausages. I had nine O levels and five distinctions.

Rosalind Crisop stuck her hand up helpfully. "I've got six," she said. Moira sighed and jerked her thumb in dismissal. "They don't want bookworms, Ros," she said.

As Ros walked off, Roger waved his hand in a gesture of advance to some other boys who'd been watching from the steps. "All right," he said. "Don't say Uncle Roger never gives you anything when you win a game."

They circled us, like Indians about to attack a wagon train. I didn't know what was happening until one of them stepped forward and tapped the girl next to me on the shoulder and took her off to the disco. The rest, who had been looking us up and down judiciously, jumped into action at that, to grab a girl before the more attractive of us got picked. There were only three of us left when a skinny youth with glasses glanced at Eleanor and the other girl then back at me. He took me by the arm.

"Hey," he said, as I started to move away. "Not so fast. I'll take you in. You're not bad looking, just a little on the thin side, but I don't mind."

I twitched my arm out of his grasp, and he staggered a bit. "Hey," he said again, aggrieved. "What's wrong with *you* then?"

"Sorry," I said. "I'm overqualified." I hadn't looked back at Eleanor as I walked off after Ros to the pub. I'd known she'd take the leavings of the rugby club ahead of me, even if he had rejected her already, ahead of time.

She was still talking about the demonstrations.

"I'd love to see all those people and the TV cameras. If me and Ian come and stay with you for a weekend could we go on one?"

"Well, it would depend what was happening," I said cautiously. "It's mainly about apartheid at the moment." *You know,* I thought of saying, *racist bastards like Barclay's Bank, like the South African rugby team and the British who still play them,* but it wasn't her fault that being chosen was as bad as not being chosen. It wasn't her fault that I hadn't liked the rules of the game. "Why don't you come and stay for a weekend anyway?" I offered. "We could at least go to a couple of meetings so you could see what it was all about."

She glanced up at Ian. "Meetings? Well we'd have to think about that wouldn't we Ian? Maybe. I'll give you a ring perhaps. Hey! What's that funny smell?"

It was my waistcoat. Someone had hung it on a chair near the fire, and the fur was scorched and stinking. I beat and pulled at it frantically. One of the boys contritely loaned me his penknife to cut away the worst parts. People tried to be kind.

"The marks won't show when you wear it. The outside is fine."

"It's really nice Claire. Where did you get it, London? It's so unusual."

"You bloody great spastic, Merve! Fancy sticking it on a chair right next to the fire."

As I drove home to the smell of scorched fur, like a dog on whom some cruel practical joke has been played by naughty boys, I decided not to go to the reunion dance at Wallingford School next week after all. When I got in, I stayed up late writing a long philosophical letter to Luke.

11.

PLEADING ESSAYS DUE AND BOOKS UNREAD, I TOOK THE BUS BACK DOWN to Yorkshire a little earlier than I had planned, arriving at the pig farm with a bag of my mother's gingersnaps, lots of her admonitions ("don't work too hard," "phone home once a week," "eat vegetables," "wear slippers") and considerable disillusion about the imminence of the people's revolution.

I came home to the Grateful Dead and the Incredible String Band, to philosophy and afghan waistcoats. I was a changeling lucky enough to have found a tribe—Linda, Sue, Peter, Big Ros and Little Ros, and finally, Luke, finally, a man of my very own, someone tall and decent enough looking to stand next to in photographs. "He's nothing to write home about," people sometimes say of their lovers, but though I didn't write home often these days, Luke was, finally, someone I could've written home about if I had wanted to. He had a rich father and a six-year-old Ford Anglia. He was musical and cultured. He was passionate about ideas, and could talk all night about Kant and Descartes, free will and capital punishment, nihilism and anarchy.

How happily we explored our shiny new world! We lived like characters from the great books I curled up with in the big Draylon armchair. Like Jack Kerouak, like Gatsby, we created ourselves as we went along, a raggle-taggle of gypsies in old army overcoats and bell-bottoms, straggling through the fields that surrounded our granite farmhouse in search of firewood, which we dragged home and stacked in the living room. Ignorant and innocent, we acted as if the world belonged to us, as though we would ever have taken the time to hang the regency wallpaper we damaged so casually with half-rotten firewood, or would have known how to hang it straight, or smooth the seams. We broke logs against the massive tiled hearth and piled them against the sooty fire back, like the logs were tradition and we were burning it, like chimney fires could never happen, like the house didn't really belong to the poor divorcee who paid the rates and the mortgage even as we sat around the flames like hunter gatherers, smoking Lebanese gold, chanting and playing the drums, dancing to the tortured music of Luke's guitar. Impelled by the rhythm, fortified by poorly digested scraps of Lao Tzu, we got up to dance, regardless of the coffee we knocked over onto the shag carpet. We sopped it up carelessly, or let it sit there as it would; later was time enough. We were committed to the moment.

Everything was easy and beautiful if you looked at it right. If someone was angry, we walked down the other side of the street, sorry and amused at their loss of cool. We avoided newspapers and television. They were full of lies, and we knew all the stuff we needed. We spent our government grants on books, dope, acid, jug wine, and cheap food from the supermarket—variegated cheese scraps bundled roughly together, white cabbage and bacon ends, dented tins of tomatoes from the bargain bin. Everything was beautiful, the stars and the sunsets, the mold that someone discovered at the back of the fridge, the cows in the fields that kicked their giddy heels up in the air and fled as we ranged through the Yorkshire woods decked in daisy chains, necklaces made of melon seeds and tie-dye T-shirts whose colors stained the bath tub forever—an eternal reminder of the rainbow generation.

We were the chosen children, the ones born to set the world to rights with our visions of peace and love. Solicitous in small ways, we were careless over the long haul. For example, we rushed with teaspoons to rescue the earwigs and wood lice that stumbled from the moldy branches of our fire, but I avoided my mother's phone calls, answering the bedside phone only by mistake one morning, thinking it was someone else, my heart sinking at the sound of her voice, plaintive and a little querulous, "Eeh, Claire! There you are! Your dad and I were getting worried. We haven't heard from you in so long."

If only she knew! What would she say if she knew?—that I had sprawled naked across the floor to seize the phone, that Luke, still in bed, was naked too, that he had pulled back the covers to show me his erection. I turned my head away so that I wouldn't giggle.

"Oh. Sorry. I've been working on an essay. It's due in tomorrow. They keep us pretty busy you know."

"Well, we've rung at least five times. We thought you might have had an accident."

"If I'd had an accident, you and Dad would be the first to know."

"Well, anyway. You're sure you're all right?"

"I'm fine. Absolutely fine, just working hard. How are you?"

A pause, then a little stiffly, "Oh, soldiering on. Can't complain."

"Pains bad?"

A slight softening. "Well, they always are this time of year. It's the damp."

"How's Dad?

A chuckle. "Oh, you know your dad. He never ails a thing. He's up at the garage tinkering on with his car. We're off to have dinner with Matthew and Andrea tomorrow. They want to show us their new fireplace."

"That'll be nice then."

"Our Matthew built it himself you know, with his friend from Stanhope."

I felt a tug at my foot. "Well that's great. Look, I've got to go in a couple of minutes. I'm off to a lecture."

"Oh! Yes! Don't be late! Just before you go, though, I want to tell you. We were driving through the village yesterday. I ran out of baking soda, and your dad wanted a tool from Halford's, so we decided to run through to Sutton. Well, who should we see but Mrs. Wilkie. She was out swilling her path, so I told your dad to stop. She gave me all the village gossip. I always get all the gossip from her you know."

"Yes, I know." Luke put his hand around my ankle and tugged. I grabbed the telephone table and hung on.

"Well, I told her all about how you and your friends were renting the house, and how well you were doing at your studies, and how you'd got yourself a nice young man, and she said she always knew you were brainy. 'Your Claire will go far, Mrs. Robson,' she said. 'Please tell her that Becky Wilkie sends her best regards.' She was most emphatic."

I braced myself against the mattress with my other foot, but I was losing the battle. "Give her mine back when you see her. Tell her I'll come and see her when I'm home for the holidays. No, I don't know when yet.

Luke and I might go camping. Yes of course we've got two tents. Look, Mam, I've really got to go. Yes . . . I will . . . I'll try and call you next week . . . Yes I promise . . . Cross my heart and hope to die . . . Yes, well maybe Tuesday . . . I'll have to see. Anyway, look I'm going to be late . . . Oh you did? That's nice . . . OK, I'll call next week. All right. Yes. Yes. Bye."

If only she knew, I thought, as I dropped the phone and Luke dragged me into bed. He rolled on top of me and probed with his penis. I reached down and separated the folds of my labia, so they wouldn't get dragged inside. If only she knew that I was researching sex as well as Renaissance poetry. Our current topic was the female orgasm. Luke was bothered that I wasn't having them.

It was not unpleasant, I reflected, as Luke started to bounce up and down, to have his prick inside me. "Unpleasant" was definitely not the word I'd use. If pushed, I would have to say that it was quite nice to have something sliding up and down in there. Apart from anything else, it meant I'd made it. I was an adult.

Luke's eyes were clamped shut, and I studied his face for a while, and beyond it his buttocks as they rose and fell. Yes, I could definitely put this in the category of pleasurable sensations. The alarm clock next to our mattress said it was almost eight o'clock. I had a tutorial with Dr. Blum at nine. I wondered what she'd thought of my essay on Milton. I didn't show my essays to Luke any more because he'd become jealous of my grades. He said English was easier than Math and Philosophy. He said Dr. Blum wasn't objective. He said no one cared about Milton, who was just a dead Puritan after all.

I loved Milton. I couldn't help myself. It was the audacity of his language, those massive metaphors, like chunks of meat. Look at that description of Satan, carrying his huge spear and shield across that flaming wasteland, rallying his troops—"Awake, arise or be for ever fallen!"

Luke was just dying to come, I could tell by the way he'd shut his eyes again, and was biting his lips. I wished he'd just get on with it, but he opened his eyes for a quick look, no doubt to assess my progress towards the mighty O. He took hold of one of my nipples and squeezed it. I was lucky, I knew. The Kinsey report said that some men didn't care whether or not their partners had orgasms. They didn't bother with foreplay. Luke wasn't like that. He was probably thinking about mathematical formula, which he said was a way to prevent premature ejaculation. He was trying so hard to make me come that his sweaty belly made suction noises against mine every now and again, like loud farting. I tried out some Miltonic comparisons, then caught myself at it, and tried to concentrate.

How would I know if I had an orgasm or not, I wondered? How did one try to have one? According to the literature, the walls of my vagina would clench in a series of rippling spasms. The spasm theory seemed validated by all those heroines I'd watched on TV as they writhed under assorted heroes. There seemed to be some initial groaning which increased in intensity until it became an uncontrolled outburst of full scale moaning. This could well be caused by some sort of spasm.

I concentrated on the walls of my vagina and realized that the pleasurable sensation I had noted earlier had given way to a dull, scraping sensation some time ago, perhaps when I had been thinking about Milton. If anything, my vagina felt bored. As I thought about this a little, I realized that the bored feeling was not limited to my vagina. The truth was that my entire being was sick of lying on its back having its vagina scraped. I wished Luke *were* one of those men who just wanted a quick fuck.

What was wrong with me?

I tried to get engaged. Maybe if I acted like I enjoyed it, I would enjoy it, like my mother said about smiling. "Oh," I cried, like an actress, and moved my hips around a little. It must be well after eight o'clock now. If we got this over with, I could grab a coffee and reread that section I'd been thinking about. "Oh," I cried again, and dug my nails in Luke's back. He pumped harder. I knew he wouldn't hold out for long. Sure enough, as I writhed and moaned a little more, he gave a long, groaning shudder and collapsed. I felt his prick shrink, as though it was twisting away from my stubborn vagina, and its reluctant walls. As he rolled off me, I felt sticky sperm smear my thighs, tickling as it cooled and dried. It reminded me of the wallpaper paste my dad used to mix up from packets of powder.

"Anything?" asked Luke as he wiped himself off. His face looked vulnerable without his glasses. I found myself wishing he'd chuck the used toilet paper in the waste paper basket instead of just letting it drop beside the mattress.

I shook my head. "It was nice though."

"Are you sure you didn't have one? You were moving like you were going to."

"I think you're meant to be able to tell when you have one," I said. "I think I would have noticed."

His face fell and I sighed and took his hand. "It was nice though. It'll just take a while. It said in that book that it might take a while."

He nodded. "Are you going in?"

"Yes. I've got a nine o'clock with Dr. Blum. Then Linda and I are going to have lunch and go shopping for tonight. It's Peter's birthday, remember?"

. . .

Linda and I went to our favorite café for lunch that day, before we went shopping. We'd started going there because it had great coffee, and a table in the corner where we could chat for hours without anyone hassling us. By now we had grown to love the plastic palm trees and the fake yucca plants.

I confessed my lukewarm feelings for Luke. "I don't know what it is," I told her. "It's freaky. I mean he's really perfect in a lot of ways. He's not, like, possessive. He really gives me the space to do my own thing, and he's creative, switched on. You've *heard* Luke on the guitar, and he's really interested in stuff, like plants and astronomy. Most men are really boring."

"So what's the problem?"

"Well there isn't a problem exactly. It's just that, I don't know, he's started to feel two-dimensional. And I'm noticing some of the little things he does more than I used to. Like, well, here's an example—he always knocks his teacup over, right? You know how we joke about that? I used to think it was his boots, and then I realized, that actually, he's just *clumsy*. He breaks things all the time. He doesn't seem to care. I used to think it was funny too, at first, but I've started picking things up off the floor when he's around, to keep them out of his way. I feel like my *mother*. Don't tell me that's normal."

"You're asking me for relationship advice?" she asked, as Hilda, our favorite waitress, set down the coffee. "I don't have a clue about boyfriends. You're the one with experience."

"Oh come off it," I said. "He's my first boyfriend for God's sake."

"Well, I expect those little things always exist between people," she said. "Everyone's got annoying habits."

"You're right," I said. "I suppose I just need to be a little less uptight."

"How's the sex life?" she asked. I slid a packet of sugar into my cup, where it piled up in a shiny brown heap, till it made a hole in the foam and sank. She looked at me over her glasses. "Well you are having a sex life, aren't you? Don't tell me you just hold hands on that king size mattress." I stirred carefully, trying to keep the foam intact.

"Yes, of course we are," I said.

"So is it OK? That side of things?" We both watched my spoon stirring the coffee.

"Oh yes," I said. "Fantastic. Far out. It takes awhile to get used to it, though. You know."

"I don't know, actually," she said. "I've never, you know, done it. I used to hear my parents at night through the wall. He was pretty horrible when he was drunk. It's sort of made me a bit wary."

"God," I said. "That's terrible."

"Yeah," she said. "I've got some real hang ups to work through around my dad."

I didn't tell her that this was Luke's theory about her—that she was hung up because of her alcoholic father. "Linda's repressed," he'd said one night, while I had been wondering aloud if she'd get a boyfriend soon. "Hence the thick glasses and all the hair. She could be good looking if she did something about herself."

"Well," I said, "to tell the truth, I don't think sex is that much of a big deal. I think they make all that stuff up about love and romance to keep women enslaved. Engels says that nuclear family stuff is all a myth."

Linda and I had started to go to Women's Liberation meetings every week. We had demanded that the men take turns cooking the bacon and cabbage and doing the washing up. "To be honest," I said, "I feel closer to you than I do Luke."

She didn't like to smile too widely, because her front teeth were crooked, but she did now, and dipped her head so that her hair fell forward. "No you do not," she said.

"I do," I said. "Honestly. Think about it. Think about just today for example. I'm spending more time with you. We talk about more important stuff, share secrets and stuff. We share Women's Lib. I've always felt really close with my friends, my women friends I mean."

"But, let's face it," she said. "We're good friends. Women can be good friends, but the bottom line is that they sleep with men. You sleep with Luke. I don't sleep with anybody."

I went back to looking at the remnants of froth crusting my empty mug.

"Claire?" I looked up to find that she was staring at me, hard. "God!" she said, exasperated. Her eyes were a little hard to take. They sort of blurred at the edges and focused at the same time, like searchlights in fog. I looked away. "It's so easy to make you feel guilty. You're so bloody arrogant that you think it's all your fault. I choose not to sleep with anyone right now. You have a boyfriend. That's normal. It's about me. Not you. Not everything is about you."

I felt uncomfortable, like I'd been caught out somehow.

"Sorry," I said.

She laughed. "Sorry? For what?"

I tried out a little smile. "Um, pass. I don't know."

"You're a nice person," she said, giving me the full grin, head up, without the hair. "Arrogant but nice. Your blind spots make you all the more endearing. Come on; let's buy the wine. It's almost four o'clock."

12.

WE BOUGHT TOO MUCH WINE, AS THINGS TURNED OUT IN THE SHORT term, or just enough, as they turned out in the long term. After all, it's just a question of perspective.

At any rate, by midnight we were all stoned, drunk, and trying to have an orgy on the floor. I remember thinking that it was funny, more than anything, all the male bottoms bouncing up and down, and their faces so serious. Sue was trying to give Peter a blow job as a birthday present, which I vaguely remembered was how the whole thing had started in the first place, but he was too drunk and giggly to get it on. She kept pulling her head back to frown at his prick as it flopped in her hand.

"Come *on,*" she told it. "It's your *birthday* present," and off Peter went into peals of manic laughter all over again.

Someone was banging up and down next to me, his hipbones dangerously close to my head, and as I began a surreptitious clamber towards the door I came across another pair of naked hairy buttocks—Luke's, I realized as I circumvented his legs. As I rounded the female feet that protruded from underneath them (they jiggled slightly on his offbeat I noticed), I came face to face with Linda. She was lying as if at a picnic, propped on her elbows with her chin on the flat of her fists. I stopped when our noses almost touched.

"Good evening," I said.

"Good evening," she said.

I got caught in the searchlight gaze.

It was like when you let yourself into a swimming pool without using the steps. At first it's a little awkward. You have to go in backwards, hold yourself up on your arms to keep your knees off that rough concrete lip, and there's a moment where you're not held up by the water yet, so your arms can't support you and you slip a little faster than you wanted. Amphibians must deal with it all the time, I guess, half in half out, always a sense of shock at a new medium. Then you're in, with a cold shock, and the water's supporting you, but you're still facing the ledge and hanging on, till you turn around. When you turn around, you don't really plan all the complex movements, the tucking up of the knees, the planting of the feet flat against the pool. The twist of your body feels natural as you drive away from the ledge, and the water is all you around you, just water, nothing sharp or rough, and you realize that it's not difficult.

It was just like that, our first kiss—no edges, and her blue eyes, like Linda was a big swimming pool and I was pushing away from the rough gray concrete to float in her and lose all sense of what was up and what was down.

If I were making a movie about it, I'd blur all the heaving bodies in the background and fade out the sound till it was just a chaotic murmur. It was like some sleepwalk scene, or maybe more like a dream, with me in slow motion, realizing that what we had done was kiss, and now she was gone. I knew that I needed to find her, and even somehow that she was waiting for me, and I walked through the dark silence of the big house, up the stairs, until there she was, exactly where I knew she would be waiting, without impatience, in the right place. She always had a capacity for that.

I must have known that women could make love—I'd seen a couple of films where it was hinted at—but I didn't know it was an *option*. I didn't know it with my body, how all those nerve endings would fire up as Linda and I lay side by side and read each other with our fingertips, like Braille. "So this is what they meant!" I said aloud, meaning how bells were ringing and whistles blowing and the fireworks display had started all through my body. So this was what the movies and the books had talked about! This is why Eve nibbled the apple and Satan fell! It hadn't been a lie after all. As certainly as if I were inside her skin, I knew how Linda felt as I traced the slope of her breasts, the curve of her buttocks.

Her white skin was marbled with blue veins. I kissed the one that pulsed in her neck, and put my head between her breasts so that I could listen to the engine that drove her. I swore that I would never forget that moment when she, inside her own skin, on the outside, affected me inside mine, and I listened to her heartbeat quicken as I slid my fingers home into the nest of her dazzling orange pubic hair.

"Wow," she said.

"Wow," I said, as we wrapped our bodies together and I felt the heat of her against my thigh.

We came at the same instant, and I expected we'd die from it, like the Elizabethans said. I would have been truly happy to do that. When I realized that we were still alive, I thought that at least the ceiling must have given way, and we'd be covered in chunks of plaster.

"We're still alive," I said.

"Barely."

I smoothed the hair back from her forehead. "It tickles," I said.

"I'll get a crew cut."

"Don't. I love your hair."

"So what does that mean?"

"What do you mean, mean?"

"Does that mean I'm not a virgin anymore?"

"I don't know what it means. I feel like I'm not a virgin anymore either."

"Do you want some tangerine?"

The light from her bedside candle flickered on her hands as she pulled the soft skin from the meat. I saw everything—how juice sprayed in tiny eruptions from beneath her nails as she separated the sections, how carefully she peeled off the white pith from each segment before she handed it to me, how she used the deep orange skin, which she had removed in one piece, as a bowl for the pips. I am ashamed to say that I saw everything and I still said, "Let's go back downstairs."

. . .

Peter looked up from rolling a joint and grinned as we came in, holding hands. "The girls look happy," he said, and patted the floor next to him for us to sit down, "Cool." Luke scooted over and sat next to us.

"I'm not jealous," he said. He'd had a shower since the orgy and put on his Arab kaftan, dabbed himself with patchouli. I could tell he was pleased with himself, presumably with his sexual performance, and now with his generosity. "I think that the more we *make* love, then the more love there is to go around."

"That's so beautiful," said little Ros. She was sitting in front of the fire, letting her long hair hang in front of her face to dry. She gave me a big smile. Luke must have given her an orgasm. I wondered how her boyfriend at Leeds would feel about that.

Peter took Luke's hand and put it in mine, closed his big hands over ours and imprisoned them there. I felt trapped, foolish.

"You guys," Peter said, giving our hands a little shake. "You're such a trip. Luke, I love you man. You want to experiment with everything, with your bread recipes and your telescope looking at the stars. You just want to know everything. And you," he turned to me, "you want to know everything too. You want to try it all. You want to see everything from both sides, even how it is to be a man, how it looks from on top of a woman. You're such explorers." He gave our hands another little shake, "Welcome home."

I tried not to look at Linda on Peter's other side. After all, Peter was right, I was in a relationship with Luke. I couldn't be in a relationship with Linda. That would mean that I was a lesbian, and I wasn't one of those. No way. The word "lesbian" sounded like an insult, or an illness, like "disabled," like being stuck in a wheelchair. Luke was right. What Linda and I just did was about increasing the amount of love in the world, and surely there was nothing wrong with that? Probably everyone was bisexual if they admitted it. Lesbians were different. They didn't like men. That was putting people into boxes. That was ruling out half the planet, while bisexuals embraced all of it. Lesbians were spinsters with hang-ups, women who couldn't hack it, women hiding from real relationships in pretend ones, women like Linda, maybe. I must be careful not to encourage her to rely on me for love.

Part Three

I MARRY FOR MY MOTHER, 1970–1973

The New York Times

TROOPS SUBDUE STUDENTS IN OHIO

Quell 3d Straight Night of Unrest at Kent State

KENT, OHIO, Monday May 4—National Guardsmen and the police drove students into their dormitories at Kent State University late last night, the third night of campus unrest. At least one student, a woman, was injured. She suffered a bayonet wound and was listed in fair condition at Robinson Memorial Hospital. There were at least 15 arrests. The sweep by the guardsmen came about 11 o'clock, after a group of about 500 students had sat for an hour and a half at an intersection on the edge of the campus facing a line of policemen and guardsmen. Helicopters hovered over the campus shortly after midnight, as the guardsmen chased stragglers into the dormitories. Shortly before 1:00 A.M., three canisters of tear gas were fired into an off-campus student apartment house. On Saturday night, several thousand students attempted to march on the house of the university president, Robert J. White, but were driven off by a volley of tear gas.

13.

"WHAT'RE YOU GOING TO WEAR?" MY MOTHER CALLED DOWN FROM HER bedroom.

"Just what I've got on."

"Oh Claire," (reproachfully) "why don't you wear those corduroy trousers and that jumper Luke's mother gave you for Christmas? You look so nice in them."

Resignedly I plodded upstairs to change, only to be captured as I passed her bedroom door.

"Can you just come and do my hair at the back, pet?"

I stood behind her at the dressing table, with its lacy doilies and glass bottles, its cheap jewelry and second-rate cosmetics. Three visions of us stared at me from the triptych of mirrors, and I ironed the impatience from my face.

"I want you just to cover that patch at the back where I've got a natural parting pet, and then put plenty of lacquer on it. You see I can't raise my hands well enough to do it." Here she demonstrated horribly, taking the brush from the glass tray on the dressing table and laboriously raising her knotted hands up towards the back of her hair. They trembled with the effort, shaking the loose flesh of her underarms. "I ask your father to give it a good brush, to really pull it through, but he's too gentle. He never gets down to the scalp. He gets exasperated with me asking him to do it harder every time."

I worked the brush through her hair, steeling myself to tug through it as she hung onto the arms of the chair, her eyes shut against the pain, but her face contented, the face of a woman at the hairdresser's, receiving ministrations. "I pray every night that you and our Matthew never have to go through being dependent on somebody else, pet. I hope you'll never know what it's like to have to rely on another person. I mean your father's a saint. He's a saint. I couldn't have hoped for a kinder man, but sometimes I see him in the mirror looking at me with his Queen Victoria face, and I can tell he's sick and tired of it, sick and tired."

I looked at the flat spot on the back of her head and understood my father's revulsion. There was something terrible about that vulnerable little patch of scalp, the hair coarsened by cheap lacquer. There was tragedy in the contrast between her neck, its vertebrae twisted by rheumatism, and the frilly piecrust collar of her blouse. I watched her fragile, stubborn face in the mirror and felt such love and horror that I wanted to throw down the brush and run.

She chatted inconsequentially about Ida and Ted, Helen and Ben, Matthew and Andrea as I smoothed hair over the patch, sprayed it liberally with lacquer, and held the mirror so that she could see the results. She twisted her head this way and that, patting the stiff helmet of hair as if it were a dog she was pleased with.

"Oh, that's just right pet! I wish you could teach your dad to do that, and it only took you a minute. It is nice to have you home. I wish you were staying longer. I know you say you've got all this studying to do, but your dad and I miss you when you're away. It would be nice if you were just a little bit nearer so that you could visit at the weekends."

"Now come on, Mam. That's not fair. Everyone has to leave home sometime. I haven't really got any friends here now. I've been left Wallingford almost three years."

"You could phone Eleanor but you never do. I always thought she was a nice girl. Our Matthew never missed a weekend at home the whole time he was at college. He's going to be best man at David Tallantyre's wedding. He's like me, a home bird. Andrea says she'd better learn how to be a proper Durham lass now they've settled up here. Well, come on. We'd better get out to the car or your dad'll be clicking his lips at us. He gets that from his mother you know. If she was cross about something, she never said, she just made that little 'tut' noise under her breath. She lived to ninety-eight though, so it can't have been that bad for her health."

I would set out on these visits full of resolve to spend my time productively—in exercise, reading and reflection. As soon as I arrived, I felt instantly leaden, and not just because of the irresistible combination of food and boredom. It seemed as if the house itself was charged with some subtle power to prevent the mind from focusing cleanly, as though the air was clogged with a dust that dissipated and diverted thoughts from their object. There was a terrible unspoken certainty my parents shared about the way life worked. Their exchanged glances and indulgent smiles when they ran out of logical arguments crippled me. I was disabled by the weight of my unspoken thoughts.

With hindsight, it was good that my mother found the letter. At least then they had to recognize the existence of a parallel universe. I was playing dutiful daughter at the time, returning from an errand to the Post Office in the Mini Countryman. I called out cheerfully as I swung in through the front door, and was surprised to receive no answer. It was cod and chips for lunch, and it should have been just about ready, but when I entered the living room, the table was bare. My father sat looking uncomfortable and solemn in the armchair, and my mother, clutching an opened letter, was slumped on the sofa. I glanced at my name on the front in Luke's squiggly handwriting and felt the sick emptiness of a child caught in the act.

"Well that's what you get from reading other people's mail," I said sullenly.

"So," said my mother in a lofty, borrowed voice, "are we to take it that you've been sleeping with this young man?"

I was enraged by the pretence. "Since you've read my personal mail you obviously know the truth, and his name is Luke, as you also know."

"Do you love him?"

"No. I don't believe in it, and nor does he."

"How can you sleep with him if you don't love him?"

"Just because I don't believe in romantic love doesn't mean I have to stay celibate all my life. Maybe what I feel for him is what you might call love. I'm not sure how I'd tell. Anyway, I'm not going to live by standards I don't believe in."

My mother gazed at my father. "She doesn't know the first thing about it, Paul, does she? Well does she? What do you think?"

"She doesn't seem to, Norah."

"Are you on the pill?"

"Yes."

She looked like she had been struck. "They should never have invented that thing for young girls. I suppose they just hand it out like aspirin at that university. I always said you should have got a decent job and not gone off to that place, but nobody listened to me. No doubt you'll be taking drugs next, and giving yourself an overdose like that terrible Janis Joplin and her screechy voice."

She glared at my dad and me, and we kept quiet, like conspirators. I felt bad that I'd somehow dragged him into all this. "An institute of learning it's called . . . Well it's certainly taught her a thing or two," she flung at him. "If she's slept with one she'll sleep with them all, and there's our Matthew and Andrea went pure to the altar. You've disgraced all of us. Paul, you'd better call them and tell them what's happened."

As he went to the phone and began to dial, she turned her face away and winced, "Paul, when you've finished that phone call could you pass me one of those heart pills from my handbag please?"

There is nothing like the helpless rage of one who fights with an invalid. Every inch of me fought to resist her. I watched impassively as she lay back in the armchair with her eyes closed, her hand pressed against her chest. Her eyelids fluttered open, and she looked towards the door, then started to take deep, quivering breaths, exhaling through her nose. I registered each detail coldly, but said nothing.

My father returned with my mother's crocodile skin handbag, and I felt a purely malicious glee. I could have told him that he'd made a mistake before my mother opened her mouth. "Not that one Paul! My other handbag that Ida brought me back from Majorca. Will you fetch me up two of the heart pills, and half a glass of water? I have to lie down. I don't know what Dr. Murray's going to say."

Laboriously, she heaved herself up from the armchair while my father went to fetch the water. She did not look at me, and I did not offer to help her. She stopped halfway across the room, made a laborious about-face, and stumped back to her chair to pick up the box of tissues that lay there. She didn't look at me as she fired off her parting bolt. "The sooner you leave that place the better, and your father thinks so too."

I sat on alone in the living room, listening to the muted voices in the bedroom. After a while my father came in, avoiding my eyes. *Coward,* I thought to myself, as he sat down awkwardly in a chair across the room. "Claire. Your mother wants you to stop seeing Luke."

I knew exactly what she'd done to get him to have this conversation, exactly how much he hated it. "I can't do that."

He sighed. "You know your mother's a very sick woman. If you go on with this she could well die. The doctor's told her to avoid any upset. You know the situation with her heart."

My voice came out flat and cruel, like a murderer's might. "I can't change my whole life just because of that. I have to live how I want to."

"We're talking about life and death, not just happiness."

I didn't think she would die, but the truth was, I couldn't let it make a difference. "Dad, I can't change. That's the problem. It's not just one thing. It's everything, and I'm not going to change. I can't."

He levered himself up resignedly from his chair. "I can see there's no point. I have to say, Claire, I'm disappointed in you. Very disappointed."

His footsteps retreated up the stairs, and I heard my mother's voice, plaintive and tearful, and my father's muffled response before the door closed. I felt a little sorry for my father, but gleeful, in a bitter sort of way, because he was in there with her and I wasn't. I sat on in the armchair, numb and strangely free. I looked around the room at the faded ink mark on the sheepskin rug that I had made when I was ten, the green velvet footstool with its little brass buttons. I got up from my chair and examined the photographs that occupied most of the vacant surfaces— Auntie Ida and Cousin Helen smiling from a wicker chair in the sun; Matthew and me at the beach, squatting beside a sandcastle; my father and mother captured by a seaside photographer, hand in hand swinging along the esplanade; Matthew and Andrea, resplendent on top of the TV in the pick of the wedding pictures.

As the faces of my family smiled at me from every shelf and surface, I became suddenly aware of the heavy tick of my grandfather's clock, as it stirred in its corner of the living room. I turned to look at its brass face, to watch the sun and moon cross in their eternal, futile journey, and to listen to its monotonous, authoritarian chime. The sharp rap of the door-knocker jolted me out of my reverie. No one else seemed to be answering it, so I did. It was Matthew. "Come on, Our Kid," he said. "You look like you could use getting out of here for a while."

I could have died with gratitude and relief. In the car, he kept his eyes on the road. "Now I'm not saying I approve of sex before marriage," he said, "because actually I don't, but it's not the end of the world, after all, and though to Mam and Dad's generation it seems a sin, I think it's more about what our Ida's going to think than anything. After all, dearest Cousin Helen had to marry Ben. It seems like there's a lot of double standards going on."

I was amazed. I had expected Matthew to rebuke me for my callous behavior towards my mother. If anyone was capable of giving me a stern talking to at this point it was he. Why was he on my side?

"Your Luke's not a bad bloke under all that hair, Our Kid," he said as we pulled into his driveway. "Don't look so miserable. Anyway, why don't you have a chat with Andrea while I put the car away?"

I shuffled uneasily into the living room. Another copy of the wedding picture smiled from the mantelpiece, and Andrea leapt up from the armchair.

"You poor thing!" she exclaimed, and actually gave me a hug. "You must have had an absolutely rotten time!"

"It's not been wonderful."

"Look, come into the kitchen, and I'll put the kettle on. We thought we'd eat at the Black Bull later on, but a cup of tea never misses the spot does it?"

I thought guiltily about all the times I had made family jokes to exclude her, because she was more like my mother thought I should be than I was.

"Your mam and dad are really nice, Claire," she said carefully as she filled the kettle, "and they've treated me like their own daughter. I don't have a bad word to say about either of them. They've been kindness itself in helping us get settled here, but they're out of the ark when it comes to some things. I mean they never seemed to even suspect that Matt used to stay over at my digs half the time in Darlington. After all, we were

engaged for nearly two years. And your mam has this thing about the pill
. . . She seems to think it's immoral. I wouldn't ever dare tell her that I'd
been taking it for sixth months before we got married."

As my brother walked in to hang up his coat I felt all sorts of
different things, but mainly a peculiar need to protect him from what
Andrea had let slip. I realized that we were all just surviving, keeping our
heads above water in our own way. I stared at him, and he sensed that
something had happened. Andrea looked from one to the other of us in
confusion. "I was just saying to Claire," she began hesitantly, "how old-
fashioned your mam is when it comes to some things. I mean we've experienced that haven't we?"

Matthew flushed. I looked away. "Yeah, well," he said. "I for one
could use a drink. What say we go to the Black Bull, Our Kid, and we'll
buy you a pint and some egg and chips?"

14.

"I THOUGHT THEY LIKED ME," SAID LUKE PLAINTIVELY. "THE LAST VISIT went well, apart from when I kicked your mother's teapot over. I played the organ on Sunday morning and impressed the vicar, and your mother wrote down my fudge recipe."

"It's not even personal," I said glumly, and not entirely truthfully. In fact, the vicar hadn't liked Luke's caftan, nor his choice of a Beatles song for a voluntary, but I wanted to spare Luke's feelings, and in any case, that was not the point. "The thing is that we're having sex before marriage, and not only do we refuse to deny it, but we also refuse to pretend that we think it's wrong. And what's more we don't subscribe to the 'Woman's Own' notion of romantic love."

Luke poured himself another cup of tea, and I watched absentmindedly as tea dripped from the spout onto the carpet. "They're hanging on to old patterns," he said, "battling old repressions. Maybe we should send them a copy of *Eros and Civilization*."

"For God's sake, Luke, be realistic."

I could tell by his bottom lip that he was hurt. It wasn't trembling exactly, but it looked like it wanted to tremble, as if his mouth was only held back from regression by the rest of his face, which was resolutely grown-up.

Linda and I had become secretive, planning long afternoons together while Luke worked in the library. A thin wedge of deceit kept our affair separate, bottled in its own compartment in the box we had constructed. I'd come across a Gay Liberation Front leaflet on a bulletin board, and suggested that Linda and I went along to a meeting. Though she'd said yes, we'd somehow never got around to going. Meanwhile, the needier Luke became, the more I slapped him away. I could have stood it if he had been a creative genius, as I had once thought, misunderstood by unimaginative academics, an original mind. Unfortunately, I had picked away at the private school veneer by now, had heard all about the concerts and the family trips to the Roundhouse Theater. I had teased at the edges of him like a scab, to see what would flake away, and now he was all pink skin and little spots of blood.

"My family's not like yours, where everybody's stuffed to the gills with *New Society* and *The Guardian*," I said. "My mother's just about illiterate, and I think my father votes conservative, but he won't talk about it. We're bacon and eggs people, none of your bloody muesli."

"Well, I was just thinking in terms of consciousness raising," he said, throwing down the latest "in" word, like a gambling chip. He was so transparent.

"I'm less worried about their consciousness than what we're going to do for money next year. Don't forget I'm still dependent on them for a grant if I want to do the teacher training course. I'm not taking money from your parents, not after your mother offered to send me to finishing school in Switzerland."

It was at this point that Linda spoke. "You could always get married," she said, quietly.

The thought was so bizarre, especially coming from her, that I almost dismissed it out of hand. "Married! Are you serious? Can you see me in a white dress?"

"It doesn't have to be like that. You can do it in five minutes in a registry office. The point is that if you're married your parents don't have to support you any more; your husband does, and if he's on a full grant then you will be as well."

"Really?" I said. "Are you sure?"

"Absolutely. You'd be independent. You're not considered their responsibility any more. You're not dependent on them."

There was something about the idea of independence that was fatally tempting. My parents could close the book on me. They'd be off my back forever.

I looked at Luke. "Well, what do you think? It would solve everything. After all it's just a load of shit. It's a piece of paper. It doesn't mean anything. There's always divorce."

He looked up from the fire, which cast his eyes into shadow. "Why not? So long as I don't have to wear a suit." He lifted his mug of tea and drank, looking at Linda over the rim of it. "You can be a bridesmaid," he said.

So we traveled up the old A1 to Glenburn to give my parents the good news. The journey took eight or nine hours in our tired old Ford Anglia. We had to keep the heater on full blast to cool the engine, but we didn't care because we were brave martyrs bearing good tidings. I had hurt my mother, but I was going to make everything OK. She could hold her head up at the church bazaar.

"Our Claire? Oh yes, she's married now you know. His parents are very well-off, not that that's the only thing. Yes, he's a teacher too."

Nothing would change. Luke and I would train to be teachers. Linda would take the Town Planning course. We'd extend our lease on the farmhouse, on the adjoining bedrooms, on the corridor I traversed between them. We could keep things as they were.

With innocent faces, conscious of doing the right thing at last, we sat on separate chairs in my parents' living room and declared our intentions. Imagine our consternation when my mother left the room, our horror when we heard the ominous growl of the vacuum cleaner above our heads, thundering across the floorboards in my brother's vacant bedroom! We sat on uneasily for a while with my father, who looked thoroughly uncomfortable. Predictably, we talked about the overheating problem on the car, though every now and again, an extra loud thump from upstairs would send our eyes rolling upwards, like saints in paintings by El Greco. Fortunately, we were just passing through on our way to the Lake District, and escape was possible. We accepted a large bottle of spare water and a rag to take the radiator cap off with, before crawling off, in the heat, to our walking holiday.

Communications from home were sparse the next term, but we continued to plan our wedding, as if following a bad script. All our friends thought it was a great joke when Linda agreed to be my maid of honor. Every now and again we received a grudging prompt from my mother. "I suppose you're going to send out some invitations soon. Who's making the cake? Where's the reception? Your Auntie Phyllis wants to know." Cheerful, blundering, trusting, we went through the motions, half serious, half flippant. I bought a secondhand engagement ring for myself, posted the banns and booked a hotel for their second-best reception. My mother was in an equally ambivalent state, reluctant to seem interested, but desperate that our relatives should not find fault. Sired by an uneasy alliance of half-baked notions and fearful conservatism, our wedding day assumed life, picked us up in its arms and hastened us towards its threshold.

15.

"Get closer," the photographer shouted, flapping his arms like awkward wings, "just a *teeny* little bit closer. Come on you mummies, snuggle up to the daddies. Let's get *physical!* Smile! This *is* a wedding." I moved closer to Luke, knowing that I was offering up a portion of my spirit to be framed and added to the collection on top of my parents' television, but glad to have it over with.

Though a wedding had sounded like a sensible idea when Linda suggested it, the reality of it was a bad scene, I reflected, as I stared at my bewildered relatives who clutched bags of confetti like life preservers. Our collective air of doom was only deepened by the professional heartiness of the photographer, who pulled and pushed us into groups as if about to stage a family war game. We looked more like guards lined up for a Kremlin execution than a wedding party.

Indeed, out of her deep sense of premonition, my mother had chosen to wear a black Cossack hat. Beneath its funereal fur, her face was pale with the stress of her desperate search for good omens on the drive to the registry office. My father wore a stiff gray suit and a smile as determined as he could muster after having been enclosed in the Mini Countryman with my mother for the last three hours. "Happy is the Bride that the Sun Shines on," she had muttered all the way down the A1, which loured with ominous clouds.

Luke's parents were better dressed than mine and dispensed well-heeled niceness, like charity. His father looked like he was already calculating how this mess would end up on his desk, along with the bill for his wife's latest car accident.

My mother and his managed not to touch as they shuffled towards each other, though they leaned their heads together graciously for the sake of good form. Each blamed the other for this ridiculous wedding, believing her child to be the innocent victim of nuptial kidnapping—as if Luke or I were the heirs to thrones or fortunes! Why else, they reasoned, would we marry so young? I was not pregnant, though my mother told me every day on the phone that Auntie Ida kept dropping skeptical hints to upset her. As for romantic love, they knew that we saw it as just another outworn bourgeois tradition, such as cooking and cleaning. Little did they know that we were tying the knot to finance next year's teacher training. Despairing of the older generation, we planned to turn kids on to revolution as soon as we were let loose in the classroom. We were "using the system to destroy the system" as Luke liked to put it.

Our sixties culture provided us with carpet slogans such as these under which we swept uncool things. "It's only a piece of paper," I told myself. Meanwhile, my unconscious life gestated in the darkness, blind and encysted like the marijuana seeds we planted in the garden and forgot to water. It was only much later that their sprouting surprised us.

Linda, my maid of honor, looked sad and out of place as usual. She was up in Doncaster now, taking the Town Planning course. Part of me was relieved and part of me was forlorn. Luke said that I had slept with her in order to explore my bisexuality, which he thought was cool. He said it was part of the whole yang openness thing we were exploring. The I Ching was his latest fad. Linda had never slept with a man, only with me. That meant that she was repressed, more of a yin kind of thing. He had cast the yarrow stalks that morning and got the hexagram about the sun shining behind a bank of thunderclouds. He said that this was a very positive hexagram, but as far as he was concerned, they all were, even the one about the man falling under the wheels of his own ox cart. I trusted my mother's brand of superstition more.

"If you're doing this for me," she'd said, just before we went in to the registry office, "then you're making a big mistake. It has to be right for the two of you. Marriage is for keeps, you know. What you see of Luke now is what you get. You won't change him." She'd cried a little, and I knew she'd be worried about her makeup. "I just have this feeling in my stomach that you might be making a terrible mistake. I don't know why. He's a canny enough lad. It just doesn't feel right somehow. Claire, it's not too late to change your mind if you have the slightest doubt about this. Your dad and I will stand by you."

I squeezed her hand and shook my head and she nodded. "All right," she said. "Just remember, pet, people don't ever change who they are, not really. My own mother told me that. I don't know what she would have thought about today, but she always told me that. People don't ever change who they really are."

And this, perversely, is why I'd shrugged away her fears and walked into the Registry Office, because people do not change. If I wasn't going to be Mrs. Right then I'd better learn protective camouflage. I needed to stage this illusion to put us all off the scent, to pose in this photograph in which I choke a bunch of freesias to death with one hand and rest the other on Luke's arm in a way that was meant to seem wifely but looks more like I just got burned. I still have that picture. Behind the fake smile, my face looks pudgy from the pill; above it, my pupils are dilated from the dope I smoked before the ceremony in the parking lot. Only Luke, with his wide young grin, looks happy, like an optimistic puppy in front of an empty bowl. He wears a leather trouser suit hand-thonged by Peter, who is there in the photo too. He grins through an acid euphoria. Matthew stands next to him with his arm around Andrea, as if to save her from a rising tide of dirty water.

I put my arm through Linda's and squeezed it as the photographer hustled us all ever closer together, but her body felt stiff through the crusty brocade of her over-formal dress. Her eyes were hidden behind the mass of orange hair that my mother never failed to criticize when I mentioned Linda's name on the phone.

"No wonder she's never been asked out," my mother always said. "She'd stand more of a chance if she tied that hair back. I think she's trying to hide behind it." She used to make disparaging comments about Luke's beard too, and the pimples that sprouted in its roots. After she had read the letter, these comments stopped, which was a relief, not because I found them unjust—quite the contrary. I had taken to shutting my eyes and faking orgasm every time Luke and I had sex, to get it done with quickly so that I could leave him sleeping and tiptoe down the hall to Linda's room.

We had stolen the hours that no one else wanted and squandered them in her single bed, reckless of assignments due and early classes. While Peter dreamed his tangled prophecies, I'd fetch his stash from the

kitchen and roll a joint the way I saw him do it—three Rizla papers and
a cardboard roach. Our stolen hours melted into perfect sweetness inside
the tent of her flaming hair, but always daylight came and the noisy birds,
staking out their territories. Time to wake to a wholesome diet—Marx
and Engels, Andy Warhol and Ken Kesey, Jack Kerouak and the Grateful
Dead, Sartre and Gide—it was a regimen of semen in the sixties and we
never even knew we were choking.

After the photographs were all taken, Linda and I met by chance in
the ladies' room. She forced a smile. "How does it feel to be a married
woman?"

"How does it feel to kiss a married woman?" I responded, and I kissed
her, angrily. I pushed her into one of the cubicles and touched her breast.

"How does it feel to commit adultery at your own wedding?" she
asked, and the champagne made me cry.

16.

THE GARDEN GATE BOUNCED ANGRILY AGAINST BEHIND ME WITH A painted metallic clunk, the teeth of its latch clenched angrily against the sneck. The thought entered my head, as it did every time I came home from work, that I would fix it after dinner; maybe it just needed a little oil. I knew, even as I had the thought, that I wouldn't act upon it. It was a peculiar thing—the two thoughts "Fix the latch" and "Forget the latch" lay side by side in my brain, as if they were not related.

Part of the problem was that I couldn't seem to believe that the cottage belonged to me in any sense, though I'd tried. I'd bought wallpaper and hung it in the living room. I'd picked dried sedge and put it in a vase.

Luke's father, James, had bought the house for us at an auction. I'd stood beside him as he bid, joyless and stubborn, against a local builder. As the price reached ridiculous proportions, the poor builder dropped out with a snort of rage. James ignored the man's rumblings about "Londoners with more money than sense" and pulled out his checkbook. "This is two thousand more than it's worth," he said as he filled in the numbers. "I just hope you like it."

"Thank you James," I'd said. "It's a beautiful house. We love it," but I didn't look him in the eye.

It *was* a beautiful house, I thought, as I opened the front door. Part of me did love the solid stone, the illusion of domesticity, the sound of Luke rattling pans in the kitchen. The other part of me, though—the part that forgot the latch—thought that the old cottage would soon outlive a pair of transients such as us, who hung wallpaper crooked and drilled holes for shelves that they would disassemble in a year or two and squeeze into a rental van.

Luke appeared in the threshold, holding a wooden spoon. He was still dressed in his teaching clothes—a tweed sports jacket and a pair of brown trousers that were a little too tight for his stocky frame, a little too short.

His once bushy beard was trimmed to a professorial point, his brown eyes hopeful, his hair cut above the collar. He looked like what I'd made him—an ex-hippy with a cheap haircut and bargain clothes, trying too hard to please. He held out the spoon for me to taste.

It tasted like everything else he cooked, generic vegetarian mush, but I feigned enthusiasm, nodding and smiling like one of the Famous Five from Enid Blyton. "Mmm!" I said, and, "That's great! Absolutely spiffing, Caruthers," I went on, hamming it up a little. "First rate! Good show!"

"It's vegetarian chili," he said, looking uncertain. "It's from that *Moosewood Cookbook* Jeremy sent us for Christmas." He nodded towards the coffee table. "There's a letter from your mother and one from Linda I think. It didn't have my name on it, so I left it for you."

I kept my face smooth as I ripped open the envelope decorated with my mother's arthritic scrawl. I began to read, and left him to stand there for a moment, deciding whether or not he dared ask to read them after me. What monsters I had made of us both.

· · ·

Claire pet you'll never guess what!! Your Cousin Helens gone off with a traveling salesman!!! Out of the blue it was but Ida says it must have been going on longer—she's livid Claire, more that she's given up the farm and all that goes with it. Ted wont even pick up the phone when she calls—she was always his favourite. Spoilt rotten if you ask me and I was sick and tired of having her crammed down my throat how many new clothes she'd bought etc etc. Not that I would wish it on anybody though—especially those poor children, they say they never recover from divorce don't they? Which is what they'll do I suppose. I never liked Ben much, for all his money he was a rude man. I once told you I think how unpleasant he was when I passed some remark on his dogs

Rain and fog for a week now, hope you and Luke are having better weather this is wreaking havoc(?) with my pains and it makes me very dependant though your dad God Bless him he never grumbles

Why on earth have you bought a motorbike???!! Your dad says they are the most dangerous things on the face of God's earth and so does our Matthew. If it's just the money Claire well couldn't you get a car loan now Luke is working and just pay it off month by month. I know its your life now—you're a married woman pet—but a mother always worries and so do I. I worry that you'll strain yourself a great heavy thing like that and everyone will talk. Not that that ever bothers you I suppose. Be very careful when you're overtaking.

What about the winter???!!!

Anyway pet I don't want to be a nag just please be very careful and wrap up well. Drop us a line when you have a minute—I know your busy with your studies—or just give us a ring. Did you get that wall-paper up? Don't forget to put plenty of paste on the seams you can always take it off after with a damp sponge.

Dad sends his love
XXXXXXXX
MAM

. . .

Linda's letter was much briefer.

She hadn't thought that my being married would make a difference, but she'd felt lonely lately and I hadn't been around for her. She'd gone on a date. It was the first time in ages that someone was interested, just in her. It was time she stopped picking up crumbs. It wasn't my fault. A clean break. She hoped that I wouldn't be too upset. Best in the long run.

It all made perfect sense.

"I'm going for a walk," I called through to the kitchen. The front gate bounced behind me as I turned left towards the open countryside. The land around the cottage was flat coastal hinterland, but the vivid sky lent it beauty. A swath of iridescent white cumulus lay across the sun, but as I walked down the lane, fingers of light streaked out through gaps now and again, like spotlights, to illuminate random objects—five tiny cows in a distant field, a cattle trough, a broken hawthorn. I walked the easy tarmac of the narrow country roads, and pondered our impact on the land. I imagined there were places in the meadows unspoiled by human feet. The nooks and crannies in the dry stone walls had lain untouched since early farmers had picked stones and piled them up to mark the boundaries of their fields. Safe places existed, hidden from history.

A mile or so down the road there was a small coppice of beech Luke and I called "the starling trees." Their branches, stripped by the blustering October winds, had been turned into charcoal by the glowing remnants of the day. Hordes of starlings gathered here nightly, filling the air with their din and fluttering wings, taking off in huge groups to circle in for a landing in a more favored tree, jostling for position, arguing in raucous voices. In the distance, three rooks flapped lazily home, but it was the starlings that drew me, with their mindless business, the weight of their numbers. I felt sad as I watched them. I picked up three autumn leaves, bright orange, like Linda's hair. The tree from which they had fallen had slowly closed down on them, launched them out into this place of piercing beauty.

Back at the house, Luke still clinked in the kitchen. I slipped the leaves inside Linda's letter and reread my mother's. *Good for Cousin Helen,* I thought. I didn't know why I'd bought a motorbike, just as I didn't know why I'd carried the Gay Liberation Front leaflet in my briefcase for all these months, but somewhere a latch clicked into place.

17.

THE LEAFLET SAID THAT THE ROB ROY WAS ON PLEASANT STREET. According to the map, that was on the other side of town from the university, the old part of town that had escaped the bombing but not the damage—the industrial side. After maneuvering my motorbike across two lanes of traffic, I swung into a wide street, pockmarked with potholes and lined with shady businesses—tattoo parlors and Chinese takeouts, heavily shuttered at this late hour. Neon streetlights on tall concrete poles stared down at collections of rubbish bins. The only other light came from the pub on the corner. A ferocious Highlander scowled at me from the battered sign on which he swung, as if from a red coats' gibbet. A waft of beery smoke hit me as I opened the door.

To my relief, the bartender didn't ask what I was looking for, though I had rehearsed saying the words on the long ride into town. He took one look at me, said, "Doonstairs," in his long-winded Scottish fashion, then glanced aside towards his only customer. This was a man who looked like he'd been installed with the furniture when the bar was first opened and had sat there ever since, consuming pints of Tartan with whiskey chasers. His buttocks engulfed his bar stool with a finality that bespoke surgical intervention in the event of a visit to the men's room. His tattooed biceps strained at the sleeves of a grimy tee shirt that proclaimed "Scots Wahey!" We eyed each other like dogs who didn't want to sniff. He looked like he knew something I didn't.

"You'll be looking for the meeting," the bartender said again, a little louder, as if to someone hard of hearing. "It's doonstairs."

I hesitated, not liking to check if he meant the Gay Liberation Front.

"They like to meet in the basement," the Buttocks said, "doon in the nether regions." He hitched his enormous trousers up by the skull that adorned his leather belt, and cocked his jowly head at me expectantly, like he was waiting for me to break into song, or sprout a second head.

Instead, I looked back at the bartender, who smeared spilled beer across the surface of the bar with what looked like a pair of the Buttocks' discarded underpants. "Could I use your ladies' room?"

He smiled unpleasantly and flung the cloth into a sink. "Either one," he said finally. The man with the tattoos smiled too and so did I—a nervous, automatic smile that hadn't got the joke.

Safely in the bathroom, I stared at myself in the mirror, and tried out suitable poses. First I zipped my leather bike jacket all the way up, and then I opened just the top part so that the plain white tee shirt showed— a James Dean sort of look I hoped. I adjusted my leather Che Guavara beret and narrowed my eyes at my reflection, composing a few descriptive lines about myself for inclusion in the short story I was writing in my head. *Claire's steely blue eyes narrowed slightly at the thought,* I wrote in my head. *Babs admired the strong bones of her face.* I made sure that the pack of Gauloise peeked out of my top pocket, took my bike gauntlets off the sink and held them loosely in my left hand. I was as ready as I would ever be.

As I walked down the stairs to the basement, I wondered how many gay people there would be, and what we would talk about—the Arts, perhaps, since I'd heard that a lot of gay men were dancers or actors. I hadn't a clue what gay women were famous for. My friend Pauline knew women in London who were lesbians and owned motorbikes, like me. Maybe some of these lesbians did, and we could all ride together. I saw us having a picnic out in the country somewhere, about ten of us, stretched out on the grass, our bikes parked in a gleaming row. We wore matching regalia on the backs of our leather jackets and laughed with our heads thrown back. I had polished my Honda yesterday in case anyone needed a ride home from the meeting. You never knew. We'd have to go to her place, of course, but if she was gay, then she'd have her own place; she wouldn't be living with a man like I was. Should I tell her about Luke? Did gay women only sleep with other gay women? No, I thought, they'd probably be willing to help someone out. It wasn't like I'd had no experience.

At first, I thought I had the wrong room. It was twentieth-century baronial, dimly lit by wrought iron sconces in the shape of thistles. A huge picture of some Highland chieftain type, presumably Rob Roy himself, hung over a cavernous fireplace in which a tiny gas log fire flickered feebly. Six heavy pine tables, stained a gloomy brown, bore menus impaled in plastic holders. There was a stale smell of ancient beef.

Two men sat on opposite sides of one of the tables. One had a battered, weary face with suspiciously black hair, an indeterminate sweater and cheap brown trousers. He sat bolt upright with a brown attaché case perched on his knees, as if at an interview. The other man was a pimply, skinny, listless youth, slouched with his legs stuck out, flicking through a copy of *Rolling Stone.* He was blue denim all the way.

I stopped in the doorway.

Blue Denim glanced up from his magazine, "Looking for GLF?"

I nodded. "This is us," he said. "So far. Not much of a turn out tonight. Marjorie'll be here in a minute. Marjorie's always late."

I must have looked uncertain, because he cracked a kind smile. "You'd better get a drink, lovey, if you want to survive."

When I came back in with my pint, a small, harried looking women had perched herself on the edge of a chair, and was sorting through an untidy stack of papers. Some of them slid to the floor, and as I picked them up, I noticed that they were about boycotting a bookstore. BRISTOL GLF CALLS YOU TO ACTION! They screamed. KEEP GOVERNMENT OUT OF OUR BEDROOMS! STOP CENSORSHIP NOW! I sifted them into a pile and handed them to her.

"Well hello," she said, flashing me a smile. "Another woman—great! We need you. Oh how we need you. What's your name?" She was an older woman, sort of lean like a greyhound, with short salt and pepper hair and slate blue eyes. I found her instantly attractive and decided then and there that I would definitely sleep with her if she were in the market, if she didn't have a girlfriend. Surely, the girlfriend would be there if she had one. I knew that if I had a girlfriend I would go everywhere with her. Everyone was staring at me I noticed, and I realized that she was waiting for an answer. The room grew suddenly hot. I felt my eyebrows and nose leak beads of sweat.

"Oh," I said, hating the sound of my voice, as I did sometimes, remembering the teasing from when I was little. "I'm Claire."

She frowned a little, not quite catching it, "Clara," she said and gave me the smile again. "Great to meet you, Clara, welcome. We were just talking about our newsletter." She turned to the denim-clad youth. "So how many articles have we got so far, Guy?"

The young man in denim feigned a start, as if he'd been lost in his own thoughts. "Well, Marjorie," he said. "Articles. Let's think." He put his hand to his chin in a stagy, thinking sort of gesture. "Not counting yours and mine?"

She who was presumably Marjorie nodded impatiently, and Guy began counting on his fingers, and then stopped and grinned at her. "None," he said.

Marjorie put her hands to her hips and glared at him.

He raised his eyebrows and assumed an indignant expression. "It's not *my* fault Marjorie," he said, with just a hint of spiteful satisfaction. "I sent *everyone* on the mailing list a reminder. If they can't even come to *meetings* what do you expect? Look at this." He waved his hands around the room.

"OK," said Marjorie, "we need to recruit. Next time everybody brings at least one other person, OK?" She looked at me sternly. "You too Clara."

"Right," I said, nodding vigorously, "at least one other person." Oh my God. I didn't know anyone who was gay. I would never be able to come back, even if I wanted to.

"Bring warm bodies," she said. "If you have to drag them here."

"Oh very funny Marjorie," said Guy, "*drag* them, eh? Well *that* might work." He spoke very precisely, in a light, husky voice. I looked closely at him. It suddenly hit me—he was *gay*. He slept with men, naked, and they took turns putting their things up each other's bottoms. I tried to imagine Guy kissing the other man, who still clutched his briefcase. I couldn't. I dressed the other man in a frilly blouse and earrings. I still couldn't, but I suddenly understood the barman's joke. What on earth was I doing here?

Another woman came into the room, pulled out a chair at one of the tables and sat down abruptly. Marjorie nodded at her, somewhat coldly I thought, so she probably wasn't her girlfriend, unless they'd argued, if gay people did argue. Linda and I never had. Even though she had dumped me, she still loved me. Even though she was going out with this bloke Allen now, we were still friends. Suddenly I wished Linda were here with me. I felt really lonely, and it would be OK if she were here with me, or, even better if we were back in her room in the farmhouse, lying in bed and eating oranges. We had been so happy together, as if there were different rules when we shut the door, or we were different people, neither male nor female, like angels. We just couldn't be who we were out in the real world. There wasn't a place for us. We weren't viable.

"Clara!"

I realized Marjorie was talking to me again.

"I was asking if you'd like another drink. I'm going up to the bar."

Wow, I thought, *she's interested.*

"Sure," I said, nonchalant.

She continued to look at me, till I started and blushed again. "Pint of Bass," I said explosively, but she continued to look expectant.

"You need to give me the money," she said, adopting the patient hard of hearing tone of voice that the barman had used.

Oh. I dug in my pocket.

Brown Trousers finally spoke, in a deep, echoing voice, as if translating from another language. "So Sarah? How is life treating you?"

I hadn't paid the new arrival much attention, because she was one of those people who I routinely wrote off as second-rate, a mousy extra to the main event. Her face looked damaged somehow, as if she'd had an accident followed by undetectable plastic surgery. She sat half-facing us, reluctant.

She glared at the portrait of Rob Roy and laughed savagely. "Life?" she said scornfully, "It's just great as usual. Paula finally moved out. With most of my money and all my furniture."

"How *terrible!*" said Guy, adopting a horrified expression.

She shrugged. "That's not even the worst part. She was meant to look after my cats and she took them to the animal rescue place instead and put them up for adoption."

"My *God!*" said Guy.

She tossed her head. "Who cares? I don't." She turned to me, her face unsmiling, "So who are you?"

I was too taken aback by so much bad luck to be self-conscious. "My name is Claire," I said. "Marjorie thinks it's Clara."

She snorted. "Yeah," she said. "Marjorie. Our fearless leader. So are you new in town or what? How come I haven't seen you around?"

"Well, this is the first time I've, you know, been to a meeting or any-thing."

She moved to the chair beside me. "Really? So where d'you live ClaraClaire?"

"Out in Dyrham—one of the villages."

"All on your own?"

It was the dreaded question.

I came right out with it. "Well, for now I'm living with someone. My husband actually."

"You have a *husband!* What are you? Bisexual or something?"

"So what if she is, Sarah?" boomed the brown jacket. "She can be bisexual if she wants."

Marjorie came back with the drinks. She set a gin and tonic in front of Sarah and half a lager in front of me, without change. "There you go Clara," she said.

I'd paid her for a pint of Bass, but I didn't say anything. She proba-bly had a lot on her mind, being such an activist and everything. Sarah gave my arm a quick squeeze. "It's cool," she whispered quietly.

We limped through Marjorie's agenda—the newsletter and the book-store boycott, updating the reading list and organizing transport to the demonstration in London. Guy told us about a movie he'd heard about where the hero beat up a gay man for making a pass at him. "Maybe we should boycott that," Marjorie said. I hadn't realized that being gay was such an uphill battle, nor that there were so few of us to fight it.

Eventually we finished. "Gotta go to the loo," I said, standing up. "All that beer."

"We use the one out back," said Sarah. "That way we don't have to deal with those dickheads at the bar. Here, I'll show you."

It was a single, but she followed me in. I was astonished when she put her arms around me, too amazed to speak. I'd only just met her! I didn't even like her! Was this how things worked? Did everyone think we'd gone off to have sex? Did Marjorie think that?

In the interim, Sarah had managed to plant a couple of kisses in the general vicinity of my mouth. She smelled of too many gin and tonics. I took hold of her hands and removed them from my waist.

"Look," I said. "I'm sorry but I can't to do this."

"Can't?" she said, "or just don't want to?"

"Well, both," I said, almost dead with embarrassment. "I'm just not really ready I suppose."

She turned instantly vitriolic. "You and your bloody Che Guevara hat!" she hissed, thrusting her nose an inch from my face. As I backed up against the sink, she took a step towards me, clenching her fists at her sides. My God, she was going to beat me up. It seemed like a cruel irony. I was going to be beaten up for being too straight at my very first gay meeting!

"Bloody bisexuals," Sarah spat at me. "You're all the same. You just mess about with people's feelings!"

Sarah grabbed hold of my arm and held me in front of the mirror. "Look at you," she said giving me a little shake, "in your bloody leather jacket!" Her face puckered into folds and creases down which tears began to trickle. I turned towards her, but she stamped her foot and tossed herself in a half circle as if I were making the pass. "Get off! Don't touch me," she said, her voice cracking. "You're just another bloody middle-class bitch out for an evening's experiment with the queers." She wiped the tears and snot off her face with the end of her sleeve and gathered herself for another onslaught. "Who *do* you sleep with if you don't want to sleep with me? I bet you fuck your husband, don't you!" She glared at me. "*Don't* you?"

I nodded numbly.

"Then you've no bloody right coming here pretending to be queer, messing people's heads up. Don't come back here. Understand? Don't come back here till you've made your muddled little mind up."

I nodded again.

She turned on her heel and left, giving me much more to think about than Marjorie's entire two-hour agenda.

18.

Autum

In autum leaves turn red and fall of the trees and my mam and I make blackberry jam. We take three pounds of blackberries and boil it for about an hour and a half with sugar. You put it in a saucer of water to see when its set and when it has my mam and I put it in the jars. My dad says our bramble jam is good as anything in the shops.

"Who can tell me what kind of writing this is?"

I was asking an open ended question, like I was meant to, but Tommy Snaithe was the only one who raised his hand, grinning in foolish parody of an eager pupil. I decided to show him that I cared about his opinion. One day, he might just come around if I didn't write him off, like all the others teachers at Hillthorpe Secondary School had, the reactionary ones.

"Well, Tommy?"

He preened for a while, milking yet another moment in the spotlight. "Miss . . ." he began.

"Mrs. Trapp," I reminded him, regretting the irony of my married name for the thousandth time.

"Sorry Miss," he said. "I mean Mrs. Well miss, I just want to say I don't like jam because it looks like sticky blood. Miss, when our dog got knocked down all this sticky blood came out its nose and it looked like raspberry jam so now I won't eat it."

I decided that the best course was to see this as a teaching moment. "Tommy, thank you," I began enthusiastically. "That's actually a really good—" but some of the class were going, "Eeewh!" and "That's disgusting!" and some were firing questions: "Which dog was that Tommy?" "Tommy, was the dog dead, Tommy?" and some were sharing stories of their own, "My dad and I went fishing once" and "chain saw massacre . . . the blood came spurting out!" Jane Goodenall looked pale and somewhat queasy. I hoped she wasn't going to cry, like she had the time I read the poem about the dead granny.

I had lost them again. I wandered round the room pretending that the chaos was actually meaningful discussion, and hoping the senior teacher wouldn't walk by my door. Mr. Hardcastle was a horrid man. He was the scourge of first year teachers like me, and ate fish paste sandwiches out of the same Tupperware box in the same chair in the staff room every day. I placed a handout on each desk—*How to Make Your Stories Real and Exciting* it said. It had quotes from Ernest Hemingway and Dylan Thomas in it. I had spent an hour on it last night, thinking of ways to shake my students out of their unfailing pragmatism, to get them writing *creatively,* about their *feelings,* to get them to use *vivid detail* . BE IMAGINATIVE! The handout said. APPEAL TO THE FOUR SENSES!

"Uuurgh," Rolly Donison yelled. "Miss! Miss! Someone's made a stinky! Tommy's farted!"

Maybe when they'd calmed down I could try to talk to them about the handout.

· · ·

After the home time bell, I strapped my book bag on the rack of the Honda and set off to Pauline's, as I did most days after work. Sometimes I felt like my friendship with her was the only thing that reminded me that I was a functional adult. She was the best thing I'd got out of the consciousness raising group in Hull, which had spent most of its time deciding how to run itself.

Pauline had been working on her run-down three-story house for five years, knocking down walls, putting up ceilings, tearing old things out and replacing them with new ones, or at least planning to. The only room left unscathed was her bedroom; the rest were chaotic with raw plasterboard, plastic sheets, and bundles of disconnected wires. Things Pauline had bought cheap or found in dumpsters stood in corners everywhere, waiting for salvation. A disconnected toilet lurked on the top landing, a Welsh dresser squatted in the front hallway, and six ornate Victorian radiators crouched in the living room like a pack of square wolves with curly hair.

I tracked her down in the kitchen, dressed in a man's shirt, dungarees, and a set of cracked amber beads. She was poring over a pile of photographs. Half a sandwich lay on the table, and by the looks of it, the rest of it was spread over the shelf of her huge bosom, in the form of crumbs. Two thin kittens prowled for scraps among the pile of dirty dishes stacked around the sink. The folds of Pauline's jowly, middle-aged face arranged themselves into a smile when she saw me. "Hi Claire," she said. "I was wondering if you'd stop by. Look at this."

I moved a pile of rags from one of the chairs and sat down to look at the photograph—a skinny black man with an Afro. He was much younger than Pauline, I noted automatically. "Who is he?"

"It's Dana and Gerta's dad," Pauline said. She chuckled at my surprise. "You assumed that they were adopted didn't you? It's OK. Everybody does. Try being a forty-six-year-old white mother pushing black twins along in a pram. It'll shake up your prejudices a little."

"Where is he now?" I asked.

"James?" she said. "He's inside. They said he was involved in the Birmingham bombings, not that he was one of the Birmingham Six, but that he was a conspirator."

"And was he?"

She dropped the photo onto the table. "The whole thing was a fix," she said. "Maybe one or two of them were involved, but they used the Prevention of Terrorism Act to pull in all sorts of people they wanted off the streets. They faked evidence." She put the picture down. "He was a sweet man. I haven't met anyone like him since."

I picked up another photograph—two women with their arms around each other. "Who's this?"

Pauline laughed. "Trust you," she said. "That's Pat and Trudy, my lesbian friends."

I peered harder.

"Wait," said Pauline, "I've got a better one somewhere." She riffled through the shoebox full of pictures, flipping out the ones she wanted. "That's their squat in Hackney," she said finally, handing me one of a big house. "They live in a lesbian separatist squatting community. We should borrow your hubby's car, go down and visit. They've fixed up these old council houses. You know, the GLC can't afford to renovate them so they leave them to rot. Usually they smash the toilet to keep squatters out, but the girls just go right in there and change the locks."

"Can't they get thrown out by the police?"

"Not if they change the locks. If your key fits the door and you have a table and chairs, a toilet and some way to cook, then they have to get a court order to prove you don't live there, and of course they're not going to bother, not till they want to tear the whole thing down, which they can't because there's still some old people hanging on there and they can't afford to rehouse them. We should go and visit them—really. Pat is one of my absolute best friends. You'd love her. They help each other out with fixing up the electricity and everything. Someone always knows someone who can do gas, or plumbing or whatever. They helped me do the ceilings in here." I looked up at the ceilings. "And the sink," she said. "Trudy is a great plumber."

What would anyone ever say that I was great at, I wondered—hanging wallpaper in my father-in-law's cottage? Screwing an obsolete husband once a week to keep him happy? Making spelling corrections on strawberry jam recipes?

Pauline's shrewd blue eyes watched me from the creases of her sagging bulldog face. Her hair was unkempt and stiff with plaster dust. I had been working hard not to think of her as ugly since I met her.

"You'd love it," she said. "There's this pub round the corner where Pat and Trudy's band plays. A women's band, just for women." She grinned at me like a shark. "Speaking of which, how's the poor old hubby?"

I hadn't said this before, not even to myself. I was amazed to hear the words coming out of my mouth. "I think I'm going to leave him."

She started to put the photographs back in the box. "I *know* you're going to leave him."

"You what?" I stared at her. I mean we'd talked. She knew about Linda, and a couple of other flings I'd had, with men and women as it turned out, but I'd never discussed leaving Luke.

"I know you're going to leave him," she said. "I've known for months. I was just waiting till you finally got the picture." She took a pen and wrote a phone number and address on the back of Pat and Trudy's photograph. "Now you've got the picture," she said, handing it to me, "just get on with it."

. . .

Snot came out of its noes and the blood was pouring out That will teach you to bite me you f****** bastard said John He put the clob away in his pocket he had beaten its brains to a blloddy pulp He cut it's head off and stuck it on the fence so that the other little doggiies wood see and behave themselves beter.

Dear Miss I hope I wont get a D agen I put some swearing in thogh not the really bad one because you said it was OK if it fit in the storey I hope there is enough VIVID DETAIL. I have tried my best.

TOMMY

"How's the marking?" asked Luke. The only time we spent together these days seemed to be an endless response to inadequacy.

"Fine," I said. "How's yours?"

"Nearly done. I thought I'd go over to Marylou's later. I said I'd lend her a book and anyway, I wanted to say goodbye before we go to Norway."

He'd been sleeping with Marylou for a month. I'd slept with her for a month before that. He always did that, I'd noticed, moved in on women I was interested in, like a dog that had to piss on the same tree that I had. Pauline was right. I had to escape this mistaken life I'd stumbled into. When the phone rang, I seized it like a lifebuoy.

"Hello pet!"

"Hi Mam! How are you? How's Dad?"

"Buggered! We've been to Barnard Castle choosing wallpaper for the bathroom and we're just sitting down for a cup of tea. How are you both? Looking forward to your holiday? Has Luke got his clothes packed yet?"

"I was thinking about doing mine tonight, but he can't. He's going out."

I couldn't stand to think of packing for two weeks imprisonment with Luke in a Volkswagen van with a foam mattress in the back and not even Tommy Snaithe to protect me from the horror of our intimacy.

"One of his friends from work is it?" my mother was asking. "I never thought he was much of a man's man. Well, that's nice."

I doodled on the cover of the telephone directory. Tommy Snaithe decapitated a dog. Blood spurted from its neck. Halfway out of the front door, Luke waved goodbye at me. I wiggled a farewell with my pen. Mam didn't seem to notice my silence. "Are you wrapping up warm in this cold weather? Remember to take care of that ear of yours now. You know what the doctor said."

"Come on, Mam. I'm twenty three."

"I don't care!" she said, heatedly. "You can't be too careful. Look at me. I can't do the washing any more. Your dad had to help me yesterday, and he does so much already. He gets sick and tired of me asking."

"Now then, Mam, come off it. You know he'd do anything for you."

"But he's not getting any younger Claire! It's not good for him to be always working when he works so hard during the day. What if something happens to him? I don't know what I'd do. I wouldn't want to carry on."

To my horror, she sounded tearful. I couldn't cope with this right now.

"I've told him what I would do, and now you know too. Don't tell our Matthew. He just gets angry with me. But I want you to know I'll never be a burden on you. You and Matthew have both got your own lives to lead. It makes your dad and I happy to know that you're both settled."

I wanted to crash the receiver into the table in front of me, to rip the telephone from its socket and hurl it into the garden. Instead, I said, "Come on Mam. You know Dad. He never ails a thing. There's no need to bury him off just yet."

I curled my fingernails into the palm of my hand, and started to draw birds sitting on the skulls I'd drawn on the phone book. She sighed. "I know," she said. "You think I'm just stupid. Tell me the rest of your news. How's that Linda? You used to be full of what she was doing, and now I never hear about her. Has she got a boyfriend yet?"

"Yes, actually, she has."

"Just as well."

"What do you mean?"

"I mean just as well. Just as well she's got one."

"Why just as well?"

She had me hooked now and backed cautiously away from the anger in my voice.

"Well, your Auntie Ida thought she had designs. On Luke you know. She was always tagging along."

"Well Auntie Ida was wrong as usual."

"She's never had a boyfriend though has she?"

Nastily, I deliberately misunderstood. "I thought she was married."

Her incredulity distorted the line. "Married! Linda! Eeh, Claire, when? Why on earth didn't you tell me? I'd've sent her a card at least. Give me their address."

My little triumph seemed cold and spiteful. "I thought you meant Ida."

"Ida. Well I know she's married. She's my sister. We were talking about Linda. I sometimes wonder what they taught you at that university. It certainly wasn't common sense."

"Well, they say that's inherited from the mother."

She chuckled, "You'd be in a poor way then, if you had to get your brains from me. No. You've got my looks and your father's brains. You always could argue that black was white, and that's probably why you've done so well for yourself. Your father's so proud of you, and I am too. We both are. Well, I should get off the phone. My program's starting soon. It's called *Thorns of Love,* and it's about this priest that falls in love with a beautiful millionairess. It's hopeless, but he can't help himself. It's on BBC 2 if you and Luke want to watch it. What are you having for dinner tonight, or have you had it?"

"He's going out, remember? He's going to see his friend in Hull."

"Oh! So you're having dinner on your own?"

"Yes. Just something quick though. I've got to finish these essays first."

"That sounds lovely. Your dad and I are having fish and chips. He'll be bringing them back from Crook in a minute, so I'd better get the kettle on and the bread buttered."

"Well, enjoy yours."

"Enjoy yours. And don't strain your eyes. Are you wearing your glasses?"

"I don't wear glasses."

"Well you should. Especially with all that reading you do. But I'll get off the phone, or you'll be saying I'm a terrible nag."

"You are a terrible nag."

"I know that's what you think!"

"Well you're right as usual."

"Mothers are always right."

"I know. It's not fair. Good night."

"We'll give you a ring before you leave pet, to wish you a happy holiday. Good night and God bless."

"God bless."

"Don't let the bugs bite."

Part Four

THE SHANGRI-LA OF LESBIAN SISTERHOOD, 1974–1975

The London Times

SEPTEMBER 6TH, 1974

House Five Years Empty Upsets Judge

A judge in the High Court yesterday criticized the Crown Estate Commissioners for leaving a property in the London Borough of Camden empty for nearly five years while there were so many homeless. "It is a positive scandal, something ought to have been done about it," Mr. Justice Templeman said in a squatters' case.

19.

LUKE AND I WEREN'T EXACTLY ARGUING WHEN WE CAME ACROSS THE lemmings, because we didn't argue any more, since the time he put his hands around my neck and I looked right into his eyes and dared him to squeeze. I'd known he just wanted to hang on to me rather than kill me. He sensed that I was slipping away. So when we rounded yet another corner on the winding coast road down to Oslo, we were probably bickering. He had made some lofty assertion about the nature of being, and I had systematically destroyed it. It was probably something like that.

There must have been a couple of hundred lemmings, their tiny brown bodies strewn across the road like bomb victims. Death on such a large scale was surprising enough to distract us from the relentless pursuit of proving each other wrong. Luke's eyes lit up. He swung the VW bus into a lay by and grabbed the camera. "Lemmings!" he said. "It must be a migration." He had read all about them in his guidebook, and now here the lemmings were, just as the *Michelin Guide Bleu* had said they might be. I followed him into the road as he knelt to take a picture of the furry corpses. I wondered what had happened to the wounded.

He picked one up. Made strangely companiable by its demise, we stood shoulder to shoulder, and examined it. It seemed undamaged, pretty enough to be in a pet store, next to the hamsters and the gerbils. "Poor little lemming," I said. "You never knew what hit you."

Luke tucked it under the windscreen wiper. "Let's take him for a ride," he said. "He wanted to travel."

As we drove on, I watched the lemming jiggling against the windscreen, throwing up its little arms now and again, as if in surprise. It wasn't the urge to travel that had killed him, I thought. He just wanted to be somewhere different, somewhere he knew in his bones he was meant to be. He'd died in search of Shangri-La. Travel was just a means to an end. I knew what he meant, because here I was, staring out of another car window, knowing I should be somewhere else too.

I hadn't escaped my mother's lot at all, merely exchanged it for an upgrade. Luke and I just drove a VW bus instead of a Mini Countryman, and spent our holiday in Scandinavia instead of Blackpool. Actually, our relationship wasn't even an upgrade. At least my parents *enjoyed* Barnard Castle and *Coronation Street,* and sometimes, when they sat close together on the sofa, or chuckled at some private joke, I could tell that they loved each other. All that made this holiday bearable was the long periods of driving when neither of us needed to pretend that we were having a good time. Luke pretended to be happy because he was afraid I'd leave him, so he was trying to convince me that our life together was cheerful and jolly. I pretended to be happy so that he would stop watching me long enough for me to contemplate leaving him. There was a ferry from Oslo to Hull. I was thinking I might catch it.

I watched Luke negotiate the winding road around yet another fjord ("Yet another fucking fjord," I swore inwardly). His Tubular Bells tape finished, and he reached over to pop the Grateful Dead in the mouth of the tape deck, like a tranquilizer. He sang along in his fake cheerful voice about Cajun women, whatever they were. I wished he'd go and find himself a Cajun woman, or any woman, and stick with her and leave me alone. His loyalty was one of the many things that made me want to hurt him.

Lesbian, I thought, trying the word out for the millionth time. I watched fir trees slip by in a green blur. *I'm a lesbian. Hello, my name is Claire and I'm a lesbian.* Being lesbian sounded like having a condition, like being a diabetic. It meant closing doors instead of opening them. It meant being a sad person in the basement of a sleazy pub. *I'm gay,* I tried instead. It seemed a much nicer thing to be. *No, I'm not married,* I told some fictitious enquirer, *I'm gay.* It was like I was building a new identity inside me, stone by stone, each time I said it. I could the feel the words piling up, becoming solid. *I'm gay. Actually,* I said, *I'm a big old dyke. I'm queer, bent as a nine bob note. I leave the fairy lights on my Christmas tree all year, because I'm* like that. *I'm a lezzy. I live with a policewoman on Lesby Avenue. Lezzy, lezzy, lezzy. I'm a big, butch, queer, dyke, bulldagger lesbian.* Each word was sharp and brought a little fear with it, like an inoculation, and a little excitement too. Each word was undeniably true. I could wind around the road as much as I wanted, but it was taking me to Oslo.

I told Luke that night over dinner. "I need to explore," I said, and, "It's not about you." I tried really hard not to feel sorry for him, but I did. I think he took it as well as he did because he sensed that I really cared for him at that moment—that moment when I was being honest, and touched his sleeve and told him that I was sorry. What were the chances, he wanted to know. Did I think that after I'd had some time to myself, I might decide to come back to him?

I said that I didn't know, but it was a lie. I was like the lemming. I felt destiny pulling at my bones.

. . .

I had never met a lesbian, a real lesbian, or if I had I never knew. Linda was with a man now, so she mustn't have ever been a lesbian. A few women had spent a couple of hours in my bed, as an experiment, but we usually ended up discussing their boyfriends afterwards, like I was some kind of asexual confessor. None of them seemed to even consider a radical revision of their sexual orientation. It was said that Dusty Springfield, the singer, was a lesbian, but she had bushy hair and makeup and sang love songs about preacher men. I didn't want her as a role model. Billy Whitelaw played a lesbian in a play on BBC 1. She fell in love with one of her students, and pushed another one off a balcony to protect their unnatural secret. It made my intense attraction to her a little confusing. I read *The Well of Loneliness*—at last, a role model! A real lesbian! A nice one! I read avidly to the end of the book, the part where she sends the love of her life off to marry a man and we're meant to think it's an honorable gesture.

Despite all the bad press, I had absolute faith in the existence of a Shangri-La of lesbian sisterhood. I knew that lesbians were good people, the kind that hold open doors for women with push chairs. Through some process of cosmic lesbian osmosis, I knew my tribe was out there. Though I had never seen a positive image on the television or a billboard, I knew that I was an ugly duckling that would eventually find swans and understand why I had felt awkward for twenty-five years. So absolute was my sense that my flock was waiting somewhere, that I needed to swim out and find them, that it never occurred to me that the swans might be busy, that they might not wish to disrupt their lives for a complete stranger, that they might not have a spare bed.

It was with this kind of faith that I took the ferry back to England and a bus to Owltree Cottage. I took nothing but a few clothes and a sleeping bag, Luke's second best rucksack, half the meager contents of our bank account, and my motorbike. I left my wedding ring on the mantelpiece. I checked one last time that the photograph on which Pauline had written Pat and Trudy's address was still in my wallet, closed the front door, and latched the gate behind me.

It took seven hours to get to London, driving fast, swooping up and down the Pennines, blasting through the Midlands. I felt free and unafraid, a cowboy with everything I owned strapped to the saddle. I roared past Sunday drivers and sang wild snatches of song. I stopped once on the A1 for petrol and fish and chips, my legs shaky from the bike's vibration, my ears ringing in the sudden silence. Two youths playing pinball in the fish shop eyed each other as I gave my order.

"That's a nice bike," one of them said, as the woman bundled up my food.

"Thanks," I said, sticking my arm through the visor of my helmet to fish in my pocket for change.

"Are you a Hell's Angel then?"

"Yes," I said, "I am."

They were impressed. "Where's all the rest? Is there a lot of you?"

I laid the change on the counter. "I'm an outrider," I told him. "The other women'll be coming through in a few minutes."

"*Women?*" the first boy said. "They're all *women?*"

"Yes," I said. "All women. It's a women's Hell's Angels chapter. Actually, they're all lesbians, like me."

There was a startled silence. I smiled. It was my first coming out.

It did occur to me, as I rang Pat and Trudy's doorbell late that evening, that they might not be home, but sometimes the universe sends a little gift when you accept an invitation, in this case, footsteps, the opening of a door.

Pat did not look like as much like a lesbian as she did in Pauline's photograph. She had a child for one thing, a little boy who peered at me from behind her legs. I was perplexed. How could lesbians have children? Pat looked soft and maternal too. The hallway of her house was clean and freshly painted, not my idea of a squat. Perhaps this was the wrong address.

"Hi," I said. "I'm Claire. Pauline Gift sent me. I think I'm a lesbian. Actually, I pretty much know I'm a lesbian." I was glad that I'd practiced this in the chip shop. "Anyway," I concluded, "I've just left my husband."

"Oh," she said, "when?"

"Well, today, or actually yesterday to be more exact. I left him in Norway."

She looked puzzled.

"We were on holiday," I said. "I got on a ferry in Oslo and went and got my bike and drove down here. Pauline gave me your address a few months ago. You do know her, right?"

"Let me get this straight," she said. "Yesterday, you dumped your husband in Norway. Today you have driven that motorbike all the way from Hull to my house in search of lesbians."

I nodded. "Bloody hell," she said, admiringly. "You'd better come in and have a cup of tea." She swung the door open. "Nice bike, by the way."

. . .

Two days later, in the wee small hours when the metropolitan police were hopefully dozing in quiet side streets far, far away, I huddled in the bushes with my new friends, Sally and Georgene. I'd arrived in Hackney just in time for Pat to get me in on the start of a new squat. Georgene knew what do, she told me. She was an old hand.

A whistle came from the end of the street, and a second shortly after from the other end. All clear. The rule was that the women who were going to live in the house did the dangerous part, the breaking and entering. That was us.

I galloped nervously down the front path with my hammer, and smashed in one the small panes of glass in the front door. I felt wildly reckless. "What on earth are you doing?" I heard my mother's voice ask. "This is a *house* for goodness' sake. You're *stealing* it from the Council!" I pushed her aside and reached through with my gloved hand to open the door latch. This was the moment that we could be arrested. Sally and Georgene darted from the bushes, their arms laden with all our gear. I shut the front door behind them, and we stared at each other, panting, for a second or two, before scrabbling in the bags for the new door lock, the screwdrivers and the torch.

It was ridiculously simple. Within ten minutes, we each had a brand new key to our front door, which was neatly mended with a piece of plywood. We shared a beer in the living room, which was furnished with three picnic chairs and a card table. We were legal.

Lesbians from the surrounding houses turned up all next day to help out and to donate furniture. Abby, Georgene's girlfriend, turned up with a special key, popped down a manhole in the street, and turned on the water. Helga fixed the electricity. Three women in a truck carried in a gas stove and installed it in the kitchen. They wore leather jackets. They had tight jeans and big boots. They wielded spanners and electric drills. They carried heavy objects. They went derry wrecking in smashed and abandoned buildings, rescuing wood and gas pipes. They knew how to do the things that I'd thought only men could do, but they were not boastful. They discussed the best way to proceed. They carried their empty cups through to the kitchen. They swept up their wood shavings. They were laconic and somewhat wry. I liked their style.

A woman called Terry hung around after the others had left. I'd bought a piece of high impact foam for a mattress, and she helped me build a rough platform bed to put it on, then stayed on for Chinese. Terry rolled a joint, and we smoked it cross-legged on the floor. She was one of those cheerful, cocky little dykes, I remember, alert like a terrier. She was courtly in the way butches like to be, like a well-mannered schoolboy with an irrepressible twinkle. She wore a denim shirt with the sleeves rolled. Her hands were quick and restless. On one bony wrist she wore a man's watch—the kind that had a metal expanding bracelet. Her hair was buzzed so short that I would be scared to be seen with her in public. I thought she was the most amazing person I had ever seen. I couldn't take my eyes off her.

"So when did you split with this husband of yours then?" she said.

I squinted against the smoke as I exhaled. "Lemme see. Four days ago." I was trying not to babble, to measure my words as she did, to make them worth something.

"But you've been with women, right?"

"Oh," I said, "Well, yeah. Three or four. But not for any length of time, you know? They usually had to get home to their boyfriends."

"Oh," she said, long and drawn out, as the penny dropped. "These women were all straight?"

"Yep. I'd never really met a lesbian before," I said, "except in the mirror, and I've only just recognized *her*."

"Wow," she said. She scooted over and knelt in front of me, throwing her arms out wide. "Whaddya think?"

I blinked.

"100 percent lesbian," she explained, throwing her chest out. "Never been with a man, actually."

"Never?"

"Fell in love with my best friend at fifteen. Never looked back. So, answer the question, Whaddya think?"

I blushed and glanced away. "OK, I guess."

"Gosh," she said. "Don't you have a way with words. We need to teach you a little small talk." She unfolded her legs and threw them over mine, one either side of my waist.

The hairs on my back stood up, the little tiny ones that are responsible for the goose bumps, the ones that fire all the nerve endings in your skin and send a charge thumping straight into your pleasure center. "Are you seducing me?" I asked.

"I was hoping so." Her eyes were bright with question, like a dog when you've taken its leash from the hook, but it's not quite sure whether or not that means a walk. She pulled me forward and kissed me, very slowly. Her tongue was bold but tender. She slid her hands around my bottom and pulled.

"Mmm," she said. "Let's make up for some of that time you lost." She unbuttoned my shirt and took it off. She had soft, warm hands and seemed completely without inhibition as she squeezed my nipples lightly and grinned when I groaned.

"It's been a while, huh?" she said sympathetically.

I took her hand and kissed the bones and sinews at the back of it. I kissed her watch and pressed it against my cheek. "I like your hands," I said. "I've wanted them to touch me all day."

"I know," she said. "Why d'you think I stuck around?"

She took my nipples in her fingers again and played with them, bending her head to lick and suck them till my clit started to throb, and I felt the length of my vagina, wanting her.

I rubbed her bristly hair. "I thought you were just being kind and helpful," I said, wrapping my legs around her back.

"I still am being kind and helpful," she said. "I stayed on to make sure your bed works OK." She rolled us towards it and pushed me aboard, unzipping my jeans and yanking them off roughly by the legs, as I hung onto the edge of the bed and raised my hips to let them slide.

When she slipped out of her own clothes, I could see that she was lean and compact. She had a rose tattooed just where her chest turned into breast. She jumped on me, growling, and I licked her smooth hard arms. She tasted of unperfumed soap.

She fitted us together, maneuvering herself till she could ride me, slowly, her arms braced, grinning her schoolboy grin as we slid moistly together. A little loop of hair flopped into her eyes and I pushed it back for her.

"You're amazing," I said.

"You like this, eh? Your straight girls didn't take you by storm with the light on, huh? They're usually a little on the shy and tentative side, I find. Expect us to do all the work."

I wrapped my arms around her back and pulled her closer, till we were moving together in an easy sexy rhythm.

"I must say," she whispered in my ear. "You take to this pretty quickly."

I reached down and brushed her clit, then eased her open with the tips of my fingers. She pushed herself over me, a little at a time, till she couldn't stop herself anymore and I took over, rolling her on her back, and filling her up like I knew she wanted it, hard, but not too rough. Her nipples were so hard I could feel each little roughness against my tongue.

"Jesus," she said. I slid my fingers out and stroked her labia, then ran my tongue along her slit, sucking up the juices.

She pulled my body up against hers and we lay facing each other for a while.

"You OK?" she said, her voice coming out a little husky.

I nodded, and stroked her face with my fingertips as we kissed, more slowly now, till she rolled on top and rode me again, pinning my wrists and pushing hard, joining our wetness together. She moved more and more quickly, her arms wrapped around me again now, our bodies sticking together once in a while because of all the sweat.

She snuck a look at my face. "You gonna come?" she asked.

"God, yes!" I said, my voice squeezed out by her insistent body slapping against mine now, her eyes squeezed shut and her top lip caught in her teeth, both of us shameless, me bucking underneath her as I came and her kissing me, filling me with her salty tongue as she shuddered against me and both of us just hanging on through it, till we were spent. After a couple of minutes, she reached back and hauled the covers up over us both.

"So that's what it's like being made love to by a 100 percent lesbian," I said.

"Actually," she said. "No, it's not."

When I opened my eyes, she was grinning at me again. She said, "That's what it's like when two 100 percent lesbians make love to each other."

20.

LEATHER CLAD AND BIG BOOTED, SPORTING A BRAND NEW BUZZ CUT, A hard street face, and a terse way with words, I clumped forward to join the ranks of radical lesbian separatists who had claimed these abandoned streets in Hackney as their empire—a no man's land you might say. I wanted to forget the past, when I hid behind a man's name and laughed at gay jokes. It hadn't been my fault, I told myself. I had been tricked and cheated. My mother had made me wear dresses and tried to turn me into a hairdresser. My father wouldn't let me use his electric drill. Society had stolen my adolescence and devastated my pride. I rarely called my parents, and I never went home. I ripped up Luke's letters and would've spat in his face if I'd seen him, because he had dared to engage me in practices that now seemed unnatural. I tried to forget that I'd let him fuck me, that I'd lain on my back for him and spread my legs, but the truth was that I'd been screwed. Even worse, I'd pretended to like it. I was furious.

Thursday nights, us big, bold dykes crammed into an upstairs room at The King's Head in Islington, a pub that had hit upon this way to make a few quid on a quiet night. We all wore blue jeans and white shirts and bumped and ground to "I Shot the Sheriff" till we found someone to go home with. I had never thought too much about why we sang along with a murderer, though I vaguely imagined that it had something to do with the fact that the sheriff's deputy had been spared. This particular night, however, the acid Georgene and I had dropped in the bathroom had rearranged my synapses somewhat, so that I believed that some wonderful truth might be found in the song's lyrics. Georgene sat opposite, her skinny denim legs propped on a chair with veteran assurance. I was lucky to have her in my squat. She knew everything and everyone and seemed happy to show me the way around. On the way here she'd told me how she'd punched out a guy who'd hassled her and her girlfriend when he saw them kissing on an underground platform. She hit him fast, hard, and dirty, she said, then grabbed Abby and ran. Looking at her contained face, framed by dark, smooth hair, I could imagine her capable of anything, like Patty Hearst.

I leaned across the table and yelled at her. "Who *was* the sheriff?"

Georgene shook her head, threw me one of her rare, sweet smiles, and spiraled her index finger to show that she hadn't heard my question and was too mellow to care, but the speed I'd taken to keep up with the acid made me persistent. I moved to perch on the edge of the chair she had her feet on and yelled in her ear. "Who was the sheriff?"

She stared at me in bewilderment.

"In the song. Why did the woman shoot the sheriff?"

She shrugged. "Who cares? He was a man. Whatever it was she said he did, he probably did it."

I imagined a man wandering in to the disco by mistake, being torn apart in seconds in a Dionysian frenzy.

"Let's dance," Georgene said.

It was a slow dance. The heaving mass of bodies had coagulated into discrete couples, and the only women not dancing were sad singles, clutching beers with awkward desperation. I shuffled my feet from side to side, thinking that I would have to spend the night alone. Georgene stepped close and put her arms around me. I must have looked flustered. "Hey," she said. "I think you're sexy. We could have some fun later."

"But what about Abby? Aren't you and she together?"

She drew back in surprise and studied my face at arms' length, as if looking for the joke. "Don't tell me you've bought into all that monogamy shit!"

"I haven't really thought about it, I suppose."

She pulled me close again, so we could talk more easily. "It's a male invention," she told me, speaking straight into my ear, so that the words tickled. "Goes back to those bloody colonialist knights. They didn't want anyone tampering with their property while they were off killing heathens. The nuclear family is the perfect chastity belt. Hang a couple of babies around a woman's neck and keep her financially dependent."

"So Engels was right," I said, proud that I was so cogent given the throb of the beat and the smell of Georgene's hair, and the wiry firmness of her arms around me, all amplified by the half tab of acid that I was honor bound to stay cool with, since no one here liked all that demonstrative hippy bongo shit any more. We were reconstructing everything along radical feminist lines. I needed to get in step.

"Exactly," Georgene said. "He had the method of oppression right. He just wasn't a woman, or a lesbian, like us." She gave me a sparkling smile and put her hand on the back of my neck so that she could kiss me. "That would be us," she said, "being lesbians, like we are."

There was nothing dialectic about the kiss. My body was ready to serve in the revolution. Subversive messages were zinging up and down my channels of communication, causing mass unrest. She pulled my shirt out of my jeans and slid her hands up my back.

"Oi! Cut that out," hissed a voice in my ear. It was Madge, of Madge and Sandy fame—the two stone-faced bouncers who kept curious men away and maintained order and decency in our ranks. The look she threw at us was partly complicit and partly hard-ass. "Go home if you want to do that stuff," she said to Georgene. "This is a dance floor." Madge and Sandy usually addressed their admonishments to the butchest looking of a troublesome pair.

Georgene giggled. "She started it."

"Oh right," Madge said. "You're such a little innocent. Pure as the driven. I know you, Georgene. You're a corrupter of youth."

"See what trouble you are?" Georgene threw a mock punch at me and I blocked it instinctively. Sandy materialized at Madge's shoulder, and raised an eyebrow at her.

"They're just arsing around," Madge told her. "I think they're smashed."

I threw a soft punch right back at Georgene. She crouched in a boxing stance and circled me, full of the devil. Madge and Sandy eyed us uncertainly as we sparred, clearing a space in the dance floor.

"Look here," said Madge, dropping a hand on my shoulder, "go home and take it out on each other a nicer way."

I was piqued. I had been branded as the femme and now I was losing the fight. Whichever way I moved, Georgene peppered me with light punches, stopping them just short of my face and torso. "This one doesn't know which hand she wants to lead with," I heard Sandy say to Madge.

Standing side by side with their arms folded, they observed me with professional interest. "Yeah," said Madge. "She can't make her mind up."

I threw myself at Georgene and grabbed her round the waist, knowing that I would have the weight advantage, even if I did get pummeled on the way in. I lifted her up and then flipped her legs aside with one of mine and decked her. We rolled around on the floor, giggling, till Madge and Sandy hauled us up, dragged us to the door and pushed us out of it.

"Fucking maniacs," Madge said, as she watched us kiss on the stairs.

A couple of hours later, back at the squat, Georgene and I lay sleepy and naked in her bed, surrounded by the smell of sex—salty and warm, like yeasty bread rising. I hoped that chemistry had made us closer, this mingling and kneading we had done, but lately I had been feeling somehow empty after sex. I couldn't get enough of it, but it was like every orgasm was like a little death, emptying the joy out of the cells of my body and leaving sadness there instead.

Georgene peeled an orange and handed me a piece. I was used up from the acid, too, worn thin and ghostly, and the burst of clean citrus took me straight back to Linda, as a taste sometimes will. I remembered the passion and purity in her blue eyes, the shock of her. A line from *The Crucible* came to me, about how there was a promise made in every bed, and I thought of Linda lying in her bed somewhere with her husband, and her children sleeping next door, her nuclear family. I wondered if she remembered the promise we had made, when we didn't have any words to make it real, and how we had broken that promise forever.

"Where'd you learn that trick?" Georgene asked. "You know, the hip throw thing you pulled on me at The King's Head?"

"My brother, Matthew," I said. "He used to do it to me all the time."

"Oh," she said, and flopped onto her back and lit a cigarette. "Mine taught me a few tricks too. Not as useful though."

"Why did you play if it wasn't any fun?"

"It was fun for him."

"But not for you?"

"He used to come into my room at night," she said. "After my parents were asleep. You know."

"God," I said.

She yawned. "God wasn't watching, I guess."

. . .

I hauled myself out of her bed next morning, feeling like shit, and arrived late and breathless for the first class of the day at Fawcett Hill Secondary School, spilling armfuls of exercise books on my way to the teacher's desk, cursing under my breath and yelling at the kids to shut up.

"What time do you call this then?" one of them called out into the sudden silence, launching a spatter of good-natured teasing. "Late night *again* then Miss? Been home at all then have yer?" The Indian girls giggled behind their hands, and then jumped up to collect the scattered exercise books and hand them round the class. Even though this was a special priority school, I got on with the students much better than I had with those in Yorkshire. It was as if they were relieved that I wasn't trying to save them, reassured that I had my own life to lead.

On the way home, I noticed some rubbish bins and a roll of carpet set out on the pavement, and throttled back the bike to check it out. The carpet turned out to be stained and filthy, but there were two big tins of white emulsion paint there, dusty but unopened. I stuck them on the carrier for Sally.

Holly, the newest resident of our house, questioned Sally's qualifications as a radical lesbian, which she could with ease, since her own were impeccable. Holly worked at a battered women's shelter by day and studied at night to become a lawyer so that she could advocate for battered women even more effectively. She read the *Times* and *The Socialist Worker* every morning over yogurt and granola. She was thus able to support a plethora of judgments with careful reasoning and well-substantiated facts. No doubt her bowel movements were equally well ordered. Since her arrival, she had instituted weekly house meetings, which she insisted we each "facilitate" in turn. When Sally or I were in charge, I noted that Holly tended towards restlessness and offered not-so-subtle suggestions as to correct procedure. After much fumbling to stay on task, we usually managed to generate some sort of rota for cooking, cleaning, or visiting the food co-op. Holly taped these neatly to the fridge and would glance at them from time to time, with a bright smile. "Let's see!" she would say, as if we were nursery school inmates with some great treat in store. "Whose turn is it to clean the kitchen this week?"

Sally was not easy to organize, being what my mother would have called "an odd duck." She spent most of her time in her room, especially if Holly was home in between bouts of making the world a better place. Sally emerged at odd hours to drink strong black tea at the kitchen table, rumpled and blinking like a bear fresh from hibernation. She drank her tea with a spoonful of honey on the side, and was given to wandering the house, setting honey spoons down and forgetting them. Holly discovered them from time to time on her preordained cleaning binges, oozing quietly on top of the fridge, or on the toilet cistern.

Though she hated the rota, Sally loved the house, and she lent it life in bursts of ecstatic energy, during which she baked bread, sewed cushion covers, scrubbed the toilets with bleach, or installed a new sink. She wore anything that took her fancy, even things with frills and flowers, pink, girly things that swirled as she danced in the kitchen. She spent hours "derry wrecking," rooting through abandoned houses, dragging home an old chair, a set of plaster ducks, a brand new toaster. She had unquenchable optimism about even the tattiest of items, noticing potential in all sorts of broken things. "We can glue the leg," she'd say, or "cut out the stained part." She clapped her hands when I staggered into the kitchen with the tins of paint.

"I can't believe someone just threw that out!" she said. "Find a screwdriver or something!" She ran upstairs to her bedroom and re-emerged with an ancient bottle of red ink. "Pink!" she said. "Let's paint the kitchen pink! We've got the whole weekend to do it. Open the paint!"

I blanched at the idea of a pink kitchen. What would Holly say when she got back from her yoga weekend? "Oh come *on!*" said Sally. "Live on the wild side! You don't have to be boring just because you're a lesbian!"

I hesitated as she grabbed the screwdriver from my hand and pried at the lid. "I dunno," I said. "Maybe we should check with Georgene and Holly."

"For Christ's sake," she said, banging hard on the end of the screwdriver. "I'm sick of living by committee and I'm sick of bossy little lists on the fridge and I'm sick and tired of Holly's power trips!" The lid of the paint can flew off and spiraled to a halt on the lino in sudden surprised silence. Sally straightened up and glared at me. "I don't know about you, but I got fucked-up by rules. I don't want to be a good girl." She unscrewed the top from the bottle of ink and raised her eyebrows at me. "Ready to make a big mess, or do you need written approval from the politburo?"

I peered into the tin. I was still burned-out from the night before, not really in the mood for excitement. "Are you sure this will work?" I asked her.

"Why shouldn't it?" she said, "Stop being such a wimp. I thought you were butch." She started to pour. I fetched a wooden spoon and began to stir. We added all sorts of things as we went along: most of the contents of an Easter egg coloring kit, some temporary hair dye and some of the felt tipped pens Holly kept for making posters. Sally stole these from Holly's room, and I broke them apart and scrunched up the inky middle parts in the blender. By nine o'clock that night, we had turned an entire wall strawberry pink. "I was going to meet Georgene for a drink," I said, glancing at my watch, "but I'll stay and help you finish."

"Hey," she said. "Don't let me ruin your social life."

Something in the way she said it made me pause. "What?" I said.

She looked down at me from the kitchen chair she was standing on. "Well," she said. "Your social life is pretty active, from what I heard last night."

I blushed a little. "Oh," I said. "That must have been me and Georgene, sorry."

She pursed her lips in concentration as she skirted a window with the small brush. "So what's it all about?"

"What's it all about, *Alfie?*" I crooned, coming along after her with the paint roller. It was a game we'd been playing as we worked: if one of us innocently mentioned a song cue in passing, the other launched straight into the first line and we suspended conversation until we'd sung as much of it as we could remember. We had christened the game "a song for every occasion." She joined in now on the "Is it *just* for the *moment* we live?" part. I liked the way Sally sang, as unrestrained and unselfconscious as an opera star, or as my mother. Actually, we'd knocked out quite a few of Mam's favorites from *The Sound of Music.* I hadn't realized how much I'd missed them.

"It's a good question," Sally said.

"I don't know the answer," I said. "How about you?"

"I believe in love," she said, wrestling open the second tin of paint.

I didn't know if she was serious, or just quoting the song. "Don't we all?" I asked her.

"I don't know," she said. "You lesbians never seem to talk about what you feel. Do you believe in it?"

"Sure." The hangover I'd suffered from all day seemed to be gathering energy from the paint fumes. I registered the "you lesbians" bit.

"What is love then, in your opinion?"

"Hell, I don't know," I said. Sally was staring to sound like my mother, with all her romantic notions. "What's your guess?"

"It's divine inspiration."

"It's *what?*" I said.

"You heard. It's not a new theory."

"Well, yeah, I know, but, hell, I don't know." I was unused to talking like this any more. I had got beyond the God thing years ago.

"Doesn't fit the lesbian dogma? Why not? God's neither male nor female. Says so right in the Bible. Politics are just a human invention."

"Yeah, but how do you know God exists even? There's no proof."

"Oh come on!" Sally said scornfully. "You know better than that. How can you prove the moon's not made of green cheese? Or that it's not OK to bash an old lady on the head with a brick? Pass me the cloth up will you?"

I handed it up to her. "That's bloody first year philosophy, that is," she said, as she wiped a drip off the window frame, "and you know it. Cut out the games."

She'd got me there. "Well, how do you know God exists then, personally speaking?"

"I meditate," she said. "I experience God firsthand."

I carried on covering the wall, cross-hatching like my Mam had taught me, buying a little time to think. Hadn't I read something about the Beatles' guru driving around in a Rolls Royce? "Are you in some kind of cult thing then?" I asked.

"There's a master, if that's what you mean," she said. "He doesn't ask anyone for money, and we don't recruit. If someone asks, like you just did, we talk about it, otherwise we don't."

"And he doesn't mind you being gay?"

She shook her head. "It's not a religion," she said. "It's a spiritual practice. There aren't any rules."

The door swung open and Holly walked through it. She dropped her overnight bag on the floor and gave the walls a long, cool stare. I felt like I'd been caught out.

"So you had a meeting without me then?" she said heavily, "and decided to paint the walls this color?"

I glanced at Sally. "Not really," I said. "Sally and I just thought it would be fun. The two of us."

It was as if I hadn't spoken. Sally set her brush down and turned to Holly. "Don't you like it?"

"That's not the point. If we can't live together and make this kind of decision jointly, what hope is there? What hope is there for the world?" She seemed almost tearful.

"Whether you like it or not is the only point," Sally said. "If you change the world by committee it'll disappear up its own agenda. People work by changing themselves. That's how people work. I understand what you want me to do, how you want us all to live. I won't do it. I'd rather die. I *would* die."

"Then why did you choose to live here?"

"I was looking for somewhere to live, and I found Claire and Georgene, who were also looking for somewhere to live. We were just people. I never signed anything that said I had to vote. I never voted to have you join the house, but you were a woman looking for somewhere to live, like I was, and now you're saying that I can't live with you."

"I can't live with you because you're antisocial. You stay in your room the whole time. You bring men into the house, which is offensive to me.

You break agreements that we've all made. You make decisions like this." She pointed at the pink walls.

"Are you throwing me out?"

"Don't be melodramatic. That's not my decision. But maybe you should consider finding some other people—people who would like to live with you."

"Hang on," I said. "Sally and Georgene and I started this squat together. That counts for something. Besides which I like living with Sally. I don't want her to leave."

Sally laughed, and dropped a hand on my shoulder. "Maybe you should find some people you can stand to live with, Holly. It's not about right and wrong, you know. It's about feelings."

21.

IT WAS A SLOW NIGHT AT THE KING'S HEAD, AND I WAS THERE ALONE.
Chilly September drizzle had kept people at home. Tammy, the DJ, was
winding us down with Natalie Cole, and the singles had pretty much
split, leaving lucky couples to smooch and a few hopefuls to eye each
other up like leftovers. Madge and Sandy had relaxed their vigilance, and
circled slowly together, Madge's stone-cut face soft and strangely touching as Sandy's head rested on her shoulder.

I had finally worked up the nerve to ask a pretty girl to dance. What
the hell. If she said no, I was too drunk to care, and she might say yes.
I'd been watching her all evening—the sad delicacy of her features, the
way she pushed her hair back from her face only to have it fall again.
When I presented myself before her, she nodded and stood up without
hesitation. I took her cool palm in my sweaty hand and led her onto the
floor. I held her cautiously, as if she were fragile, did the dance, asked a
few questions.

Jane. Her name was Jane. Yes, she'd been here before. Yes, a couple
of times. The china department at Harrods, actually. Well, it was OK
and, yes, it paid pretty well. Yes, some of it *was* quite interesting, actually. Well, like how you found out if china was good by flipping it with
a fingernail. Sometimes there were these little bubble things hidden
inside there. Flaws, they called them. When you pinged something with
a flaw, you could hear it didn't sound quite right. Well *she* couldn't. No
really she couldn't. She'd only been there six months.

Her voice was very BBC, husky, as if out of practice. After a while,
she put her arms around my hips and pulled me into her. "I know all
about *you*," she said. "You don't need to tell me anything. Let's not talk
any more."

I had been radicalized by this time. I'd descended deep into lesbian
grunge, quit my teaching job to sign on once a week and spend my dole
money on beer, drugs and a tank of petrol. I was wearing my cleanest

jeans, my leather jacket, and an Incredible Hulk T-shirt I'd bought for fifty pence at Oxfam. I had washed this so many times it stretched across my skinny frame just like the Hulk's clothes did when someone crossed him. This was when The Hulk told his truth, when his bulging muscles ripped his sober, everyday clothes apart, and he stood naked before his startled tormentors, puzzled at their injustice, baffled by a rage that could destroy them.

"Me Tarzan. You Jane," I told her, stupidly, and she smiled for the first time and tilted up her head so I could taste the surrender in her lips, exotic with lipstick, the milky whiteness of her neck, touched with perfume, feel her hair against my cheek, soft, perfumed, conditioned.

I remembered that smell from when I was a kid, shopping at Binns or Debenhams for Mam's Christmas present, how I'd sneak warily into the cosmetic department, one hand in my shorts' pocket to clutch my saved up pennies so they wouldn't jingle and disrupt the cathedral-like calm. Girls just like Jane sat frozen in elegant attitudes behind the ranks of perfume bottles, studiously avoiding the eyes of customers. Instead, they gossiped acidly and shot furtive glances towards the ugly old doyen crouched at the cash desk. After an agonizing eternity, one of them would lift a penciled eyebrow at me. "Can I help you?" Her friends curled their glossy lips in barely disguised contempt as I stood there, scabby-kneed and tongue-tied, not knowing how to find out what I could afford.

Such women had left me with an urge to rumple their composure somehow, to tousle them. I was at once drawn and repelled by their skill at putting themselves together, the seamless, impervious femininity that defied criticism at the same time as it invited my scorn for their girliness. Now here one of them was, crippled by her heels, immaculate as the Virgin Mary, waiting for me to scribble my address on her beer mat, while her *sois disant* friend Angela stared off into the distance, as if in search of a non-existent waiter. Angela was pretending that she wasn't really there, slumming it at The King's Head disco, and I colluded, happy to ignore her because I was desperate to despoil Jane, who I guessed had talked Angela into the whole thing—finishing up their evening's entertainment at an East End dyke bar so she could pick up some dirty, drunken, mindless fuck, which was me.

Jane took a taxi back to my place, claiming to be scared of catching a cold in the chilly drizzle, but the truth was that her quest for the wild side probably didn't stretch to getting wiped out riding pillion with a drunken lesbian on the Old Kent Road.

If you're wondering why lesbians like to ride motorbikes, then let me tell you—there's no cure for rage like burning it up and blowing it out behind you. There's nothing like pouring those wasted years into the engine between your legs and blasting them into smoke. There's nothing like twisting your wrist to blow off that man who guns his engine at you, grinning at his girlfriend across a pair of fuzzy dice. She clutched his arm as I idled beside them now at a red light, hungry to get home to Jane. As we pretended not to look at each other, I saw her snigger at the interlocked women's symbols stenciled on my helmet.

High on speed and promise, I left them behind, but five minutes later, I took the turn onto E11 too sharply, and skidded in the slickness. For a few horrible moments, I clung to the bike as it weaved and twisted along the wrong side of the road. I had just enough presence of mind to stay away from the brake. A police car appeared out of nowhere and pulled alongside as I stopped at the curb, sweating.

"Park the bike," the policeman said and opened his door. Brusque male voices crackled on his radio as he clambered heavily out to stare at me as I wrestled the bike onto the stand, washed in the accusation of his circling blue light.

"Ever thought of getting something you can handle?" he asked, slow and casual, taking his time. "Something a bit more ladylike?"

I said nothing, as he looked me up and down with a grin. "But then you're not much of a lady, are you? What's that thing on your helmet mean?"

"Oh," I said lightly, "It's just a feminist badge."

"Oh really. So what does your boyfriend think of that?"

"Are you allowed to ask me that kind of personal question?"

He took a step towards me and dropped the grin. "Do you know how fast you were going, on the wrong side of the road, out of control? Do you?"

"I skidded."

"Because you were out of control. You're totally out of control, you and your kind. You don't have a boyfriend do you? And you think I'm stupid, don't you? Well I'm not. I know what that symbol means sweetheart. It means you crawled out from under some fucking stone like all the other fucking queers." He took hold of me by the front of the jacket and pulled so that my toes lifted off the ground slightly. "You're thinking this is harassment aren't you?"

I nodded. "Well spotted," he said, and let go. He dusted his hands off against his trousers. "Bugger off," he said. "When you kill yourself, try not to take anyone normal down with you."

I drove home demurely, signaling at every turn. Jane was shivering at the door when I got there. "Christ," she said. "This is a bloody awful place to keep me waiting for half an hour. I hope to God you've got something to drink."

I opened the front door without speaking and led her upstairs to my bedroom. I poured two big glasses full of scotch from the bottle next to my bed and handed her one. "I got stopped by the fuzz," I said. The incident seemed more romantic now that I was drinking scotch with Jane.

"God," she said.

"He was a fucking pig," I said. "He tried to intimidate me. The only good thing was that I didn't really show any weakness." I was already reframing the story.

"I always cry," she said. "Everybody lets you off if you cry."

"He let me off anyway," I said. "He pretty much said he hoped I'd kill myself if I kept riding the bike."

"You have that air about you," she said. "Like James Dean or something. It's why I picked you up."

She put her drink down and took mine away and set that down too and kissed me, arching her neck and pulling me down against her with her hands in my hair. I took her clothes off carefully, opened her up slowly, like a gift, till she lay back, naked and passive, her body gleaming in the streetlight that reached out to stroke her from the uncurtained window.

I took her in my arms, brushed back the heavy fall of her hair to kiss the porcelain curves of her ears, inhaled the smell of her, exotic in my unmade bed like spices from the Orient, costly and rare.

"You're gentle," she said, as if surprised. I touched her nipple, and she tensed.

"Don't bother," she said. "They're wired up wrong."

The more I touched it, the more her nipple tightened up inside her, pushing downwards toward her heart. She took my hand impatiently and pushed it between her legs, but when I slid a finger into her, she was dry. I kissed her there, tried to kick start her with my tongue like she was a cold engine, but though she thrust against me and shuddered I could tell it was fake.

We lay in silence for a while, till I said, "You faked it."

She sighed. "I'm sorry."

"What happened? Was it me?"

She rolled onto her back. "I had a sort of breakdown thing two years ago." Her voice was matter of fact. "My boyfriend broke up with me, and there was some other stuff. Stuff I don't want to talk about. Anyway, I ended up in hospital. I got better, but since then I've been like this. Frigid."

The word lay there between us for a while.

"Do you enjoy sex?" I asked her. "I mean did you? Just now?"

"It's pleasant," she said. "My body's just not wired up right any more. Once in a while I check."

"So that's what you were doing with me—checking?"

"Sorry," she said again. "At least I'm telling you the truth." She kissed the end of my nose. "You're sweet. Too sweet to be a diesel dyke."

The next morning I found a Harrods bag tucked inside the orange crate. Inside it was a brooch, made of tiny china roses.

I set it aside, thinking I'd give it to my mother for Christmas.

22.

THOUGH SOME PEOPLE LIKE TO STEREOTYPE THE BRITISH, THE MORE knowledgeable will love to tell you that the British Isles are made up of four different countries, England being only one of them. A lesser-known fact is that England itself is divided into two discrete regions—the North of England and the South. The line that divides them is variously defined. People on the south coast believe that the North of England begins at the River Thames. Londoners claim that it lies beyond Watford Gap. For their part, Northerners claim that the true North begins much higher up, somewhere in the Midlands.

I would set it at a point on the A1 where six cooling towers dribble smoke into the flat gray sky like lazy sentries. As one barrels past them, due north along the old Roman road, the landscape eases out into rolling moors and hillsides, scattered with rusting coal mines, ragged sheep, and grimy towns, where all the back-to-back houses are for sale, and unemployed men in shapeless raincoats gather outside betting shops to thrust their hands into their empty pockets.

In our hotchpotch of a household I initially gravitated towards Sally because she was a Yorkshire Lass, with the same long, stubborn roots as mine, like those on the tenacious, wiry parsnips my dad pried out of the frosted garden in November. Georgene, Australian by birth, had created herself anew, shucking off the patriarchy like dirty underwear and ironing out any ethnic wrinkles in her smooth lesbian persona. For all Holly's radical veneer, she was a nice, middle-class girl at heart. Her parents owned a Range Rover and lived in Milton Keynes. She ate bean sprouts and washed them down with Earl Grey tea. There was a terrible earnestness about her activism that brought out the worst in Sally and me. She was relentlessly diligent, as if she expected a prize for achievement. What really pissed me off was that she would no doubt win it. Her nice parents and her good school and her law degree would see to that, as Sally pointed out. "The battered women will stay battered, and Holly will make a nice living. It's as clear as the nose on your face. It'll stay like that till people change." She poured more tea into her mug, picked up the Rizla reds and started to construct a cigarette, her capable fingers seeming to have eyes of their own as they packed tobacco into a smooth cylinder and nipped away the shaggy ends.

Sally and I had established a sort of northern enclave in the kitchen, and spent an increasing amount of time smoking endless roll-ups, drinking strong black tea, and arguing about the most effective way to set the universe to rights. An old door with four-by-fours screwed on it for legs served as a table on which we had piled the necessities of a good long chat—a massive black teapot, full of well-stewed PG Tips, a bottle of milk, several mugs, a bowl of sugar, two packets of Old Holborn, the cigarette papers, and a packet of gingersnaps.

"That's all very well," I told her, sprinkling a little grass into my roll-up, "but society doesn't change by itself. This policeman stopped me last night. He was Neanderthal, Sally. You've got no idea."

She looked a little skeptical. "Well, you want people to think you're scary, don't you? Why blame him for doing what you want? How do you think you'll change anyone if you scare them shitless and act out their darkest fears?"

"Hell, Sally! I've got a right to be who I want to be. He's meant to respect everybody equally, not pick and choose. It's a bloody democracy after all!"

"Yeah, but you're the one that's talking about change. What's your grand plan to change that policeman then?"

"Well, I thought I was going to do it through education. Start with kids before society got to them, help them see through all the advertising bullshit."

She jammed her plastic national health glasses back up the bridge of her nose with her forefinger. "But you quit your teaching job."

"We all did," I said, firing up a Swan Vesta and setting it to the twisted end of my toke. "It was a protest against underfunding. Besides which I didn't really see how making those poor kids write essays about poetry was helping anything. But people are still doing useful things. I mean, look at Holly. Say what you like, but at least she's out there fighting for abused women."

"People don't change because a bunch of lefty teachers leave their jobs, or Holly marches about with a banner. God." She cackled, shook out her match, and dropped it into the overflowing saucer we used as an ashtray. "Holly's an *incentive* to batter. I'd batter her myself if I wasn't a pacifist."

"Well at least she's doing *something*. I'm trying to decide my next step. What are *you* doing?"

She gave me a strange look, complicit and assessing, then leaned back in her chair. "I'm going to be an osteopath," she said.

"An *osteopath?*" I was flummoxed.

"I've been accepted for a course in Kent. I just got a letter yesterday."

"My God," I said, astonished.

"Well come on! It's not like I'm saying I want to be an axe murderer when I grow up."

My poor little brain cells were rushing around like ants trying to reassemble a nest that some clodhopper had put his foot into. A course in Kent, she'd said, so she was moving. .

" . . . changes people at a deep level," she was saying. "It's holistic. If that policeman's lying on my table with all his anger making his back hurt, maybe he'll be ready to change. He *has* to change to get better. I can help him cut through all the crap." Her face had lost all of its funnygirl cheeriness. She looked serene, somehow, powerful like a priestess or something. Her green eyes were intense, very deep somehow, and luminous, like there were tunnels in there and people with candles.

I stared at her, surprised that I hadn't expected this, even in our revolving door of a community. I felt a little chastened, as if I had been remiss in some way, too casual, too sloppy.

She leaned forward and propped her elbows on her knees to look me in the eye. Her eyes were wild, like a goat's. "Speaking of crap. Isn't it about time you got yourself together?"

Now, as I stared into Sally's wild green eyes, I felt like Kirk Douglas in *The Vikings*—that part when he's the captain and he's standing at the front of the longship with the wind whipping his face. Behind him there's this big ox of a man with a bald head, and he's beating on a drum and the poor slaves are straining at the oars. They're pretty scared because they're chained to the deck and these enormous waves are crashing over their heads and if the ship goes down they'll go down with it, so they keep rowing, even though they're pretty scrawny looking and underfed. The other sailors are hanging on to ropes and spars and things for dear life, peering ahead into the murky waves, watching for the edge of the world, which they believe they are about to reach. They think that when they reach it they will fall off it into some kind of Viking hell and fry there forever and lose their chance of reaching Valhalla. The trusty first mate, who has followed Kirk Douglas into battle etcetera and has scars and probably even missing body parts to prove it, even he shakes his captain by the arm. "Turn back, Captain! You must turn back! It's the End of the World!" A huge wave lifts the boat up and sends it plunging downwards, and I sat there like Kirk Douglas, staring into the abyss.

"I don't know, Sally," I said, after a while, wrenching away from her gaze. "It's all fucked-up."

"Of course it's all fucked-up."

"I don't have a map."

She ground her roll-up out in the ashtray. "Of *course* you don't have a map. Of course it's fucked-up. This is the temporal plane. It doesn't matter where you start, not really. It's about intention. It's just about taking responsibility for your own actions. You can only change yourself."

"Oh great," I said, crossly. "So what do we do? Just sit back and let some poor woman get the crap beat out of her because it's her karma?"

Sally glared at me and put her mug down on the table so hard I jumped. "Don't be so fucking patronizing! Shoot him! Lock him up! Educate him! Frankly, I don't bloody care, as long as you do *something!*"

"I do! I have!"

She stood up without comment and brushed gingersnap crumbs from her jeans.

"*What?*" I asked her.

"What what?"

"Well, come on. Don't just walk out. I can tell you're just dying to say something."

"All right," she said. "Since you ask. It seems to me like you're on a hiding to nothing. I feel miserable just watching you. You've got so much talent, and you've just numbed it all." There were indeed tears standing there in her eyes.

I tried to stay afloat by clinging to semantics. "What *is* a hiding to nothing?"

"You've got no job," Sally said. "No proper home. No sense of direction. You've cut yourself off from your family. You're always stoned or drunk. You never sleep with anyone more than once, and you don't really seem to have any passion even about that. Everything your mother always warned you about—that's a hiding to nothing."

I looked away. "Oh," I said, "that."

"That," she said.

"Well, Alfie," I asked her, trying to appeal to our common language of song. "What *is* it all about?"

"I told you already," she said.

"Love?" I thought about poor fucked-up Jane from last night and her inverted nipples and how I couldn't reach her. I thought about all the women I'd slept with, and how I was starting to feel stretched out and thin, somehow, each time I had sex with someone. "You sound more and more like my poor old mother," I said.

"Fuck you!"

I stared at her.

"Hey!" I said.

"I bet your mother makes more sense than you do!" She was shaking with rage. "How dare you belittle her? You make me sick sometimes!" A piece of spit flew out of her mouth and landed somewhere on my cheek. "You're so fucking cool you're brain dead, Claire. Wake up! Do something! If you want to be a radical lesbian guerrilla then fine! I'd respect you! But all you do is spout half-baked politics, drop acid, and moan about being oppressed!"

I stared at her, speechless.

"Jesus!" she said, finally. "You're living off people who work ten-hour shifts to pay their fucking taxes!"

Holly walked quietly into the silence. She ignored Sally, who was

LOVE IN GOOD TIME

standing over me, fists clenched and shaking. "Everything all right?" she asked me, all her training about battering clearly firing up.

I nodded shakily. "It's fine. We were just having a heated discussion." Sally stood motionless for a second or two longer, then walked off upstairs.

Holly stood there uneasily. "Look," she said finally. "I know you and Sally have got something going together, but I think she's crazy. You listen to her too much. If you take my advice you won't get too involved."

"Me and Sally?" I said. "Oh no. It's not like that. We just like to talk."

"Oh," she said. "Well it doesn't really matter. I want to move out."

"OK," I said. "I suppose it was on the cards. When are you leaving?"

"Well," she said. "That's what I wanted to talk to you about. I met this woman, Julia, at the shelter. Her husband half killed her when he found out that she was a lesbian. She wants to start a new life."

"So you're moving in with her?"

"We want to start a squat. There's a house just became empty two streets down."

"Oh," I said, wondering why she was telling me all this.

"Julia can't afford to get arrested," Holly said, significantly. "She's got a kid."

"Ah," I said, seeing where she was headed. "You want me to help."

"It's in a good cause," she said.

"OK," I said. "Why the heck not?"

23.

As I crouched in the bushes next to Holly, all I could think was how we were like actors in a bad movie. The whole thing was so fucking predictable—two policemen crunching around in a dark city garden chasing skulking villains. Only the scratchiness of the forsythia and the ache in my knees reminded me that this was actually happening—the darkness punctuated by crisscross flashlight beams that illuminated random trees, ominous branches waving obligingly against the bilious half-lit London sky—me hiding from the cops. Somehow, I had blundered into another wrong script, and I was the bad guy.

It was all Holly's fault. We should have left when the next door neighbor heard us, when the window stuck and I'd tried to force it and a woman's tremulous voice had called out from next door. "Who's there?"

I hadn't wanted her to be frightened. It seemed ridiculous. It was just me. I knew that I wasn't frightening. I'd glanced at Holly, who shook her head as she continued to struggle with the window.

"Who's there?" the woman had called again, shrill with false bravado. "Get out of here before I call the police!"

Unable to stand the fact that she was pointlessly upset, I walked towards her across the common garden and stopped in a pool of street-light so she could see me through the crack in her back door. "It's OK," I called out. "We're just trying to start a squat in this empty house next door to you. We're not burglars or anything."

There was a startled pause before she yelled, "Get out of here! I'm calling the police." The door banged shut and I stood there, dithering about whether to go and knock on her door and try to talk to her. It's difficult to reassure someone when you're lurking in their back garden at 2:00 A.M.

In the end, I'd walked back to tap Holly's shoulder and jerk my head in the direction of the gate. She was still wrestling with the window, which had opened for six inches and then stuck. If we could crawl inside and change the front door lock there was nothing the police could do except go to court and have us evicted, and we knew they wouldn't bother. "You go if you want," Holly hissed. "It's just stuck. It'll only take a minute." When I took her arm, she jerked away like I was the enemy.

I tried again when I heard the sirens in the distance. "Christ, Holly," I'd said. "It's the police. She must have called them. They're almost here. Christ. Come on. We're going to get nicked."

Holly turned to face me, her lips compressed, her face white and set. "They can't touch us for starting a squat," she said reasonably, as if she were conducting a house meeting. "We haven't damaged anything. I've shut the window again. I'm just going to wait till they leave."

"You're crazy," I said. "They'll *find* us, Holly! This is *reality!*"

Her eyes filled up. "Julia *needs* this house. She's counting on me." She walked away from me and sat in the bushes with her back to me, like a recalcitrant child. I walked to the fence, stopped and turned to look at her. She hadn't moved. "Shit!" I said. "Shit!" I stumped back and plopped down beside her, so angry that I couldn't speak. We sat in stony silence as the car drew up, siren off, headlights dimmed. Two big black shadows vaulted the fence and began an efficient search. When they were almost on top of us I stood up.

"We're over here," I said. "You can stop looking." My voice came out bored, a little contemptuous. The first one ran over, all shiny metal badges and bristling efficiency, as if we were real criminals. He reached for his handcuffs, and I was vaguely amused. "Don't bother," I told him. "We're pretty harmless." They cuffed us anyway. They dragged us to the car, put their hands flat on top of our heads and pushed us in, just like on an American cop show.

I thought we had a chance with the desk sergeant who booked us. He was an older guy, with crinkles that betrayed the fact that he smiled a lot. Right now, his crinkles were arranged in a somewhat forbidding frown, but I could see their potential. His nametag said that he was Sergeant Billings.

"Come on, Sergeant Billings, " I encouraged him. "We were just trying to start a squat for a homeless woman with kids. We didn't damage anything, unless you count a scratch on the windowsill. We didn't steal anything. We didn't even get inside."

He pointed his pen at Holly, who glared back at him as if he were the Gestapo. "What about her then? Why won't she tell us her name? She got a record or something?"

"No," I said. "I don't know what's wrong with her. I think she's just freaked out. Come on," I told her. "Just tell him your name. They're going to find out anyway."

She shook her head again.

Sergeant Billings tapped his pencil on the desk. "Last chance, darling," he told Holly. "You'd best listen to what your friend here's telling you. If you won't give me your name, I'll have to book you."

"So book us," Holly said.

He gave her a long hard stare. "Attempted burglary," he told her. "Carries quite a nice little wallop."

"Don't be daft!" I cried. "We weren't trying to steal anything. The house was empty."

He turned his shrewd blue gaze on me. "That's where you're wrong. There was furniture stored on the top floor. That's why the owners fitted window locks."

Window locks. So that's why they wouldn't open. Sergeant Billings's baggy eyes were still assessing me. "We didn't know about the furniture," I told him earnestly. "We thought the place was empty."

He chuckled and raised his eyebrows stagily at the policemen who'd brought us in and still stood there, like big trees. "Oh dear," he said. "They're innocent. What were you thinking, lads, bringing in two innocent young girls who just happened to be hiding in someone else's garden with enough tools to start a do-it-yourself shop?"

"I dunno, Sarge," one of them said heavily. "I dunno what we was thinking."

The sergeant jerked his head towards the door. "Take them down," he said. "Book them. Keep them separate."

The cell was breezeblock, painted with pale brown cat puke emulsion and illuminated by a single bulb hanging from the ceiling in a metal cage. A tubular steel cot bore a thin mattress and a couple of khaki blankets,

neatly folded. The only other item of furniture was a stainless steel com-
mode that held a tasteful splash of milky Dettol. It was bolted to the floor.
Next to it lay a packet of that cheap scratchy toilet paper that you pull out
of a flat box, like Kleenex.

I sat down on the edge of the cot and took a couple of shaky breaths.
I had been arrested. I would have a police record. I'd never be allowed to
teach again. I didn't have any money and I'd have to stay in jail or call
my parents to get bail. I'd made bad decisions; worse than that, I'd made
no decisions. I was on a hiding to nothing, and this cell was the ultimate
nothing. Sally was right.

I lay on the cot and pulled the blankets over me. The naked bulb
glared down, and a drunk mumbled incessantly from a nearby cell.
"Angela!" he said. "You've gotter call Angela! She's waiting on the corner. I shouldn't have left you Ange!"

Why hadn't I walked away? I had known that woman was going to
dial 999 as certainly as if I'd seen her do it. It's what my mother would
have done. Christ! This was going to kill her!

After a while, I sat up and pulled the blankets over my shoulders,
dropped my head into my hands. What else did Sally say? What would
she say now? She'd say that I had myself, that that was all we had in the
end. Sally would be self-sufficient. She would cope with years of solitary
confinement and stay sane. She'd meditate, like Ghandi. She'd work out
an exercise program. She'd knead beads out of bread and string them on
strands of her hair to make an abacus, like that woman in the *Reader's
Digest* article I once read. I yanked my legs up onto the cot and sat in the
lotus position. OK, so this was what I had. Myself. OK. What was in
there then? What was inside this self that I had? I closed my eyes, took
a couple of deep breaths and pulled my concentration up and into the spot
just above and between my eyes. The books Sally had loaned me said that
this was the seat of the soul. For once, my system was clear of dope, so
maybe this was a good time to try.

For a long while, images of our arrest swam before me—the tree
branches swaying, and the strip search, when they'd emptied the tools out
of my pockets and tied little tags onto them. The young WPC had been
quite amused as I brought tools out of my pockets one by one like a magi-

cian. "Quite the Houdini darling, aren't you?" she'd said. "Now, you'll have to take your clothes off, but don't worry, I've seen it all before. Don't get silly on me like that friend of yours." I saw Holly's stubborn, stupid face. "Stupid. Stupid," I mumbled to myself, and twisted a little on the cot. For a second, it seemed like there was something emerging inside my head, like a tickle. I felt peculiar. Perhaps I was about to have a divine revelation. I had no way of knowing what they felt like.

I concentrated on the peculiar feeling. It was not pleasant or unpleasant, more like an alert—a red oil light flickering on a dashboard or that feeling right before you sneeze. I realized that the feeling was not new. It had been lurking there a while without me noticing. It was somehow connected with the empty feeling I'd been trying to shake off for a while. This new feeling had been hiding behind the empty blankness. It was connected with Sally. Good grief! Shazam! As soon as I put the feeling and Sally together in my mind, it fitted like a glove! A triumphant "Aha" feeling washed through me! I was having a strange feeling about Sally!

I felt like I had never ever really thought something through from start to finish like this before. I had been following other people's scripts and suddenly stumbled upon my own. I pulled the rough blankets a little closer. I needed to think about this some more! No sooner had I settled down for another think, then a policeman, a new one, jangled open the door. I smiled at him. He smiled back. "You must be our burglar," he said. "Time to answer a few questions."

He took me up to the interrogation room and made a great deal of fuss with his bits of paper and pens and the business of my name and address. He was alert and scrubbed-looking, like he'd just got out of the shower. Must be from the morning shift. I tilted my head to sneak a glance at his watch, but it was obscured by the fluffy ginger hairs on his wrist. "Well now," he said finally. "You proceeded to number nine Willington Crescent with the declared intent of breaking into that property. Is that correct?" I wondered if they taught them how to talk like that in policeman school.

"Not exactly," I said. "We went to start a squat for a homeless woman."

"OK," he said, in a concessionary sort of way, "but you needed access. You were planning to force an entry, correct?"

"Correct," I said.

He scribbled on his notepad and I waited politely.

"So you had tools concealed about your person. What were they for?"

"To fix the house up. For the homeless woman," I prompted, but he didn't write it down.

"But you used them to try and effect an entry," he said.

"Only because of the window locks."

"So you took the tools to force the window locks?"

"We didn't know there were any window locks."

"But if you had known, it was your intent to use the tools to force them?"

"I don't know what I would've thought. I might've thought that that would be against the law."

He scratched his head with his pen. "Why didn't you bring a ladder?" he said.

"I don't have a ladder."

"But if you'd had one, you'd have brought it?"

I needed to talk to Sally about this feeling I had discovered that I was having. Maybe she would understand. "Can I make a phone call?" I asked him.

"Tell me about the ladder first," he said. "If you'd had one, you're saying that you would have brought it?"

"Hang on," I said. "Why would I do that?"

He leaned forward, pen poised. "Why don't you tell me?"

"Well, I wouldn't. A ladder wouldn't have helped."

"But surely you could have gained access through the upstairs windows?"

I thought about this for a second. "Oh," I said, "so there weren't any window locks on the upstairs windows."

He wrote busily on his paper.

"Just a minute," I told him. "I didn't know about the window locks. I don't have a ladder. This is like an alternate universe."

He set his pen down neatly on the pad and pushed back against the edge of the table with his arms, as if I were a map and he needed some distance to read me. "What do you mean by that then? Are you saying that you believe in an alternate universe?"

"Well, I'm not sure," I said. "I'm beginning to wonder."

He stared at me, hard. "Is that what this group you belong to believes in then?"

I was baffled. "What group?"

"This group." He held out the address book that the WPC had taken from me. A little cardboard tag dangled from the spine. The policeman pointed to an entry with a big forefinger. "L. teachers," it read.

"Oh," I said, uncomfortably. "That's just a teacher's group. They don't have anything to do with this."

"What's the L for?"

What else began with L other than 'lesbian'? "Leytonstone," I told him. "They meet in Leytonstone."

"What about this lot?" he said. "C. Party. You wouldn't be a communist now would you?"

"What if I was? It's not against the law is it?"

"Well are you or aren't you?"

"No," I said. "I'm not." It'd been one of Luke's phases. I'd torn up my card when I left him.

"Let's get back to the ladder," he said.

"There isn't a ladder," I told him. "You made it up. Look. This is silly. Don't I get a phone call?"

"Do you want a phone call? It's six o'clock in the morning. Your lawyer will still be in bed."

"I don't have a lawyer. I don't have a ladder, or a lawyer, and I'm not a communist."

"I'm glad we got that straight. Now let's go back to those non-existent window locks."

"I never said they didn't exist. I just said we didn't know about them till the desk sergeant told us. Like trees falling in the forest."

"Oh come on," he said. "They were right there on the window. You tried to force them with the crowbar you had concealed about your person for that sole purpose."

"How did we get off the subject of the phone call?" This was like a bad trip.

"You said you didn't have a lawyer to phone."

"But why can't I call someone else?"

"Well you only get one call. I thought you said you wanted to wait till your lawyer was awake?"

"This is like the Twilight Zone," I said. "Look. Just try to concentrate for a second. In this universe that we are actually in, am I allowed to make a phone call?"

"Well," he said. "Technically, yes, you are."

I stood up. I was capable of thinking things through. "Then I want to make it."

24.

"DON'T SAY ANYTHING," SALLY TOLD ME, HER VOICE CRACKLING ANGRILY into the earpiece. "Not a bloody thing. I'm coming to bail you out. They can't keep you now you've been charged. I'm phoning for a taxi. Jesus, how *fucking* stupid!" I wasn't sure if she meant me, or Holly, or the police, and I didn't care. Sally was on her way. My interrogator shrugged when I told him I wasn't answering any more questions, and brought me up to the front desk, where I watched Sergeant Billings's daytime replacement clean his nails with a penknife for a while. Finally, a taxi drew up, and Sally exploded from it into the lobby, by the look of her white, angry face, ready to battle her way past every policeman in the building.

"I'm here," I said, just in case she might start tearing down walls.

"Are you all right?" she snarled without looking at me, her eyes fixed on the desk sergeant as if she were a cowboy who'd just walked into a saloon and he were a gunslinger. "They've had you here for hours."

"I'm fine," I said brightly. I hadn't felt like crying up to this point.

Sally walked over to the desk and slapped down her checkbook. "Some bloody democracy," she hissed at the sergeant. Fortunately, the daytime sergeant was a bland and stolid individual, more concerned with the seemingly complicated business of getting Sally's address and phone number than taking offense at her indignation.

When we got home, we made tea, then Sally picked up the phone and scrutinized the neat list of phone numbers Holly had taped next to it on the wall. Her face was still set and full of purpose. "What are you doing?" I asked.

"Calling Holly's parents," she said. "Her rich and no doubt influential parents. So they can get her out."

"Hey," I said. "Do you think we should be doing that? I mean what if Holly doesn't want them to know?"

She barely glanced at me. "Don't be fucking stupid!" she said again, and continued to dial.

They turned up at the squat some time later, with Holly and a lawyer in tow—a young legal aid guy with John Lennon glasses and a ponytail. After we told him our story, he rubbed his hands together and grinned. Suddenly, our ignominious capture was a victory! We were heroines! "They brought the wrong charge," he said. "Breaking and entry, maybe, but not burglary. They haven't a bat's chance in hell. They were pushing it, hoping that you'd plead guilty, or maybe that they'd squeak it by a conservative magistrate. We'll insist that they try it in the high court and they'll look like idiots."

Some months later, that's how it all turned out. Our lawyer persuaded Holly's girlfriend Julia to let her hair grow and dress up in a skirt. She told the jurors her sad story of homelessness and abuse while her two kids sat neatly in the public gallery. The furniture in the empty house turned out to be a load of junk the owners couldn't be bothered to get rid of. The next-door neighbor confirmed that I had told her we were planning to start a squat, and the high court judge threw the case out of court, with a stern reprimand to the police for wasting taxpayers' money. Holly wrote an impassioned article about the whole escapade for *Spare Rib* and became a minor celebrity in squatting circles.

Meanwhile, when I finally got to bed after the lawyer left, I fell asleep instantly, but woke with a bang at 4:00 A.M. and sat up in bed. Something had happened. Something was different. I listened to a car rumble by in the distance. From even farther away came the wail of a speeding ambulance. Not that. It wasn't that. Those were other people's concerns.

The events of the night before rushed into my vacant consciousness and arranged themselves into the most recent construct of my life—I was a felon awaiting trial. What had I been thinking? How had I got here from there? But no, it wasn't that either. It wasn't my legal status that was bothering me, and in any case, the lawyer had said that it was going to be all right.

I watched my room take shape in the gloom—a table and chair emerged, and a dark shape on the floor gathered itself into the heap of clothes I had thrown off the night before. Here I was. It was going to be all right. Everything could rearrange itself comfortably. I had time to pick up that train of thought from the cell, that strange feeling, which was somehow connected with Sally.

When I let myself think about Sally, I realized that I felt rather strongly about her. I felt like she understood me, like she really cared, like I needed to spend time with her, like I would be devastated if she moved and left me. These feelings were not those of generic good sisterhood. Could it be that—surely not! We had never touched, let alone slept together. On the other hand, Holly had thought that—and last night, when Sally had snatched me up, she would have torn down the walls, and she was the one I'd called, the one I trusted, the one I needed in my life. Wait a minute! Good God! How come I'd never seen it? It was obvious! It was as plain as the nose on my face! Talk about not seeing the wood for the trees!

I WAS IN LOVE!

I sat up in bed as the truth shot through me like a bolt of lightning. All these years I had scorned romantic love as a bourgeois invention, a manifestation of the patriarchy! But here it was, unmistakable! This was what I was feeling! This weird thing—it was love! How absurd! How fabulous! It was like the stuff that happened in films, that made my mother cry at the end, whether Joan Crawford lived happily ever after or died of leukemia. That's what my Mam had meant by those corny promises. "When you do fall in love, you'll know," she'd said, and, "There's no mistaking it. It's not like anything else." Amazingly, overwhelmingly, I knew that this was exactly what she had been talking about. There I'd been thinking it was just a trap and now here it was—my own real version of it! This was it all right!

I WAS IN LOVE!

I must tell Sally. I clung to that idea as I groped my way through the sleeping house with a hand stretched out before me, like a cheap movie spook. Past Georgene's door I fumbled, then past Holly's to follow the banister up the stairs to Sally's room. I couldn't do anything else or talk to anyone else until I had told Sally that I was in love with her. I didn't care about what might result. It didn't matter. I just needed to share my revelation with Sally, who would know what to do, who would make sense of it all, who would spring me from this prison I'd been locked inside, with my cynicism and my critical distance, my ironic detachment. The love that I had for Sally was like the wrecking ball I'd seen them swinging at buildings they'd finally got rid of. Once in motion, there was nothing anyone could do to stop it.

I cracked Sally's bedroom door open gently and slid inside, closing it behind me. Standing in the darkness, listening to her breath, I suddenly felt panicky and hysterical, like I was hiding in the garden again and the police were looking for us. There was that same sense of the inevitability of it all—that "destiny" thing. Once Sally had woken up, nothing would be the same, and here was I, alone in the moment, the only one conscious of its immanence. I could sneak out of the room. No one need ever know how close we had been. Sucking in a breath and holding it there, I reached out and touched her shoulder, as it rose and fell under its flowery eider-down.

"Sally," I whispered. "Wake up."

The room was dimmed by heavy velvet curtains, and I could just make out Sally's face in the half-light as she rolled it around towards me and opened her eyes, startled. She didn't have her glasses on, so they gleamed green and owlishly. She gazed at me, not quite knowing who I was yet, I realized. Good gracious! How beautiful she was! How come I hadn't noticed that before? I giggled and she started to chuckle too, trusting that something would be funny soon.

"I've just realized something," I said. "It's very important." My voice was that of a castaway, unused to speech.

She struggled to sit up and fumbled on top of the packing crate at the side of her bed. "Hang on," she mumbled. "I can't hear without my specs on," and then she chuckled some more at her own joke, then chuckled some more as I giggled too and watched her, fondly. She stuck her plastic national health glasses on her face and blinked through them dramatically to prove that she was awake. "OK," she said, "ready for the very important news."

"Well," I said, "I've been trying to work out why I've been feeling so peculiar lately."

"Peculiar," she said.

"Yes," I said, still whispering. "Peculiar. Remember how I was saying last week how I felt peculiar?"

She thought for a while, then nodded.

"Well I've worked out what it is."

"Good," she said. There was a long pause. "What time is it?"

"It's early," I told her. "It's very, very early." She frowned.

"Look," I said. "Try to concentrate. This is important. I think I'm in love. Actually, I know I'm in love."

"In love!" she said loudly. "Who with?"

"Shh!" I whispered.

"Why are we whispering?"

"It's a secret," I said.

"Oh," she said, lowering her voice obediently. "I see."

"I'm in love with you."

She stared.

"I've fallen in love with *you*," I said. "Don't worry. It's not a *bad* thing. I just wanted to tell you."

"What happens next?" she asked.

I considered this for a moment. "Well," I asked. "Are you in love with me too?"

"I'm not meant to fall in love," she said. "I'm trying to get to heaven."

"But have you? Are you? Are you in love with me?"

She pursed her lips and thought about it. "Yes," she said. She put up her arms to pull me under the covers.

We were ruthless and unrelenting about probing the depths of each other, reinventing naked. Being in bed with her was like being an egg in a nest, or a bear waking up in the spring, or someone in a science fiction movie traveling to a new dimension. It was dark and mysterious; everything was new. Making love was not even about sex, it was about transcendence, creation, God. I hadn't believed in love, and now here I was, in it, cleaving to a wonderful woman who was my soul mate! Suddenly, I was no longer alone, but joined together with this other person. We would journey together. Of course Julie Andrews followed Christopher Plummer across the Alps. She loved him.

25.

IMAGINE THE CHILL WIND THAT RIPS AWAY THE LEAVES OF THE CALEN-dar in an old Hollywood film. Time is passing. Let yourself feel its uncharitable grasp, as it probes for things that are not well attached then plucks them from you and leaves you to shiver. Know that time is just another bully—out to teach you a lesson, whether you deserve it or not, ready to snatch your hat and hurl it into the river, to blow your umbrella inside out. The old know his unmannerly ways. They expect the worst, plan for disaster, feel carefully behind them before they sit, look for the next safe step on the pavement. They are alert for uneven paving stones, slippery leaves, dog shit. They fear for the young, who hurl themselves forward, eyes on the goal, pivoting past opponents as if by magic, kept aloft by the angels who watch over them, who charm their lives.

In the entire history of the universe, nobody had ever been in love like Sally and I. Everything was possible. Everything became easy, even major life decisions. We packed our bags and boxed up our chipped dishes, untouched by Holly's righteous scorn and Georgene's weary cynicism. This wasn't just about us; it was about the Truth. Everything else belonged to Maya—the world of illusion. We packed our scant boxes into the back of a one-way rental car, drove to Maidstone, and knocked on the door of the first house we saw with a For Rent sign in the window. The bed-sit was affordable and close to the Osteopathic Institute. The fact that it was cramped and dingy seemed appropriate somehow. We embraced monasticism. The blue flame of the single gas ring was holy. The rice and lentils we cooked there were enchanted. We needed nothing but each other and Simran: the Five Holy Names.

By now, I'd taken the vows of Sant Mat. I'd given up drugs and meat and alcohol, because they were impediments to my steady climb towards enlightenment. Every morning at 4:00 A.M. Sally and I struggled out of bed, drowsy and half-conscious, in order to meditate for two and a half hours, cross-legged under our separate piles of blankets, me next to the table and Sally tucked away in the broom cupboard so our auras wouldn't get tangled. After breakfast we headed off to work, Sally to osteopathy college, and I to teach English at the secondary school, dressed in the classic tweed skirts and slightly worn blouses that we scrounged at jumble sales and the Oxfam Shop. We were honest and upright in all our dealings. We turned the other cheek. We worked hard and avoided temptation. At night, I graded piles of papers, while Sally worked the late shift at Tesco's supermarket. At nine o'clock, we fell, exhausted, into bed. Although we were meant to be detaching ourselves from the dictates of the body, this was a long-term goal. Meanwhile, the knowledge that we should be striving for celibacy seemed only to fuel our passion. I inhaled Sally, her confidence, her juiciness, her big cackling laughter, her ability to turn the world upside down, to turn me upside down. We became a universe of two. Our goal was heaven. The rules were simple. We had permission to turn our backs upon the world.

Once a month we took the train into London and sat in a beige hotel room with other satsangis. We ate samosas and gulab jaman, then listened to tapes of Charan Singh Ji, the Master, a dignified old Sikh from the Punjab. He said that it is better to marry than to burn, that we must render unto Caesar what was Caesar's. First, there is desire, and then there is suffering. There would be no pain if we desired only the Lord. We were here to learn how to die. Nothing seemed to make more sense. The other satsangis saw nothing odd about two young women living together. They assumed that we were avoiding temptation. Homosexuality was never mentioned in the teachings, and we never brought it up. Our cloistered life and sense of purpose made us extraordinarily productive. Sally aced her tests. I was made second in department, then head of year. We scraped together enough money to buy an old terraced house, which we renovated at the weekends. Keeping our little secret seemed a small price to pay for a tidy vegetable garden, an ordered life, sanity, acceptance, love. After all, sex was only about procreation, a trap to chain us to the material world. It was a small piece in the grand scheme of things. Finally, I could call my parents every week with good news, and they were happy to hear that I was doing so well. I couldn't compete with Matthew and Andrea's three fine boys, but at least I had a house, and a job.

Time had bleached my father's hair snow white and plucked it slowly from his skull, leaving its smooth surface to be bronzed by the sun that ripened the tomatoes in his greenhouse. My mother's duodenum ulcerated, ruptured, ulcerated again. A blood clot congealed in one of her veins, and the arthritis continued to blossom in her joints, causing them to swell and buckle. Beaten into submission, my parents retreated into their rituals, deriving satisfaction from the certainty of the same cups on each bedside table, the regular weekly reappearance on the TV screen of Len Fairclough, Bob Monkhouse, and Bruce Forsythe. When one of her TV personalities or film stars died, my mother called Sally and me in Kent to let us know, as if they were mutual friends, or relatives.

"You'll never guess who died," she would say, her voice filled with tragedy, "Claudette Colbert. Your Dad and I saw every film she made when we were courting. They're not saying what it was, just 'a long illness.' It must have been cancer."

Once a year, they visited us in Kent. They planned for weeks, months, in advance. My father took the Lada in for a service, and then polished it from bonnet to boot, using the lamb's wool mitt from the eggshell blue box. It took a week for my mother to clean the house, a day to shop for the new clothes necessary to make a holiday real, another day to shop for the things they needed for the journey, such as boiled sweets, tissues, paper serviettes, potato crisps, chicken, Marks and Spencer's salad. My father dug out the wicker picnic hamper, in which nestled the picnic stove, two plastic mugs, the aluminum kettle that they boiled up for tea in a lay by.

Sally and I de-dyked the house: set up a bed in the study and moved Sally's clothes there, hid the photograph of us kissing on the beach. We rarely discussed telling them. "They are old and frail," I told myself. "They wouldn't understand." In any case, why cause them pain around the issue of sex, which wasn't important anyway, which we had less and less often as we settled down, became more involved in meditation, work, the garden, the wallpaper, satsangi meetings, when we fell into bed exhausted and woke early to do it all again? Why rub their faces in it? What was the point? Ironically, the less we were lovers, the more they treated us as such, buying us a Welsh dresser for the kitchen, sending us joint Christmas cards.

For twenty-seven years my father had launched the unwilling youth of Glenburn on their educational journeys, and schooled them to entertain their parents at Christmas in the customary manner, the boys with striped bath towels tied around their heads, the girls with spray painted wings, the Chosen One smugly clasping plastic Baby Jesus. In his years at the school, my dad had dug through snowdrifts in order to place hot water bottles strategically around the fish tank. He had listened to the woes and endured the miscalculations of an endless series of school clerks, buying each, at her departure, a small wedding present, selected by my mother. He oversaw the change of seasons, making Easter bunnies, sheaves of corn, snowmen, and spring flowers appear on the classroom windows in endless succession. As children passed from ABC to long division, from Chief Shepherd to compere in the Young Farmers' Review, from first job to first mortgage to first child, my father was constant.

When he retired, the local paper ran a photograph under the headline: "Glenburn Headmaster Retires." As photographs do, it froze time, preserving it for irony. The sharp black-and-white print my mother framed so proudly is yellowed now. The neat black suit he bought for the occasion is outdated; the smiling young children the *Weardale Clarion* photographer placed around him have got married, given birth, moved away, bought caravans, divorced, started riding schools in Surrey. In the photograph, Sally and I stand next to my brother and Andrea, and we all stare affectionately at my father and mother, who study a small brass clock, as if they are about to take it apart. The caption says that Sally is a "friend of the family."

Sally graduated at the top of her class. I applied for a deputy headship at a prestigious grammar school. When I was appointed, a reporter interviewed me for the local paper. Under the headline "Youngest Deputy Head in Kent," the local populace learned only that I liked cats and gardening. With the money we saved by living so frugally, we bought a big Victorian house. It was far enough away from my school to avoid gossip. Sally started her own practice in the spacious downstairs rooms. It was a posh house with thick carpets and stained glass and a walled garden—the poshest anyone in my family had ever owned. I couldn't wait for my parents to visit, but when my mother finally struggled out of the Lada and hobbled into the hallway, she seemed alarmed by our house's unfamiliar opulence, and tiptoed around, as if expecting to be evicted. She feared that I was tempting Providence by having so many good things without a man.

"Are you sure you can afford this?" my mother whispered, as we put away the dishes after dinner. "I hope you're not running yourselves into debt. What if something needs to be fixed? What if Sally finds a boyfriend? I know you're divorced, but what if Sally falls in love? I hope your money isn't too tangled up together," she said. "She's still young enough to get married and have children."

It was my secret, unacknowledged fear. "Sally doesn't *want* children," I told her, crossly, and she shut up, but the set of her lips told me that she wasn't convinced. Undeterred, I took them to see my school, with its weathered brick and ivy. I used my master key to let us into the sixth form center for which I was responsible. As we entered through the main assembly hall, its shining parquet floor struck awe into their hearts, as I had intended. The walls were lined with stone honors boards into which were chiseled the names of those who had found posterity in acceptable ways, graduating from Oxford or Cambridge, dying in a war. Every morning, clad in academic gown, I stood at that carved lectern to read the prayers. Ten senior tutors sat behind me, and in front of me sat the two hundred sixth formers whose lives I could enrich, or make miserable, who ran after me with the handbag I left everywhere, because I was unused to carrying one, or who tapped on my door to tell their troubles, ask permission, discuss their progress.

At last, I felt, my parents must be impressed. I earned more money and wielded more power than my brother or my father. These trappings must confirm that I had made it.

As we walked across the hall towards my study, our footsteps echoing hollowly, we saw Copper, the assistant caretaker. He was a cheery, amiable soul, always willing to take on the little extra jobs I gave him, and ready for a chat. Occasionally, he complained about the state of a classroom, though he was reluctant to get anyone into trouble. When he did, I visited the class in question. I took a firm line, keeping students in after school to tidy up. I was morally indignant.

"Hello Copper, it's only me," I called.

"Hello there, Miss Robson. Not working today I hope. It's sunny out there."

"No chance. I've just brought some visitors to see the place. Mum, Dad, I'd like you to meet Mr. Jenks, our assistant caretaker. He's the reason the place looks so immaculate."

Copper used to work with the gentry, and his manners were excellent. He shook hands with alacrity. My father complimented him on the polished floors. Overcome by the size and strangeness of it all, my mother was bursting with the need to say something. She felt that it was like something from a book, or perhaps one of those serials about the aristocracy on BBC 2.

"It's very nice to meet you Mr. Jenks," she managed finally, with her most refined accent. "It's a wonderful place you have here. Our Claire tells me the school goes back four hundred and fifty years."

"Yes, Mrs. Robson," said Copper, "I believe it does."

"Well," said my mother, "I hope my daughter isn't causing too much trouble."

Before she was to meet the Headmaster, I took my mother to task. "Just remember that I'm grown-up," I said.

"I know you're grown-up," she said indignantly. "I was only joking. He took it as a joke too."

"Of course he did," I said. "I'm his boss. I'll be living it down for weeks. It's just as well I get on with him OK."

"Well, I'm not stupid," she said. "What do you think I'm going to say?"

"I want no remarks about my cleft palate, or how I behaved at school, or my divorce. Try and think that I'm his deputy head, not just your daughter. I'm grown-up."

"She's right, Norah," my Dad said quietly.

My mother behaved immaculately in the headmaster's study, sipping her sherry quietly, while my father and Evan chatted desperately about education, the drive down, the North of England. I watched her eyes take in the leather books, the framed photographs of Cambridge rugby teams, the silver letter opener. Evan was gracious, impressive, kindly, offering alternative chairs solicitously for my mother's better comfort. With apologies to my parents, he consulted me briefly, but unnecessarily, about a matter raised in a recent letter from a parent, slipping into a crisp professional manner for my parents' benefit, questioning me briskly, then listening attentively to my opinion.

"Well, we'll do that then, Claire," he said eventually, "and trust to your judgment in the matter."

We were acting out a little scene for my parents' sake, like eleven year olds playing at being in grown-up jobs. He was the good boss, attentive, considerate, listening to the views of others. I was his efficient lieutenant, capable, well informed, upon whose judgment he relied. As we played out the game, I watched him adjust his spectacles to look at me over the top of them, a gesture he had copied from television actors pretending to be wise. He had only had them for a few weeks, and I had observed him trying them out various attitudes, taking them off to emphasize a point, waving them gently in one hand for emphasis.

I listened to myself abandoning my northern accent and trying to sound BBC, affecting a cultivated laugh and crossing my legs at the ankle. I looked at my father smiling a little too much, and my mother, small and intimidated in a big leather arm chair. She was holding her sherry glass somewhat gingerly by the stem, and I knew she was willing her arthritic fingers not to lose their grasp. Her head was tilted to one side in an attentive attitude, and I could see the flat bit at the back of her hair with which she fought her daily battle. We seemed like a roomful of sad, frightened children who had slipped out in our parents' clothes, shuffling along in huge shoes, clutching massive handbags, trying to act dignified. Filled with sudden tenderness, and distaste for further pretence, I reached across, and put an arm around my mother.

"Do you want me to get rid of that glass for you, Mam?" I said, consciously using the familiar Durham endearment.

"Thanks, pet," she said with dignity, as she handed it to me and looked directly at my boss. "Paul and I are very proud of our Claire, Mr. Williams, and very pleased she's working in such a good school. I know she enjoys working with you, and we think that's one of the main things, working with people you get on with. We feel very happy for her now we've seen everything, and met you."

Evan smiled genuinely for the first time.

"She's good at her job," he said. "I'm glad we appointed her."

I felt five years old again.

Part Five

A STATE NOT TO BE
STRIVEN FOR, 1984

The Times Educational Supplement

JUNE 1984

The pink triangle

Congratulations on your "Young and gay" feature (TES, June 1). Attention to homosexuality and gay issues in the educational press is long overdue.

The hitherto lack of coverage has served to reinforce the pervasive silence on gay issues in schools and the youth service. Generally, teachers and youth workers are singularly shy when it comes to a serious consideration of sexuality. Insufficient knowledge and confidence prevents them from sustaining a meaningful dialogue with young people who are struggling to develop their identity and self esteem, in a society obsessed with sexual stereotypes, along with the myth, prejudice and fear that go with them.

—*Peter Kent-Baguley is Senior Lecturer at Crewe and Alsager College of HE.*

26.

KEEPING MY FACE DIPLOMATICALLY BLANK WAS ONE OF THE MANY skills I had acquired in the last six years as Deputy Headmistress at Sir Henry Mansfield's School. Under the cover of my inscrutability, I amused myself with close, critical scrutiny of our Head of Religious Education. Ken Sitchell was an interesting subject—a plump, tweedy young man with a much older, even stouter one lurking deep inside, I suspected, trying to get out. He was the type of pompous misogynist that flourished at Mansfield's, which had been a boys' school for four hundred and fifty years till the girls and I had arrived six years ago to swell the diminishing rolls and sweeten centuries of stale locker room sweat. Ken was a man who would have been happy as an ambitious vicar in a Jane Austen novel, currying favor and blind to irony. When he wasn't sending me prissy memos about the length of the senior girls' skirts, or quoting St. Paul in the staff room, he could be found knee to knee with sensitive seventeen-year-old boys, dispensing sound advice about staying away from girls, none of whom were worth it. The less sensitive ones ordered catalogues for sex toys in Ken Sitchell's name, or at least their cruel approximation of it. Brown envelopes addressed to "Mr. Ken Sexual, Headmaster's House" plopped through the massive wooden door on a regular basis.

Begowned for morning assembly, massive behind his littered desk, Evan cleared his throat to address us. "Well, as you know, I've called us here because we need to take some sort of position on the issue of homosexuality." He mouthed the word as if it were a piece of gristle in a beef sandwich. "One of our new governors has pointed out that we don't have a written policy."

Arthur, the other deputy head, shifted uneasily in his chair and glanced surreptitiously at his watch. We all knew he would rather be helping the first years make wrought iron pokers and wooden coat racks than here, talking about homosexuality, a topic that had probably never before entered his kindly, patrician head. To his credit, he enjoyed helping the first year girls make pokers as much as he did the boys, and had accepted me quite happily as his equal, particularly since I did most of the work and covered for him when he went off to the workshop.

I was struck, not for the first time, by the difference between what we all knew and what we pretended to believe, the image and the reality. The headmaster knew that I had lived with Sally for the six years I had been at the school, and never went out with men, although I strategically pretended to be uncertain about the wisdom of instituting a policy that might declare my lifestyle acceptable. I knew that one of our senior teachers—a pillar of the community, with a wry wife and an elderly Labrador and a seat on the magistrate's bench—had a crush on our school secretary. I knew this because the secretary in question had gone through half a box of Kleenex in my office just yesterday, wondering if it was her fault that the senior teacher kept begging her to kiss him, because she liked to wear pretty blouses and short skirts. I knew much more than I wanted to know about what happened in the boys' boarding houses late at night, about lonely little boys who drank vodka, who bullied and buggered each other in endless Dickensian intrigues. I knew how Roger Wilkinson, head of Boys' PE, got drunk with the 1st XI hockey team and confided in them about his sexual exploits, how Bill Jaffey, commanding officer of the Combined Cadet Force called our lone black student "the darky" and all women except me "dearie."

He had called me that once, too, until I had taken him to one side and asked him not to. Clad in what Sally called my Margaret Thatcher uniform—a Jaeger suit and well-made shoes—I was girded with the knowledge that even the most bellicose of our male staff were afraid of women. They didn't understand how we were put together, our delicacy and deviousness. Every moment of every day I slipped under their guard, around their stiff, warlike posturing, following a few simple rules of battle. I never raised my voice. I never engaged in an argument I couldn't win, and when I won, I always helped my opponent up, made some small concession, handed him his dignity back in one piece.

Evan glanced at me as I sat impassively at the edge of a leather armchair, my leather Filofax open on the immaculate tweed platter of my knees. "These are certainly more enlightened times," he offered. I nodded, but didn't help him out, held his gaze without blinking. "Well, since we are a religious foundation, I've asked Ken here to give us an update on the church's current thinking." He threw himself simultaneously back on his chair and on organized religion.

Ken Sitchell threw one plump little leg over the other and leaned back too, in unconscious parody. As ineffectual men will, he worshipped at the altar of robust masculine power. "The Bible is quite clear, Headmaster," he said, glancing at the weighty tomes on the bookshelves in Evan's study, as if for confirmation. "Leviticus tells us that homosexuality is wrong. It's quite clear."

The fact that no one chose to look at me told me exactly where I stood, what the rumors were. Evan cleared his throat. "Yes," he said, "but doesn't the Bible also preach compassion, Ken?"

Ken's pudgy face turned a rosy pink. "Compassion for the sinner, headmaster. Not for the sin. I believe that we have a sacred duty to help our young men toward normal family life. I don't need to remind you, headmaster, that we have boarders here. We have a duty to give them firm leadership, especially when there have been so many changes, with the girls joining us, and all that that involves." He glanced at me for the first time. "There are enough temptations in their path, and enough modern influences."

"Yes, of course Ken," Evan said, rolling his eyes briefly up toward the ceiling as he did when he was uncomfortable. "Of course. We all want to set a clear example. That's why we're here." He shifted in his chair slightly and came at it from another angle. "Now in terms of a written policy, Ken, something concrete that I can take back to the governors—I wonder where the church stands officially? Do you happen to know what the most recent Council of Bishops said, for example?" Evan loved written policy. The school had a ton of it, written up in a huge staff handbook that the staff used as bookends and paperweights.

Ken pursed his lips. "There are liberals, of course," he said, "in the church, as well as in this school. They're making inroads. As far as I remember, they said that it wasn't a sin, neither was it a state to be striven for."

I was filled with unholy mirth. How would one strive to be a homosexual, I wondered? Would one gaze determinedly at members of one's own sex, hoping to eventually feel some attraction? Would one read gay erotica before going to sleep, or repeat some kind of mantra? "I *will* be gay. I *will* be gay." Had I striven to be gay? Was I striving not to be? I couldn't remember the last time Sally and I had made love.

Evan looked at me, and raised his eyebrows questioningly, inviting me to speak. "There was an interesting article in the *Times Educational Supplement* last week," I offered. "It was about teen suicide. Did anyone see it?" Evan shook his head but looked hopeful. He loved newspaper articles almost as much as written policy. "Well," I said, "it suggested that gay students run a much higher risk of taking their own lives, about four times, I seem to remember. Given that one in ten of our students probably identifies as gay, according to the *Times Ed*'s figures, I'm just wondering what message we should send them? I'm wondering about our moral responsibility to them, and our legal one I suppose."

I had played several trump cards at once here. I had read the newspaper article and my colleagues had not. I had statistics on my side and had gently invoked morality too. Most important, I had summoned the awful specter of one of our boarders suspended by his neck with a damning suicide note pinned to his jacket.

"Which day did you read that, Claire?" Evan's pen was poised.

"Er, Tuesday, I think. I might still have it over in my office," I told him, knowing damn well that I had. The only reason that I hadn't made copies for everyone was that it would have been impolitic to seem too eager. I decided that it was time to offer the compromise. "How about saying that although the church believes that homosexuality is not a state to be striven for, we nurture all our students, regardless of their sexual orientation?" I said. "Maybe that would get around the problem. We wouldn't actually be encouraging them to be gay," I glanced at Ken, "or encouraging them to *strive* to be gay. We'd just be saying that we'd nurture them, as we would all wish, I'm sure, to nurture our students. Nurture is a pretty vague word," I added. "It leaves us plenty of rope, if you'll pardon the expression."

Evan glanced at his watch. "Well, unless anyone's got anything else to say, I think we've gone as far as we can today. I should get ready for assembly." He picked up his copy of the little book that told headmasters how to stand at the lectern and strike a good moral attitude. "I'll give it some more thought and let you know what I've decided. Thanks for your input everybody."

I followed Ken out and caught up with him in the staff room, where I found him sitting next to Major William Jaffey, Officer Commanding, CCF, who was squeezed into a khaki uniform with a polished Sam Browne belt stretched across his paunch, ready to march at the front of his pimply battalion in the weekly parade. I didn't need a crystal ball to know what they were talking about, but sat down next to Ken anyway, knowing that he'd feel less threatened in the presence of an ally. "Well, Ken," I asked him, "What did you think? It's a vexed question, isn't it?"

He turned to me angrily. "So I suppose we're going to throw out centuries of Christian teaching, just because some bloody liberal lawyer on the governing body wants us to be nice to homosexuals?"

"Well, I don't know what position the head's going to take, Ken," I said, neatly distancing myself from the decision. "I thought you argued a strong case."

"Know what they do with queers in the Army?" Bill leaned forward heavily to ask me. He had one of those wet slobbery mouths, only partly concealed by a military moustache.

I braced myself. "Dishonorable discharge?"

"Only in peacetime," he said. "In wartime they discharge them permanently with one bullet. It's cheaper."

I touched Ken's sleeve gently. "I wanted to ask you a favor." He swung stiffly around in his seat, his face stormy. Bill Jaffey smirked, ready to enjoy my defeat. "What?" said Ken.

"Well," I said, making my voice nervous and hesitant. "The Head has to go to court next Friday."

Ken's face gathered momentum, his mental fist raised to smite. "If you're asking me to cover his classes, the answer is no," he said loudly. Heads began to turn toward us. "I teach every period but one that day. I'm not giving up my preparation time." He flushed and picked up his coffee mug, pretending indifference. He knew that I had the power to make him do it, but that it weakened every time I had to invoke it. I pretended horrified confusion.

"God, no, Ken!" I told him. "I'm sorry. I should have been much clearer. I know your timetable is a nightmare this year. That's why I've kept you off the cover list this term, or at least so far. No, no, the Head was meant to be taking sixth form assembly for me, and I was wondering if you would consider standing in for him."

There was nothing Ken liked so much as to be up on the stage delivering passionate homilies. It was a place usually reserved for higher moral authority, in the form of Evan or us deputies, resplendent in our academic gowns, which the other staff were only allowed to wear once a year on Speech Day. I watched Ken struggle to keep the gratification from his face.

"Come on Ken," I said, pleadingly, as if I didn't know how much he wanted to preen at that lectern. "I know you're really busy, but the sixth formers are tired of my face. They keep asking me when you're going to be taking assembly again. They loved that thing you did on missionaries in China." (Actually, the truth was that I had had to ask the Head of Maths to sit at the back to stop them from sniggering.) I delivered the coup de grace quickly, before Ken had time to capitulate. "Look. How about if I get the student teacher to take one of your classes this week, to give you time to prepare? Would that help?"

The wheels in his brain ground to a halt and he nodded huffily. "I suppose so. But I'll need to have some prayers photocopied. I don't like that modern book you're using."

"Thanks Ken," I said, letting out my breath as if in relief. "Just give the prayers to my secretary, and let me know which class you need the student in for. Thanks so much for helping me out." I stood up and headed for the door, turned as though I'd just had a thought. "Oh . . . would you mind wearing your academic gown? Just to maintain the tone, you know, just for the sake of consistency."

27.

According to Sally's appointment book, which was spread-eagled next to the telephone, she was finishing up with her last patient when I got home. I made tea, cleared the jumble of client cards off the coffee table, and set the tray down with two mugs. I heard her huge laugh from the treatment room next door. "I'll see you next week," she said, then her voice dropped to a murmur. Something in the quality of it made me listen closely, but all I could hear was a muffled male voice, and then Sally again, still speaking softly, and then normally again, saying, "I'm not sure. Maybe. I'll phone you later on, all right?" and then another male mumble and her laugh again. "I'm going to keep you to that, OK?"

The door cracked open and she burst in, a patient file clasped under her arm to restrain the pound notes that dangled from its clutches. Her glasses were perched on the very end of her nose. Wisps of hair hung from the elastic band she wore around her ponytail. She wore one of the starched white cotton medical tunics she kept lined up in her wardrobe, and the Dr. Scholl sandals she swore by for her feet. Once Sally found something she liked, she stuck with it, invested in it, bought it in quantity.

She seemed surprised to see me. "You're home early."

I poured her tea out as she plumped down and rolled a big messy cigarette on Mrs. Jones's case history. "Who was that?" I asked.

"Jeff."

"The young kid?"

"He's not actually a kid," she said. "He's twenty-three."

"The runner?"

"Yeah. How was your day?"

I curled my stockinged feet up underneath me. We really needed to do something about getting the couch recovered. The whole house could do with sprucing up actually.

"It was a day. We decided that homosexuality is not a state to be striven for. It's official."

She lit her cigarette and brushed at a fleck of tobacco that smoldered on her chest. "Oh."

"So we can stop striving," I said.

She stood up and took her white coat off. She'd put on a little weight lately, and her breasts strained against the fabric of her bra.

"Nice pair," I said.

"Thanks," she said, waggling her jacket in the air in parody of a stripper.

I pretended to grab at her and she swung away and picked up her T-shirt. "No touching the merchandise."

"You look nice," I said.

"Thanks," she said again.

"Fancy a nap?" I sounded much too casual.

She shrugged into her shirt and made a wry face. "You don't mean a nap."

"I'd settle for a nap," I said, hating myself for being abject, knowing that this whole conversation was a mistake, but powerless to rewind it.

"Don't you have work to do?"

"I always have work to do," I said petulantly. "I'm tired of being a good girl." I tried to put things right. "Tell you what. Let's do something fun. Kick over the traces."

"I need to do my accounts."

"We could burn them in the wood stove."

"I don't want to take a nap."

"Well forget the nap. How about watching TV, or renting a video, or deciding on a new color scheme for the living room? Come on, we haven't had a night off together in weeks."

She sighed. "I'm going to meditate for an hour, then have something to eat and then do my accounts. Why don't you meditate too?"

"I really need to mark these essays for tomorrow."

"So you could spare the time to take a nap or watch TV, but you can't spare the time to meditate?" I felt the weight of another fight coming on, and I'd only been home thirty minutes.

"Well, I shouldn't do either, actually. I do have to do these essays and then I really should work on the staff meeting agenda."

She stubbed out her cigarette and stood up. "Then do it."

"I will."

She walked to the door, stood there for a moment, then turned, her face a strange mixture of feelings I didn't recognize. "I'm going out for a drink with Jeff tomorrow night."

Something squeezed my heart, like a cold hand. "So you can go out for a drink with someone else but not me. I'm not invited presumably."

"He needs someone to talk to."

"I thought you didn't like to get involved with patients."

"I'm not getting involved with him. I'm just going out for a drink."

"Are you attracted to him?" I sounded shrewish, even to my own ears, like some jealous husband from *Coronation Street*. God. How had we ended up in such a tired script?

"It's not about that."

"Then what is it about? What is it about, Sally?" I hadn't invented it then—the way she'd changed in the last few months, the separate bedrooms, the irritation in her voice.

She began to cry. It was something that she did easily. "Try and understand. Don't be angry. I need you to understand. If you don't understand, who will?"

The phone rang but neither of us moved. The answering machine cut in at the third ring. As Sally's cheerful message boomed through the speaker, I wished we could go back to when she'd recorded it, hopeful and optimistic, the brand-new treatment tables waiting in the freshly painted practice rooms, the rest of our lives standing ready for us to inhabit them.

"What is there to understand?" I asked her. "Tell me."

"I'm meant to do this," she said.

"Meant to?" I heard my voice spiral up a couple of decibels. "You're meant to be letting go of other people. You're not meant to be getting involved with some fucked-up kid. What are you doing, Sally?"

"I'm doing what I have to. Try and understand. It's not really about Jeff. It's about us. We're not lovers, Claire. I'm not a lesbian. I want to have sex with men."

I'd seen it coming, but it was happening too quickly. It was too predictable, too fucking predictable for words. "After seven years," I said.

"You're going to leave me for some spotty little dipshit, just because he's got a prick. No doubt you want me to sit around and do your laundry, wash the semen off your sheets. Well do your own fucking laundry."

Sally held up a hand to stop me, her face suddenly intent, and I heard my brother's voice on the answering machine, gruff with the embarrassment of having his voice recorded, and with something else. "Claire? It's Matt." There was a long pause. "Sally, if you're with a patient and you get this, you need to find Claire. It's Dad. He seems to have had a stroke."

I snatched up the phone.

28.

THE COAL FIRE BURNS BRIGHTLY AT THE CENTER OF MY CHILDHOOD
memories of Pond House. Every day, Dad filled up the coal box with
lumps of assorted sizes selected from the big pile in the coal shed at the
bottom of the garden—small pieces were for starting the fire, larger ones
for length and endurance. Some cheap coal, smuggled into the bottoms
of the sacks delivered by the coal man, sputtered and spat out sparks that
landed on the sheepskin hearth rug, burning quiet, smelly holes as we
frantically searched its tangled hairs for culprits. Judiciously, my dad
selected and dispensed the coals as the evening wore on. It was a trust he
guarded jealously, as if in obedience to some inarticulate tribal memory.
When I was little, I used to watch in awe as the blue flames licked at the
newsprint, ate yellowy into the sticks, drawing steam and gray smoke
from the coal dust, and finally consumed the coal itself, burning blue at
first, then bright orange-yellow, causing minor explosions and avalanches
as the combustible shoring collapsed. Tending the fire was a manly business, and my father took refuge in it as his private place, a retreat from
my mother's incessant restlessness, her anxious observations. He met each
of the fire's demands in the same meticulous, organized way, in personal
rituals that never varied, protecting him from anger at his lot, or the will
to change it. His little shovel, its front edge shiny and ragged from use,
his kindling hatchet with its worn, smooth handle—all knew him, and
soothed him with their familiarity.

The morning of the day that Sally decided to go for a drink with Jeff
and the headmaster of Sir Henry Mansfield's School decided that we
should not, in any case, strive to be queer, my father had been sweeping
the hearth, his mind already full of the day's projects, when his legs suddenly went on strike. He collapsed, astonished, into his armchair. His first
reaction was exasperation. He would have to call my mother, who was
still in bed, waiting for her tea. She might think it was one of his early
morning jokes, and refuse to come. When she did come she would make

a fuss. The kettle began to mutter to itself in the kitchen, and he found that he couldn't get up to turn it off. After careful thought he called, "Norah!"

No reply.

"Norah!"

"Yes?"

"Can you come down pet? I don't feel too well."

To his relief, he heard the sounds of the bedsprings creaking, and her feet on the floorboards above, trying their best to hurry. He had heard these noises so often, the little squeak of the wardrobe door—she was getting her dressing gown—the plop of her slippers landing on the floor as she dropped them ready to step into, unable to bend down and pull them onto her feet. He heard my mother's heavy, halting tread on the stairs, as she labored down them, clutching the banister. Everything was as it should be; everything was in place: the horse brasses gleamed on their leather straps; the fire crackled cheerfully.

My mother appeared around the doorframe, a picture of worry and concern. She was in that state that old married couples no longer really notice about each other. Her hair was stuck thinly across her skull; her eyes were dazed with sleep and worry, and a thin trail of dried saliva marked one side of her mouth. She looked as frail as a child in her nightie and dressing gown, though age stuck out in the angles of her bones and dragged at her limbs.

Norah May Robson and Cecil William Robson were not unfamiliar with mortality, which had after all been visited upon all four of their parents. My mother enjoyed recounting stories of sudden death, and told them with horrified intensity. "She just turned over in the bed . . ." "She found him in the chair, so peaceful, like he'd fallen asleep . . ."

But now, here they were! Nothing clean and easy! It was all a terrible mess! My mother was supposed to be sick and useless and die. My father was meant to live on quietly and dig the garden, and do the crossword and have a rest—he who had always pruned the roses and clipped the edges of the lawn, though it was tempting to leave them every once in a while. And those mornings when he had felt like skipping church, when he had got out of bed in the cold and gone off to dig the car out! It was all wrong. It wasn't what was meant to happen at all.

My mother gazed at him helplessly, as he sat there in the chair, very white, his eyes filled with tears. But he never cried! He was her rock! He took the tops off jars, and killed wasps with his rolled-up newspaper. He pulled the washing machine out from under the shelf, and sorted the clothes into piles at her direction. He wrung them out with his strong hands. He knew what to think about what they saw on the news. She felt terribly alone. What was she to do? Should she try and walk around to Gwen's, or stop George on his bike? Unsteadily, she walked across the room to my father, her lip trembling. His eyebrows had got all out of shape as he slept on his face, and, unthinkingly, she licked a finger to smooth them back.

"Well," he said finally, "You'd better call our Matthew at work."

29.

ALL I HAD RETAINED FROM MATTHEW'S PHONE CALL WERE HEADLINES—
Prepare for Shock, Paralyzed from the Waist Down, Severe Stroke. For a moment
or two, as I walked the length of the ward to my father's bed, I wondered
if I'd heard my brother all wrong, if Dad was going to walk out of there
in a couple of days after all. Propped up on a snowy expanse of hospital
pillows, his face beamed like a beacon. "Hello there. Fancy coming all this
way to see your poor, gray-haired, old father! What a nice surprise.
Where's Sally?"

I kissed him on the cheek to hide my face, the sharp stab of realization that I didn't know where Sally was right now, that she might be with
Jeff. "Poor old father nothing. You look loads better than I expected."
Indeed he did. His cheeks were rosy; his eyes sparkled. "Sally's working,"
I told him. "She's booked solid with patients till late Friday night, but
she might come up on the train at the weekend. She sent her love." It
wasn't a lie. Sally had been filled with concern, packed me off with sandwiches and clean clothes and a hug, as if I were a child going off on a day
trip. "I'll call Evan," she'd said. "Don't worry about anything here. Just
go and take care of your dad. I love him too you know, both of them, and
I love you, you great cabbage, so don't go thinking that I don't. We'll
talk about everything when you get back."

"Send her my love when you call her," Dad was saying, "and tell her
she won't need to come all the way up here. I feel much better, much better than yesterday." He glanced at my mother, who was crumpled silently
in the unyielding plastic chair, like Duncan's ghost. She had cried a little when I arrived, but on the whole had been unsettlingly passive, as if
drugged. She seemed to sense rather than see my father's gaze now, and
stirred herself to look at him.

"Did they say why they took you all the way to Sunderland?" she said.
"It's such a long drive in that bumpy ambulance. We've always gone to
Sutton. The nurses are better there too."

He smiled at her, encouragingly. "The physiotherapy department's the best in the county," he said. "My girl's called Maureen, and she was telling me all about it while she was working on me. Listen Norah, she was pretty certain there was some movement in my feet—one of my toes. She was pretty certain, she said. She's looking for a good recovery." I glanced at the plastic bag hanging at the side of Dad's bed, at the mysterious white humps that were his useless legs, then looked up quickly as he said, "Sally would like her. They'd have a lot in common, with Sally being an osteopath and everything. I'll be out of here in the shake of a lamb's tail, Claire. Wait till you meet this girl. Only twenty-two, but she doesn't half know her job. These two male nurses were trying to move me from the chair to the bed, and they were having a real struggle. Actually, they hurt me a bit. Maureen was furious! Told them to clear off out of it and did it herself in five seconds. She braced my feet against hers and just leaned back and swung me round. I didn't feel a thing. Marvelous. She really is. Marvelous." He looked earnestly at me, his desperation barely concealed, begging me to join his fiction.

The collapsed folds of my mother's face assumed a stern expression. "Did she tell you to fight, Paul?" she asked. "That's what you have to do in these places, you know. Fight."

She tightened her grip on the handle of her walking stick, causing it to shake gently. She straightened her back, and looked at my father sternly. "Every time I came in I thought I would never come out again except for in my coffin, but I did. They said I must have a stubborn streak. I was a fighter. Now it's your turn. You mustn't let this get you down in the dumps."

He stared at her earnestly. "Don't you worry about that, Norah. Now I'm feeling better, I'm going to work at the exercises Maureen's given me. You just take care of yourself. There's no sense in you making yourself ill too. I'll be back home in no time."

"Is there anything you want while you're in here?" asked Matthew. I could tell he needed to escape my Dad's painful efforts to cheer us up.

"Well, there's just my pen," Dad said, deprecatingly. "Someone's taken my pen. You know my green Parker that the kids gave me for my retirement. I loaned it to that staff nurse to do her crossword with, and she's forgotten to give it back. I've asked her for it twice."

"Is that the one I spoke to yesterday?" asked Matthew. "The one whose son worked for Jimmy Weir?" My father nodded, and Matthew strode off.

"Some of these young nurses," said my mother, shaking her head, "they need chasing for everything. That man in the bed at the end wanted his water jug filled at the start of visiting time, and they still haven't done it. You'd've got much better treatment at Sutton. I'm surprised they didn't take you straight there."

"On the whole they're marvelous though, Norah. I've had no complaints, no complaints at all, apart from my pen." With some common ground safely restored, he was off on some story about a young nurse who'd been at Eppleton School, the unnatural brightness of his eyes and high color an unsettling contrast with my mother's tired grayness. Beneath his determined cheerfulness, I guessed at the horror he must feel, his scarlet embarrassment at being so exposed to intrusion, to the paraphernalia of illness. He had been so unerringly correct all his life, so proper, and now here he was, hoping that good behavior would earn him a reprieve, worrying about my mother, about the things he'd left undone. "There's some church stuff I should look at," he was saying. "Peggy Heavisides will need the order of the hymns for next Sunday, and then there'll be the next parish magazine to get ready for the printers. I was going to call Ronnie about it today."

"I'm taking everything down to the vicarage," I said suddenly. "The vicar can deal with it. You're not lying here worrying about it." I was surprised at how angry I felt.

My father looked up in surprise. "Norman?" he said. "He's new. He won't know how to organize things. He's only been in the parish two months."

"Maybe our Matthew should give him a ring and discuss things," my mother put in nervously.

"Norman will have to learn," I said grimly. "I'm going to find every last bit of paper in your desk to do with the church, and I'm going to give it to Norman, and that's that." I was tired of how the good guys got screwed.

My father looked me in the eye. It felt like the first time he had ever looked straight at me, like an equal. He gave me a strange complicit smile. "I suppose they can't expect too much of me now," he said, glancing at his shrouded legs. "They can hardly say I'm making it up."

My mother and I were staying with Matthew and Andrea while my father was in hospital, and Sally would stay there as well, if she came, as she offered. I preferred to shelve that whole mess for now. There were enough complications as it was. My three young nephews were suddenly exposed to a grandmother who slumped in an armchair for much of the time and seemed hardly aware of them. She hated being away from her things, and had already accumulated a list of items necessary to her daily well-being: her sheepskin slippers, her second-best anorak, her address book from her other handbag. Accordingly, I drove her over there in my father's Lada the next morning. I had my own agenda. "Now listen, Mam. We need to sort things out a bit. It looks like the house is going to be empty for a little while, and we should make sure it's OK to be left."

"Well, your dad will tell you and our Matthew what should be done."

"I don't think we should worry Dad with it. Right now he needs to have the rest of us take care of things for a while, till he gets better. I think everything's got on top of him a little bit lately."

"Why?" she said sharply. "What has he said to you?"

"He hasn't said anything."

"Has he said something to our Matthew then?"

"No, he didn't say anything. But our Matthew thinks Dad's been looking tired lately. He's had all the business of the new vicar's inauguration and the garden and everything. He's not getting any younger, Mam. These things take their toll."

"Everybody's going to think it was looking after me," she said. Tears started to roll down her face. "It'll be all over the village by now that Mr. Robson had a stroke looking after his wife because she was so helpless. He wouldn't be lying in that hospital now if it wasn't for me."

"Everyone knows how much you do," I said gently, "the washing and the housework and all the cooking." I held her hand as her chest shook with smothered sobs. "It's not your fault, Mam." I started to cry myself, at the way none of it was our fault, how we had all done the best we could and never intended any harm, and hoped for better endings, greater rewards. I went and got her hanky from her handbag and she blew her nose.

"Why don't you get all the money together from out of your teapots while I look through Dad's papers?" I asked her. "Where would Dad keep them?"

She looked evasive again, "I don't think he'd want you to look through those. He's always been very private about those things."

"He certainly wouldn't want them stolen, Mam. The police said we should take anything valuable into safekeeping. He could keep them with him in hospital if he really wanted. Matthew and I talked about it last night. We both think we should take them."

Appeal to higher authorities did the trick, and ten minutes later I had collected a gray tin box from under their bed and was looking through his upstairs desk. Anything to do with the church I put in a large manila folder, anything to do with money or insurance in another to look at later. Matt and I had no idea how much money they had, and we'd need to make some decisions soon, about what was to happen to them. Working methodically through the bureau, I came across a set of small blue notebooks. The front covers read "Durham County Council—School Notebooks," and in the space left for the pupil's name there were dates in my father's neat copper plate script: "September to February 1982," "March to June 1982." Leafing through the earliest, I found neat columns filled with household accounts and records. He had noted every gas bill, every time he had the oil changed on the car, the date they bought the new stair carpet, and its price. He kept track of my mother's payments on her catalogue purchases, the date that they pruned the roses, and how much fertilizer they had put on them.

On impulse, I turned to those covering the last year, only to find a steady decline in the quality of his entries. At first they were briefer and sparser. Next, the handwriting became erratic, hurried, harassed, and finally, occasional notes gave way to books that were dated and ruled into columns, but otherwise blank. I put all the notebooks back in order in their cubbyhole. I felt blank myself.

I went back downstairs. "I'm off to the vicar's then to give him this church stuff. Will you be all right for half an hour?"

She was busy watering the plants on the kitchen windowsill, and looked up somewhat puzzled. "All right? Of course I'll be all right."

"Do you need to go upstairs?"

"Well, I was going to get some clean pajamas for your dad, and I could do with my angora sweater and my brown walking shoes."

"Can we do that when I get back? I don't think it's such a good idea for you to go upstairs."

She bridled. "Why not? Is it a mess up there? Does it need dusting? Maybe I should just run the vacuum cleaner over it."

"No. It's just that you're a little unsteady on your pins, what with all the upset. I don't want you to do a header down the stairs."

She chuckled at my bluntness. "I hold on to the banister rail, pet, and I only do one step at a time."

"I know, but I'll be worrying all the time I'm at Norman's."

"All right. I've got my plants in the conservatory to water anyhow."

"Promise?"

"I promise."

When I got back an hour later she didn't answer when I called. I scouted around downstairs, sticking my head around each successive doorjamb, calling for her. I ran out into the back garden—maybe she had gone down to the greenhouse. Finally, I went to the bottom of the stairs and called up, trying to decide whether she'd gone to see Gwen next door, or broken her promise to stay at ground level. I heard her answer from upstairs, and to my relief, she sounded quite composed, if surprised. "Claire? Is that you?" Her voice was strong again, like it was before all this had happened. She'd obviously needed to be back among her things to get her grounded I thought to myself, as I bounded up the stairs in relief.

At first, I thought she was trying to get something from underneath the bed. She was lying on the floor next to it, but seemed strangely unconcerned, amazed and happy rather than hurt or miserable, as if nothing had happened. "Claire!" she said. "It *is* you! I thought I was dreaming! Here, help me up." I put an arm under each elbow and hauled her onto the bed, where she stared at me in joyful surprise. "What on earth are *you* doing here!"

I stared back. "What do you mean? I've been to the vicarage, like I said. I came up to see Dad . . . you know I did. What were you doing down on the floor?"

"Never mind that," she said, with some of her old exasperation. "Why do you want to see your dad in the middle of term time? You haven't resigned have you? What's wrong? Has something happened? Don't tell me you're moving again! What about Sally?"

"Mam, I *told* you. The staff are covering my classes. They knew I needed to see Dad. Are you hurt? You were on the floor when I came in. What were you doing on the floor?"

"On the floor? I don't remember. But wait. Just tell me why you're here first. It's not a holiday. Why have you come to see us in the middle of term time?"

"I've come to see Dad in hospital."

Her mouth dropped open, as if I had hit her. "In hospital! Your dad! What's the matter with him?"

There was a small bruise on her forehead. I suddenly realized what must have happened. "Mam. You've had a fall. Try to stand up." She obeyed automatically, and winced with pain. "I can't move this leg. It must have stiffened up."

I took her by the shoulders and held her eyes with mine. "Listen Mam. Try and concentrate on what I'm telling you. You've had a fall. I think you've banged your head and hurt your leg. I'm going to call an ambulance. I'll only be gone two minutes, then I'll come back and tell you everything."

"No!" she said. "Wait! Don't call an ambulance. I'm all right. I'm going to get up in a minute. Just sit down and tell me what's going on. Why have you driven up from Kent? Where's Sally?"

"Mam, Dad's been taken ill. He's not very well. He's in hospital."

"Your dad! Your dad's in hospital!" She began to push feebly at the bed with her arms, struggling to get up. "When did he go in? What's wrong with him? Has he had an accident? It's not his heart is it? We have to go and see him!" Her breath came in panicky little gasps.

"He was taken ill suddenly, Mam. Don't you remember? You've been in to see him, with our Matthew. He's had a stroke."

"A stroke! What are we doing here then? I have to go and see him!"

We seemed to be moving in the right direction. "Yes," I said. "I'll run down and call Andrea."

"Yes," she said. "Call Andrea. Talk to her, or maybe our Matthew's home from school. What time is it?"

I was on my way to the door when she cut me off with a wail. "But you haven't told me anything! No! Claire! Don't go! Just tell me what's going on first. Where's your dad?"

I tried to distract her, to change the subject, but always she returned to her questions. Why was I here? Where was Sally? Why wasn't I at work? Sometimes she would be distracted by her inability to walk, and would make me help her and I knelt on the floor and picked her feet up one by one, moving them inch by inch as I broke the news of Dad's illness to her again and again and she collapsed with the shock and horror of it again and again, as if we were caught in some existentialist play about hell and would never escape, as if it were some cruel joke God had decided to play on the weakest people He could find—my mother, crippled and alone, myself, tormented and scared, locked together in a room in a nightmare of suffering and isolation.

I didn't have the courage to leave her, and somehow I ended up carrying her down the stairs in my arms, praying that nothing was too broken in her, that I wouldn't stumble. As I staggered down the front path, I saw Martha Braithwaite coming up the village. Her pace quickened as she saw us and, as often happened, my mother and I were united by the most ridiculous of motives.

"There's Martha Braithwaite," I hissed at her as I squeezed her into the car.

Amnesiac or not, she knew the implications of that one straight away. "Quick," she said, "I can shut the car door. Just get this leg in. I can't lift my foot."

"I've got to shut the front door," I said, fumbling to get her skirt tucked in. "I think I saw Gwen looking out of her window too." I felt like screaming.

Sure enough, as I sprinted up the front path, Gwen's door opened. "She's just had a bit of a dizzy spell," I called as calmly as I could. "I don't think it's anything too serious." On my way back down the path I waved cheerfully at Martha, who was approaching at warp speed, considering her bulk. "Hello Martha!" I yelled. "I really can't stay. Mam's not feeling too good."

"Close the front gate, pet," my mother called from the car. "I don't want those bloody ducks eating my crocuses."

Fortunately, Martha was still too breathless to speak as I hopped into the Lada, executed a neat three point turn in front of her concerned gaze, and set off for Matthew and Andrea's. My mother's short-term memory seemed partially, though not totally, restored by our victory, from which she derived great satisfaction.

"What did you say to Gwen?" she asked. "Who else did I hear you talking to? Oh no! Not Martha Braithwaite! It'll be all over the village. Thank goodness you just said I wasn't feeling too well. Did you make sure the kitchen taps were all turned off?"

"Yes, they were all off."

"Did you close the front gate? I don't want those bloody ducks of Trevor Turnbull's eating my crocuses again."

"You've already asked me about the bloody ducks," I said.

30.

"THEY'VE MOVED HIM TO A SIDE WARD," I TOLD SALLY ON THE PHONE. I was perched on the edge of Matthew and Andrea's double bed, staring blindly at their wedding photograph on the bedside table, my ear pressed to the telephone, as if to inhale the clink of Sally's teaspoon against the cup, the sound of a match flaring.

"Why did they do that?" she asked.

"I don't know," I said. "Nobody will tell us what it means. I don't think it's good though. It's his lungs, Sal. He can't clear them properly. He's on antibiotics, but I think they're worried."

"How's he holding up?"

"Oh God. He's still being the model patient, as if that's going to help. Those Geordie bus drivers I told you about, the ones in the main surgical ward, keep him entertained. They took the dinner trolley apart with their knives and forks yesterday and hid all the bits in their beds. The nurse thought she was going nuts when she couldn't find it. They come and chat to him, you know. Tell him they know what he's up to— just pretending to be paralyzed when all the time he's sneaking off to the men's room for a crafty smoke."

She didn't laugh. "Have you and Matt thought about worst-case scenarios?"

"Do you think he's going to die?" Her silence told me exactly what she thought. "Just tell me the truth, Sally," I said. "We need to know. Jesus, if he dies, we need to think about her."

"It doesn't look great," she said. "There's probably a chance, but it doesn't look great. Look. We'll do what we need to, you and I, right? If he does die, and you have to take care of her. We'll work it out. Don't worry."

"I'll try."

"I love you."

"How's Jeff?"

"Jeff's fine."

"So you had that drink with him then?"

"Yes."

"I see."

"I just had a drink with him Claire, that's all. A drink. We'll talk about all that later."

"It's over though Sally, right?"

I crouched over the phone, waiting for the inevitable, staring at the picture of Matthew, tall and proud in his tails, his top hat in one hand and the other arm around Andrea. How awkward I had been at their wedding, how out of place in a miserable pink satin dress. My life was ruined.

"It's been over for a while," Sally said finally. "We just didn't notice."

"OK."

"Look. I'm sorry about the timing. I'm sorry about everything. I'm just . . . sorry."

Match of the Day was on TV the last time I saw Dad—Tottenham Hotspur v. Sunderland at Roker Park. We had brought ice creams, and Dad said it was like being at the cinema, what with the noise and the dim light. He said that they just had the one TV set for the whole ward of thirty beds, so he wouldn't let us turn it down. He said it was just a pity it was right outside his door. Sunderland lost, as usual. Later, one of the bus drivers attributed my father's demise to their poor showing on the field. "Poor bugger couldn't stand to watch that forward line arsing about any more," he lamented. "It was enough to make anybody pop his clogs."

We knew exactly how my mother would react to Dad's death because it was one of those gloomy eventualities she picked at constantly, like a scab. "He's a saint, Claire," she was fond of telling me. "Everyone in the village knows he's a saint, and it's true. I don't know what I'd do if anything happened to him."

"Now come on, Mam," I'd say, trying to catch her eye, to force her to see reason. "Why on earth are you worrying about that? Dad's never ill. He doesn't even get colds. When was he last in bed for a day? He's as fit as a lop. Give him the crossword every night and he's happy."

"You don't know the half of it," she'd say, avoiding my earnest gaze. "He has his worries. You won't know till you've a husband yourself. You don't know because you've always been closer to women. Men are different. They don't like to discuss these things. Your dad acts like it's immoral to let on what he's feeling. He'd rather die. It's like prizing it out of him with one of those crowbar things. I've told him I won't outlive him though. Thank God my heart wouldn't stand the shock, and if it did I'd take all my pills. I've told our Matthew I'll never be a burden to either of you. You have your own lives," and she would begin to cry quietly, clenching her teeth till the tears rolled down the creases in her face.

Matt and I made our way along the miserable gray hospital lino to the rehabilitation ward where'd we'd placed her temporarily, till her pelvis healed from the fracture. I wondered where my mother's pills were, and whether they were truly lethal. We were terrified, but we had a plan, as usual. Matthew would break the news, and if she survived the first shock, I would steal her pills at some later moment. She was already dressed, hunched uncomfortably in a black plastic chair, her crocodile skin handbag by her side. My guess was that the pills were somewhere in there, probably in the little black leather box I had brought her back from Florence. She looked up slowly, the handle of her walking stick beside her knees like a scepter.

Matthew cleared his throat. "It's bad news I'm afraid Mam."

"It's your dad," she said flatly. "He's dead isn't he?"

"I'm afraid so. It was this morning, in the early hours. The hospital called us straight away."

"I thought he looked poorly last night when we gave him the ice cream," she said quietly. "He didn't half enjoy it didn't he? He ate every last little bit. I'm glad we gave him that." She looked up at us. "Have you come to take me out of here?"

"Yes," said Matthew. "We thought we should all be together at Stanhope tonight, then maybe you and Claire can go back to Pond House, if that's what you want."

I spent the next two weeks almost exclusively with my mother. Most of the time she sat listlessly in her armchair, like someone already dead, and roused herself slowly if I spoke to her, as if swimming up from a great depth. She made a few simple requests: a cup of tea, cheese on toast, an extra cardigan. She watched some of her usual programs on TV, but her face never moved, even during comedies. She didn't want to speak to anyone who called, though she read her sympathy cards carefully, before stowing them away in a big manila envelope. When I asked her if I could look after her pills for a while, she asked me why, then told me not to be silly. Her eyes were very dull.

Every morning I went to help her get dressed, as my father had done. I tiptoed across the hallway to open her door stealthily, holding my breath. She seemed to have such a weak grip on life that I was certain it would slip from her one of these dark nights, and I would find her dead. I wanted to know before I looked at her, and so I listened for her breathing. Sometimes I thought it had stopped, and would be horrified to feel my heart leap with something like relief. She was helpless, crippled, couldn't even walk to the end of her front path without assistance. How could she go on? What would happen to her? Sometimes, when I heard the quiet snore of her breath, I crept across the carpet to stare at her collapsed face, the way her wrinkled eyelids twitched as if in pain or consternation, the way her mouth hung open, empty of teeth, and her cheeks sagged down into space. When I touched her shoulder, she'd murmur my father's name. Even when she was awake she'd call me "Paul," automatically, as if I'd stepped into his shoes.

The other night Sally and I had asked her what she thought about living with us in Kent. After all, we had nothing to hide now. We were getting along, had settled into another routine. We were still close, still cared for each other, still kept everything going. Sally was here right now, up for the funeral, asleep in my brother's old room, while I reinhabited my own old bedroom, stuck in a time warp of virginal teenage innocence—floral wallpaper and a dressing table with ornate gold knobs. "You could help out, if you wanted to, Norah," Sally had told my mother, "make tea for the patients in the waiting room, answer the phone and things. You wouldn't have to, of course, only if you wanted. I'm around all day. It's not like you'd be all on your own."

I'd end up like Auntie Phyllis, just like Mam had always said, taking care of my mother while Sally had Jeff's babies. I'd join a book club and volunteer at the library and buy useless gifts for my nephews and always be cheerful and careful not to stay outstay my welcome. I'd touch myself under the covers late at night, and take out my spite on silly girls in the third year who'd make cruel jokes about spinsters behind my back.

"Maybe," my mother had said, patting Sally on the hand. "It's nice of you to ask pet. I'd miss seeing Matthew and Andrea though, and the lads growing up. We'll see. There's plenty of time for all that."

At the funeral home a voiceless man in a black suit, like a cross between a butler and a mime artist, ushered me into a tiny room. The body in the coffin looked like Dad, except that everything had shrunken slightly. His cheeks were hollow, and it made his face look rodent-like. I saw with displeasure that they had trimmed his bushy eyebrows, and dressed him in a sort of white surplice with a gold trim, his hands crossed on his chest, like a medieval angel. I sat in the single chair and looked at him for a while. I wondered what other people did on such visits. I wondered if the funeral home took the robe off before the cremation, and used it on some-one else's corpse. I wondered where they ordered these strange garments from, and in how many different sizes. I imagined small factories dedicated to sewing clothes for dead people, and wondered if the fashions changed, if they put out annual catalogues with new styles. I leaned forward to touch his hand. It felt like flesh, but cold and unyielding. I wondered how long they let visitors stay. Maybe desperate lovers climbed into the box to wail and beg the dead to return. Maybe our movements were being mon-itored by hidden cameras. In the end, I kissed his cheek, but he remained unmoved. Although my mother hadn't wanted to see him, she quizzed me at length about how he looked. I said he looked just like the Pope, and she derived great comfort from this, as I had known she would.

"Our Claire says he looked just like the Pope—dignified. They'd put him in a white surplice. I think they must have known he was a church warden. Our Matthew must have told them. The only thing Claire didn't like was they'd trimmed his eyebrows. He'd have hated that. He'd never let me near them with the scissors."

. . .

The morning of Dad's funeral I lay in bed, dreaming that I was lying in bed on the morning of Dad's funeral. In my dream, I was woken by my mother's heavy, crippled tread. There was something mysterious and terrible about the sound of her halting steps. It was the sound of the monster, dragging itself up the stairs, when you know there's nowhere to hide. It was the moment when actors in horror movies sit bolt upright in bed and pull the sheets around their necks. I held myself rigid, pressed against the headboard, and listened to an awful silence as my mother stopped outside my bedroom door. For long seconds, I felt her listening, pregnant with intention, before she called my name.

"Claire. Claire pet, are you there?"

Even in the dream, I did not understand why I was so afraid. Nothing was more familiar, more homely, than the sound of my mother's voice. She called me so often, to do up her shoelaces, to comb her hair, to fetch her handbag, her purse, a letter, her coat, that I responded without thought, as if her brain was connected to my muscles. Calling me was so instinctive, so casual for my mother that sometimes when I got there she had forgotten what she wanted. Since we were all schooled in patience, not a sigh or a grimace would escape me at the end of such a wasted journey. We all knew how helpless it made her feel to be so dependent. Our code of honor prevented complaint.

In the dream, she sounded querulous, as if wondering whether or not she'd made a long painful journey across the hall only to find that I was not in my room. I held my breath. "Claire! Claire! I need you for a second. It'll only take a minute."

It was only when she moved again that I realized what was wrong. It was the noise—not the footsteps, but the other noise—a rustling, like bats stirring in a cave, or the shirring of insects' wings. The door swung open and she appeared, shrouded in mourning clothes, her short and dumpy figure swathed in Victorian widow's weeds. A heavy taffeta skirt hung in grotesque layers from beneath a nebulous arrangement of shawls and frills, all of the deepest black. She wore a coalscuttle bonnet fringed with beads of clicking jet, and a heavy veil clouded her face. As she shifted slightly on her unsteady legs, she staggered under the weight of her garments and put a hand out for balance. Everything about her swayed and sighed. She was a ridiculous aberration, like a monkey dressed to kill, like an insane child in grown-up clothing. As I stared at her in horror, her eyes suddenly transfixed me. They blazed at me, consumed with inconsolable suffering.

Suddenly I was jolted awake by a huge noise. The big brass knocker was hammering on the front door, and I leaped out of bed, stupid with sleep and fear, aware that my heart was pounding too. As I stumbled downstairs, still half dreaming, I heard my mother, shaken loose from her own dreams, calling again. "Paul! Paul! Where are you? There's the door. There's someone knocking."

I wrestled open the door to find a man framed there, as if in a surrealist painting. He wore a black Magritte suit and bowler hat. Without speaking, he held out a huge floral cross. I stared at him wildly, wondering if he would disappear. After a few seconds, he whispered something, placed the cross gently in my arms and closed the door. "Claire!" my mother called. "Is that you? Who was that? What time is it?"

Sally appeared at the top of the stairs, sleepy and concerned. "Is everything OK? It sounded like an earthquake." I wished that I could crawl into her bed with her, in Matthew's old room, and pull the covers up over our heads like we used to. I wished that she would come downstairs and give me a hug. I wished that we could make a pot of tea and talk about this, about how I was feeling, but my mother was still calling. "I'll go and get dressed," Sally said, "and then I'll put the kettle on."

I went to my mother's door, holding the white cross. It was at least five feet long, and very heavy. I stared stupidly at the door handle, with no hand free to open it. For a while I walked around helplessly, maneuvering my burden around corners, looking for a surface large enough to hold it. I was struck somehow dumb, like the ancient mariner when his tongue was withered at the root and the guilt of the dead albatross lay heavy around his neck. I was unable to call up the stairs to Sally. My mother was still calling my name, increasingly worried, as I rejected the coffee table, the couch, the draining board. Finally, I put it down on the stairs outside her door.

"Cooperative Funeral Service," I finally realized. That's what he had said. For some reason the Co-op had sent the cross for my father's hearse on ahead of his body. Flowers and corpses—they must be different departments, I realized—different storage conditions.

. . .

Funerals are an ideal recipe for hysteria, and those organized by the Cooperative Society—Sutton's oldest department store and dividend club—are even more ideal than most. First, take several traumatized adults and face them with the prospect of lengthy public exposure to a harrowing religious service. Then place them in a well-polished black car, where all they can do is stare at each other. Next drive them along at a snail's pace for seventeen miles. If it is a Co-op funeral, add a driver who is clearly an exotic minor character from a Dickens novel. Ours looked like he had been taken from the public bar of the Three Tuns and forced at gunpoint into a black suit. He seemed incapable of speech, and held his eyebrows clenched together in what he must have imagined to be an attitude of grief and respect. When we attempted to enter the funeral car, he clasped each of us firmly by the elbow, considerably hindering our progress. As more and more people climbed in, he silently operated folding seats to accommodate us, causing them to spring from concealment, like a magician.

For the first mile we stared in ghastly silence at the driver's short back-and-sides haircut, and at my father's coffin, laden with its weighty floral tribute, as it crawled ahead of us through Glenburn in its lonely hearse. Finally, Matthew cleared his throat and we all turned to stare at him, hollow-eyed. "I wonder what Dad would have made of all this?" he tried.

"He'd probably have enjoyed it," I said. "He'd have liked those folding seats."

We all glanced at Mam.

"He would've," she said. "He'd have had those seats up and down a few times by now to see how they worked. He could fix anything, bless him."

"That driver!" Andrea said. "When Matt and I got to Pond House he was having a quick smoke down Turnbull's back alley."

"He never was!" said Auntie Phyllis, looking shocked. "Was he? Well that's disrespectful. You should complain to the Co-op then, shouldn't you? That's not right. At least *I* don't think it is."

"I don't know Phyl," Sally said, wickedly. "I could have done with a crafty smoke myself. It's not as if the poor bloke can light up now can he? It would look a bit off if he was driving along with a woodbine hanging out the window."

My mother was staring at him through the glass screen. "His shirt collar needs soaking in a bit of bleach," she said suddenly. "I wonder if his wife does them, or if the Co-op sends them out to a laundry." By now, Sally was pink with repressed mirth. I didn't dare catch her eye.

"I wonder if they give them an allocation of clean hankies?" Andrea said, "to hand out to mourners, like headphones on aeroplanes."

My mother started to chuckle. "Don't be stupid," she said. "It's the Co-op, not British Airways."

Andrea began to snuffle into her hankie, her shoulders shaking with repressed giggles. Auntie Phyllis was getting anxious.

"He'll hear us," she hissed. "Whatever will he think? He'll think we're showing disrespect for the dead."

My mother couldn't pass up a chance to show Auntie Phyllis what was what. "Paul wouldn't have cared," she said. "He'd have been worse than any of us. He'd have had us all in stitches by now."

"He'd have been up front having a bit chat with the driver," said Matthew. "They'd both have lit up by now. Dad would've given him one of his Embassy filters."

We giggled our way down Hollin Bank and chuckled all through Everley. By Toft Hill we were groaning and fighting for breath, and we only had to look at one another to start another painful bout. Sally was moaning quietly; Andrea's face was scarlet and tears were pouring down my mother's cheeks. Matthew was clutching his chest in agony, and I whimpered helplessly. Even Auntie Phyllis had cracked. As we entered Darlington, her shoulders were heaving and her teeth were bared in ghastly laughter. On the last mile of our journey to the crematorium, people stopped respectfully in the middle of the busy High Street. Men pressed their doffed hats to their hearts, glancing at our reddened eyes, our tear slimed cheeks. They were impressed by the depth of our sorrow.

Part Six

REBOUND, 1984–1986

The Kent Chronicle

June 1984

Martina Wins Grand Slam

Martina Navratilova won a cherished niche alongside other tennis immortals yesterday by becoming only the fifth player to win a Grand Slam. She easily beat her rival Chris Lloyd 6-3, 6-1 in only 63 minutes.

During the first five games of the second set, Lloyd won only two points, and though the darling of the center court showed typical fortitude, she was steamrollered by the Amazonian Czech powerhouse. In the first set, Lloyd, trim as a hospital sister in all-blue, kept as deep a length as she dared, knowing that her muscular rival would pounce like a tigress on anything too short. But in the short second set, Lloyd was almost brutally outclassed. Navratilova carried all the big guns, mixing up heavily sliced backhands with thundering forehand volleys to annihilate the ever-popular Lloyd.

The special bonus of $1 million presented to Navratilova was just so many bubbles on her brimming glass of champagne victory. "Most of it will go in taxes," she grinned. "My next goal may be another Slam, or may be to bankrupt the Federation." There are fears that she is getting so good that she might bankrupt women's tennis.

31.

MRS. MARSHALL DID NOT LOOK LIKE AN ANGEL WHEN SHE FIRST
appeared on our front doorstep—a bustling, steely, gray-haired attack
missile of a woman, clutching a folder and a large bag of those rubber
things you stick on the end of walking sticks to prevent them from slipping. How typical of Durham County Social Services, I thought, to imagine that what my mother needed right now was a large collection of
well-shod walking sticks! But I could tell that my mother liked her. By
the time I'd made us all a cup of coffee, they were on first name terms
and swapping stories about the deaths of their respective husbands, with
my divorce thrown in for good measure.

"So, Norah," she asked finally, setting down her empty coffee cup.
"What do you think you'll do?"

"Do?" my mother said. "You mean in terms of living?"

"Yes," said Mrs. Marshall.

"Well, we've talked about me moving to Sally and our Claire's house
in Kent," said my mother. "Our Matthew and Andrea haven't got room,
with the three lads growing up."

"I see," Mrs. Marshall said slowly, glancing at me. "And who would
Sally be?"

"She would be my roommate," I told her. My ex-lover, I added silently.

"They're career girls," my mother told her. "Sally's an osteopath you
know. She came up for the funeral but she's gone back to her practice now.
They have a beautiful house in Kent. Our Claire's a headmistress now."

"Deputy head," I corrected her, automatically.

"They both work too hard," my mother said. "They're married to
their careers, you know."

Mrs. Marshall looked at me more kindly. "I see," she said. *No flies on
her,* I thought. She knew what was what.

"Is that what you *want* to do then Norah? I mean right now. If I asked
you what you wanted to do right now."

"Well," said my mother slowly. "Right now I want to stay here. It's all been such an upset you see. I just want to be with my own things." Bravely, she tried to inject some briskness into her voice. "Claire tells me I could take them to Kent though. It's not really a possibility is it? Staying here I mean."

"Why is that then?"

"Well, as I was telling you, I'm housebound, you know. Paul did everything for me. He was a saint, Enid. I think that's partly what killed him you know."

Enid Marshall seemed unaware of my mother's sudden tears. "What did he do?"

My mother fumbled in her sleeve for her hanky. "Well, like I say, he did everything. I couldn't have coped without him."

"Did he cook?"

"Well no. I did all the cooking, but he opened all the tins and the jars for me."

"You'll qualify for a home help, if you want one, Norah. She'd do that. You'd just have to plan your menu in advance and tell her what tins you wanted her to open before she left. The service isn't free, but it is subsidized. I think you'd have to pay about ten shillings a week. That would take care of any of the housework you can't do."

My mother looked at me dubiously. "I don't think I would really need a home help, would I Claire? I mean it would take some thinking about, wouldn't it? We'll have to see what our Matthew has to say."

"What are you bothered about?" I asked her. "It's not the money, is it? Is it having someone you don't know coming into the house?"

She gave me a warning glance and smiled at Mrs. Marshall. "No, pet, no, it's not anything like that. I'm sure they're all very nice. It's just that it would be a strange person. In the house. Paul didn't like that much, you know."

"Well," said Mrs. Marshall, "to be a bit blunt, Norah, you need to be more worried about your children right now. Claire here's got to go back to Kent, and she's going to be worried sick about you."

"Oh," said my mother. She looked at me in surprise. "I'd never thought of it that way. You're not worried are you pet? What on earth is there to worry about?"

"Of course I'm worried!" I said crossly. "I'm three hundred and fifty miles away, for goodness' sake. I'll be worried sick."

"You know, Norah," said Mrs. Marshall. "It's up to you. It really is, but here's my three penn'orth for what it's worth. It's usually a bad idea to move. You need to grieve Paul, and you're absolutely right—it's best to do it in your own home where you can remember him properly. They've done studies. Another thing—it often doesn't work so well when widows move in with their children. I've seen good relationships ruined. Besides everything else, what would you do in Kent? Who would you know that's your own age? Your life is here, love, isn't it? This is where your community is. The best advice I can give is to stay here for a year, then see how you feel. There's a big change after the first anniversary. I know you don't think that now, Norah, but I've been through it. The first year is always the worst."

My mother's eyes had filled up, and I put an arm around her as Mrs. Marshall turned to me. "Talk about it with her, and don't act out of guilt. It's fatal. Meanwhile, I'll get one of my best ladies out here. I think Janet's free at the moment." She stood up and brushed biscuit crumbs from her chest briskly. "Now then, let's look at what else you might need Norah. What about the cooker knobs?"

"Paul used to turn them for me."

"Come and watch this," said Mrs. Marshall. Five minutes later, she had fitted rubber walking stick knobs to all the cooker controls. "They're a godsend," she told us, as she stood back and looked at them in satisfaction, "far better than all these fancy devices the scientists have come up with, though I'll show you those too." She was right. My mother didn't really need a pincer arrangement to pick things off the floor, but she could now operate the cooker and open and shut the front and back door, something she hadn't done in years.

"Well who would have thought?" my mother kept saying. "A simple thing like that. All the times I had to ask your dad to come and turn a pan down, or open the back door."

"Norah," said Mrs. Marshall, "you're by no means the worst case we have, not by half. I'm actually assessing you as highly functional. You've got all your marbles, for one thing. Just think about how blind people manage, and people in wheelchairs. I've worked with a *deaf* person in a wheelchair. It's just a question of thinking things through." She looked at me briefly, "Got a pen? Right. For a start, get rid of that coal fire and get some electric radiators. They're not the cheapest things to run, but then the price of coal's going to go up with all this business with the miners' strike, and the electric heaters are very convenient. What else?"

My mother furrowed her brow and looked at me. "Is there anything else pet?" she said. "Matthew and Claire have been wonderful," she explained to Mrs. Marshall. "They've thought of everything for me."

I was slowly realizing that this wasn't the point. "Just run through a normal day, Mam," I said. "Think about what Dad did that you couldn't."

"Get up," she said. "Put my clothes on. I can do that. He used to take me shopping. I'd tell him what to buy, then he'd run in and I'd sit in the car."

"Well what about your daughter-in-law?"

"Andrea's wonderful," said my mother, "but I wouldn't like to be a burden."

"You're eligible for a travel allowance to take a taxi to the shops," Mrs. Marshall said. "Give it to Andrea, and your laundry allowance. Pay her to do your shopping and your washing. She can drop it off at the same time. She can just do yours when she does her own. You'll both get something out of it, and you won't feel so dependent."

My mother was getting into this. "I can vacuum with that little Bex Bissel we bought," she said. "Let me think what else . . . light the fire, oh no, I'll have the radiators. I wish we could move that hallstand."

For a moment, I was irritated that all she could think about was moving furniture, but Mrs. Marshall went to look at it. "The phone," she said. "It's in an awkward place isn't it Norah? Do you stand up to make calls?"

"Paul used to fetch me a chair through from the living room," Mam said.

"I'll get an extension lead," I said, "and how about one of those little tables you can swing over the arm of a chair? The phone could stay on there, and maybe it would be handy to eat off."

My mother looked pleased. "I find it hard to balance plates on my knees," she said, "and it's bloody freezing in winter trying to have a nice chat to someone in that hallway."

"You'll be on the phone a lot," said Mrs. Marshall, "so you may as well be comfy."

I cleared my throat. "What if Mam falls?" I said. "She's not great on the stairs."

Mrs. Marshall tilted her head to look at me. "What's that room off to the right, as soon as you come in the front door?" she asked.

"The sitting room," I told her.

"Use it much?" she asked Mam, "or is it just for company? You can move your bed there."

"My God," I said. "In fact the whole bedroom. She wouldn't need to go upstairs at all."

"What about the upstairs dusting!" said my mother, horrified.

"To hell with the dusting," said Mrs. Marshall, "that's what about it. Forget about upstairs. Pretend you live in a bungalow. Nobody will ever go up there. Claire and Sally can give it a spring clean when they come to visit."

Mam chuckled. "To hell with it," she said. "I bet our Claire approves of that."

"Too damn right," I said. "But just going back to the idea of accidents for a minute. My brother and I saw an ad in a magazine for a personal alarm system, and we thought, you know, she could wear it around her neck, and we thought—"

"You thought it would make you feel better," said Mrs. Marshall, "but can you imagine wearing one every waking hour? What's the message you're sending to Norah? We could all fall, but we don't think about it all the bloody time, and if I'm not mistaken, Norah doesn't want to think about it either, do you Norah?"

My mother shook her head emphatically. "It would make me feel like a helpless old biddy," she said. "Even if I am one, I don't want to feel like one."

"Write up the emergency telephone numbers nice and big by the phone," Mrs. Marshall continued. "If she can't get to the phone she can yell or bang something as well as you or I can, and in any case, someone will be in every day." She scribbled a couple of notes and bundled up her papers. "Now look, Norah, I think you've got the hang of the sort of things you're looking at. Buy yourself a smaller kettle, one you can lift. When your daughter-in-law leaves your shopping, get her to loosen all the jar tops and lids for you before she puts them away. She can put them back on gently. Call me about the home help, and let me know what you want to do." She put her hand on my mother's arm. "If you have any questions at all, just pick up the phone, Norah," she said, "but I think you'll be fine. I'll pop in and see you when your daughter's gone home."

"Talk about a white tornado," said Mam as she closed the door on Mrs. Marshall and leaned on my arm back down towards the living room. "She was just like that Ajax advert." She sighed. "When I think of all those things that Paul did I feel terrible. We could have done all this before. We just never thought. He used to push that heavy mower every week, and our Matthew's found one of the village lads to do it for a few shillings. He might still have been alive," she said, "if we'd just thought."

I remembered the way in which the neat columns in my father's diary had fallen into disarray, and Matthew's face when I'd showed them to him. "We should have done something," he'd said. "We should have asked if he needed help, if things were getting too much."

"He was very independent," I said to my mother. "It's easy to look back and see what we should have done. I feel badly, and I know Matthew blames himself too, but Dad was so proud. Maybe he would have felt insulted."

My mother brightened a little. "He would," she said. "He'd of been furious, actually. Remember when you asked him if he was all right to drive all the way to Kent? He was mortified."

"The main thing," I said, "is that we know how to make things easier for you now. As Matthew would say, we have a plan."

"We'd better get cracking," said my mother.

I emptied out the fire grate, and carried its dismantled parts down to the garden shed, while my mother swept up the remainder of the ashes, and washed and scrubbed the gloomy hole that remained. "Maybe if he hadn't had to light this damned thing every morning, and carry coals up from the shed, he wouldn't have died," said my mother. "He would insist on going down there with his carpet slippers on." Preventing people from going outside with slippers on was always high on her list of priorities, and from now on became such an obsession that I would look guiltily at my feet whenever I heard the phone ring.

"I don't think it was any one thing, Mam," I told her gently. "It was just his time. He had a good life. You looked after him very well. You know you did."

My mother began to cry. "Do you think so?"

"I remember him sitting there waiting for his supper, doing the crossword. Not a care in the world, and you coming in with his egg and chips. Or off down the village to buy your mint humbugs and gossip with Donnie in the post office. Or in his greenhouse pottering around nipping side shoots off the tomatoes for ages. He was happy as Larry."

My mother's eyes shone as she chuckled. "Eeh, Claire. He was, pet, wasn't he? He was so proud of you and Matthew, and Andrea and the lads. He loved going over to Stanhope. Those boys are going to miss their Granda. We all are. I just can't get used to it. I wake up in the morning and he's not there. You've no idea. I keep thinking I'm going to hear him whistling, or see him, coming in the back door from the coalhouse with his shovelful. I keep forgetting he's gone, and then I have to remember all over again. I feel so lonely, so lonely."

She was crying again. I put my arms around her, and cried too. "I miss him as well. I can remember just what his face looked like, all wrinkled and smiling, and how it used to go bright red when he laughed. He used to make such awful jokes, and I'd hit him, and he'd pretend to be badly hurt and call for you to help him. He'd say I was beating my poor old father who'd got gray hair."

After we'd finished crying, we poured ourselves some of Dad's homemade wine, and settled down to consider finances. Mam thought of all the outgoings she could, while I wrote them down on a piece of paper. I was emphatic about the need for a new system. "No more teapots," I said. "It's not safe keeping all that money in the house. You can cash your old age pension every week, and if you've got any left over you can give it to Matthew to put in the bank. Then when you want to buy something special, you can just write a check."

She looked surprised. "Can I?"

I got out the checkbook and showed her the two names on it. "It's a joint account see? Mr. C. W. Robson and Mrs. N. M. Robson. Either of you can sign."

She squinted at it rather mistrustfully. "But I'd have to fill these other bits in too."

"You mean you've never done that?"

She shook her head. "Your dad did all that. He tried to show me once but I couldn't do it right."

"Good God. It's easy. I'll show you."

"Let's do it tomorrow. Or I'll get our Matthew to write them out."

"Just watch for five minutes. Then if you want to stop, you can. Here, have some more wine." Patiently, I showed her where each bit went on the check. She was made stupid by fear, but eventually was amazed to see how easy it was.

"Now we can imagine we're buying something, and write one out. No! Even better, let's pay that phone bill that just came."

She balked at this. "Eeh, no pet. Let's leave that to our Matthew. I might make a mistake."

"So what if you do? We can just tear the check up and start again."

She looked at me suspiciously. "How do you know?"

"Come on Mam. I've had my own checkbook since you and Dad dropped me off that day at York University. I countersign all the checks that go out from our school."

She shook her head in exasperation. "You always could argue black was white. Well I'm not using that old biro. Pass me that presentation pen of your dad's out of the bureau."

An hour later, we had paid all the outstanding bills and moved on to the cash accounts. Soon we had a neat row of Dad's Durham County Council brown envelopes lined up in a Tupperware box. It was the modern Slim Line version of the teapot system. Each envelope was labeled: "Papers—1.20" or "Milk 2.75."

My mother sat and carefully counted shilling pieces into her envelopes, till the week's bills were organized. "It's a wonderful system," she said. "I can see what's in here easier than the teapots."

She was well set up by the time I left for Kent. Her cupboards were stocked; her house was fully functional, and Matt and I had spent the last three days just watching her do things, looking for loopholes in the system. Of course, it is the nature of loopholes to be well concealed, and we didn't find them all. Three months later she called very late one night.

"Claire, pet. Guess what? I can't get my shoes off."

"Why on earth not?"

"Well, the other day I was talking to Martha Braithwaite, and I was telling her about that little toe of mine. The one where the nail is twisted round."

I was used to my mother's need to put situations firmly in context, which usually meant starting anecdotes three days before the main event. I waited patiently, knowing that there was no point in rushing her, even if I did have to get up early tomorrow.

"Well, Martha was telling me that there's a kiropo . . . shiropo . . . shiropodist. Do you say shiropodist or kiropodist? People seem to say both, and I never like to ask."

"I think it's kiropodist. Anyway, you went to one did you?"

"Well, Martha Braithwaite told me there's one comes to the Village Hall the first Monday of every month, and it's free if you're on the old age pension. Your dad and I could have gone all this time. He had terribly cold feet you know. They maybe might could have done something."

"How did you get down there?"

"Gwen Batty asked her Malcolm if he'd drive me and he did. Wasn't that nice of him? Your dad always did like Malcolm, even if he was a rough diamond. Anyway, the shiropodist . . . or did you say it was kiropodist?"

"Kiropodist"

"Well, he was ever so nice. From Surrey originally, and so well-mannered. I was trying to do my shoelaces up and he said, 'Let me help you with those, Mrs. Robson. You seem to be having a bit of a struggle.' Can you believe Claire, he got down on his knees and did them up for me, and I didn't think anything about it."

Realization was dawning.

"So I came back, and Gwen came in for a cup of tea. She asked after

you. She always does you know and then, well, after she went, I watched
the film. It wasn't any good, all shooting each other then jumping into
bed the whole time, and I must have dozed off, because when I looked at
the clock it was half past eleven. So I came to get my clothes off and go
to bed and here they are."

"Too tight, eh?"

She chuckled. "Too bloody tight all right. I can't budge them. He
wouldn't think, would he? He just did them up nice and tight like he
normally would. He was just being helpful."

"How about cutting the laces?"

"I tried. I can't get the scissors gripped properly. I tried that big bread
knife with the serrated blade too. I got it underneath the laces but I
couldn't saw through them. Listen, this is what I called to ask. I don't
want to call our Matthew, or wake Gwen up; it's too late. So I thought
I'd just go to bed in my shoes and tights, and the home help can undo
them tomorrow. What do you think?"

"Are you sure you'll sleep?"

"Oh yes. I'll get Andrea to wash the sheets, but I'm not going to tell
our Matthew. He'll be cross I didn't phone him."

"Well I wish I could be there to undo them, but since I'm not, I think
yours is the best plan."

"I know. It's a shame you didn't live just a bit nearer. Anyway. I just
wanted to check. I'll let you get off to bed now. Night night."

"Night night. Sleep tight. Shoes and all."

She chuckled.

"Aren't I stupid Claire? You'll have to tell them all at school so they
can have a good laugh."

"You're not stupid."

"Wait till I tell Martha Braithwaite. It'll be all round the village that
Mrs. Robson's lost her marbles now her husband's died."

"Mam. You're not stupid. It's not your fault. I'm actually quite upset.
I don't think it's funny at all."

"Come on now pet, there's nothing to be upset about. I'll get them
off tomorrow."

"Well, stop saying you're stupid."

"All right. I'm Brain of Britain. Good night."

"Good night."

"Don't let the bugs bite."

32.

MAGGIE PERKINS WAS A SHORT WOMAN, ABOUT FIVE-FOOT-TWO, BUT close-knit, with the look of a pocket pugilist or an economy-sized Olympian—coiled and ready to execute a handspring—as she perched in the hot seat on the other side of my office desk. She seemed irrepressibly bouncy, like Tigger in Winnie-the-Pooh. Her boxy blue interview suit was all wrong on her. My guess was that she'd bought it just for this occasion, from Dorothy Perkins or some other cheap high street boutique. I imagined a couple of maternally minded roommates digging in their wardrobes to find her suitable accessories—the pretty gold chain, the polyester blouse, the excruciating shoes with the smallest possible heel. Despite their best efforts to feminize her, she looked like she was in drag—just like I was. The only difference was that I had a bigger budget and more practice, would've known better than to wear a digital watch with an expanding metal strap that was just too wide to be acceptable, would've shaved my legs and carried a handbag.

These days, I'd say that my Gaydar registered an incoming missile, armed and dangerous. All I knew back then was that the sharp lines of Maggie's face scrabbled at the veneer of my professional persona in a way that was exciting, but a little uncomfortable. I felt suddenly unsure of myself, dry and brittle, like the chrysalis of my pretensions was about to split. Though she answered my questions intelligently and politely, there was an underswell of irony in her Atlantic blue eyes, as if she thought that we were playing a rather silly game. I ploughed through my stock of questions anyway, as forbiddingly as I could, and confirmed what I had already suspected from her application. She was the perfect candidate— bright, up-to-date, energetic, and efficient.

At the end, when I invited questions, she asked how long I had been there. "Everyone else seems a bit. . . . well . . ." she struggled only briefly for a polite way to put it, "primeval."

"I've been here six years," I told her, ignoring the last part of her question.

"Do you play any sports?" she asked, with her head to one side, like a bird sizing up a worm.

"I used to," I said, already feeling myself unbend a little, wanting to impress her. "County hockey, distance running, a little basketball."

"Basketball!" She sat up in her chair. "Have you been to the women's league in Canterbury?"

I smiled a little. "I haven't played in years. I'm a bit long in the tooth for that kind of thing these days."

"Oh, come on," she said, tossing her heavy black hair. "How old *are* you? No more than thirty seven or so I'd guess, and you look pretty fit."

I steered the conversation back to the physical education curriculum for a few minutes, then walked her over to Evan's office, where she'd no doubt endure his standard interrogation about her capacity for unremitting toil. Later, when he and I were comparing notes, I tried to warn him off, but without conviction. "There might be trouble if you appoint her," I told him. "She'll be good at her job, but I think people could find her abrasive. My guess is that she has a low tolerance for bullshit, and that could be quite a handicap here at Mansfield's, as you know."

Evan laughed. "Good," he said. "I'd rather have her than that lumpy creature from Nonnington who seems to think that she should take orders from Roger Wilkinson. We need someone to shake things up a bit. If she upsets that lazy bastard she'll be doing her job."

My excuse for finally taking up Maggie's repeated offers to play basketball was that I was lonely. Sally and Jeff had progressed from drinks to overnights, tactfully arranged at his house. It was almost a relief to find that the house was empty, as I did this particular Friday night, because I hated to hear Sally stop whistling in the kitchen when I came in, or to notice that she was wearing something new and snazzy. I was tired of feeling like an elderly aunt. It was spring again, almost a year since Dad had died. The crocuses were blooming in the garden, and our neglected cats scrabbled against the French windows, turning their heads to mew at me, wanting to hunt nesting birds in the lilacs. I threw my bag of exercise books onto the sofa. I should change out of my school clothes. I should take food out of the freezer. I should settle down to grading papers. The phone rang, and from the scrabbling noises, I realized that my mother was fumbling with the receiver. Her voice was strong and excited. "Hello pet! Guess who sends her regards to you!"

"I've no idea."

"Mrs. Wilkie! You know, the one who lives in the council houses. She was married to Road Jack."

I remembered them both. Road Jack worked for the council road crew and could normally be found sitting by a hole in the road on his neatly folded yellow jacket, hand-rolling cigarettes. His wife, Ada, conducted most of her business transactions through local children, banging on her window to attract their attention, or running into the street with her slippers on when this failed.

"I want you to buy me a bag of bull's-eyes," she'd demand. "Here's two shillings, and bring me the change. I'll give you one for going, but don't you dare open that bag on the way home, because I'll know." Most of the adults in my life spoke in slow, pragmatic Glenburn sentences, as carefully weighed as if talk were a dangerous and costly commodity, but when I was little, Mrs. Wilkie and I would sit on her sofa sucking bull's-eyes, and rattle on for hours about ghosts, God, the new people down the street, film stars, and dogs. Sometimes Road Jack would be there, spread in an armchair like laundry, but we pretty much ignored him after I said, "Hello Mr. Wilkie," and he smiled back.

"Mrs. Wilkie!" I said. "How is she? Tell her I'll come and see her when I come up for Christmas."

"Eeeh pet, she had me in stitches. She's a real tonic. I laughed so hard the tears were rolling down my face. It's the way she talks. She was telling me about this miner's wife kept her dead husband's ashes in a vase on the mantelpiece. One winter's day she couldn't get down her front path, so she took the ashes and threw them on the ice. 'The bugger was no use to me when he was alive,' she says, 'so he can serve a purpose now he's gone.'" My mother cackled heartily. "She said old Vicar Smith told her it was acceptable to swear if you didn't take the Lord's name in vain, so she says 'bugger' and 'bloody' are all right but 'God' isn't. Mavis

Brant-Jefferson can't stand her you know. She told me Ada used to be in the Women's Institute, but she fell out with everybody and handed in her resignation."

"Ada's worth ten Mrs. Brant-Jeffersons."

"Do you really think so? Your dad never liked her. He thought she was vulgar."

"She is vulgar."

"So you think I shouldn't have her in the house?"

"What on earth do you mean?"

"Well your dad would never have her in the house."

"What do you mean? He wouldn't let her in if she came to the door for a glass of water?"

"Don't be silly. I just mean we didn't invite her in. The same way we never invited Martha Braithwaite in. Your dad said we had to maintain a standard."

I ran through a mental checklist of people who visited Pond House. There was the vicar, and Mr. Robinson, the insurance man. There were always relatives of course, Grannie Robson and Auntie Phyllis, Auntie Ida and Uncle Ted. The Brant-Jeffersons would occasionally come by to discuss church business with Dad, and there were some shadowy friends from Houghton-le-Spring—the Hennises, who left witty notes on the door ("We came. We saw. We did not conquer."). When we came home and found these, my parents would engage in lengthy gloating sessions. "Thank God we were out," they'd say. "Trust Jack Hennis to drive all the way from Houghton without telephoning. Serves him right."

"Are you still there?" my mother asked finally.

"Yes," I said. "I was just thinking back. Is that why we never had many visitors?"

"Well of course. I was brought up very differently at Station Road. My father was a very social man, and my mother had a lot of her own friends too. When we lived in Houghton I had Mrs. Carr next door. I told her everything. She was always there to give me advice, you know, when your dad was overseas, and to talk to about problems. I remember the first time your dad and I had a bad argument, I went round and talked to her over the fence the next morning. 'It'll blow over,' she said. 'It's not the end of the world. You'll see. He didn't mean that.'" She sighed. "It's nice for a woman to have someone to have a bit of gossip with. I got out of the way of it a bit in Glenburn you know, because your dad had his position to maintain."

"Mam, I think it's fine if you want to invite Mrs. Wilkie in. She's a good person."

"Our Matthew doesn't like her."

"Only because she told him and Lonny Turnbull off years ago for looking through the Village Hall windows when they were doing their Weight Watchers exercises."

"She's got a sharp tongue."

"Look, what on earth can be the harm if you have her in the house? Invite her for dinner."

"Oh no Claire. I could never do that."

"She's not infectious for goodness sake."

"Oh Claire. You don't understand. I don't want to let myself go like some do when they lose a husband, or a wife for that matter. I'm losing my routines. You'll never guess what I did yesterday."

"Probably something absolutely terrible, like leaving the washing up for half an hour."

"Eeh Claire, no. It was worse. Promise you won't tell our Matthew."

"Mum's the word."

"Well, I stayed up till two o'clock in the morning watching this film on TV. It was Lana Turner, and your dad used to love her. She couldn't marry the man because she thought she had leukemia, but she never told him in case he stayed with her out of sympathy, so he thought she was having an affair with Cary Grant. I sat with a box of tissues and ate a whole quarter pound of those licorice allsorts. It was a lovely film."

"So what on earth was wrong with that?"

"Well Claire. I didn't wake up till 10:30, and Kenny Armstrong was knocking on the door for the milk money. I didn't know what to do. He knew I was in there because I can't go anywhere. I thought he might think I was dead or something and break the door down. But then I couldn't have gone to the door in my dressing gown at that time of the day. The whole village would have heard about it. You know what a gossip his mother, Florence, is. In the end I called through the letter box and told him I'd just got out of the bath, and he came back on his way down the village."

"Oh really Mam! Is that it! You made it sound like you'd murdered somebody!"

"I felt so guilty. What would your dad have said?"

"But Mam! You can do what you like. You've worked hard all your life, and now you're allowed to have some fun. Stay up till two o'clock and have wild drinking parties with Ada Wilkie! Get Martha Braithwaite round and play bingo!"

She started to chuckle wheezily, coughing as she built up pace, like a rusty engine turning over. "I should've known better than to call and ask you for advice. You're worse than I am!"

"Chip off the old block," I retorted. "Oh go on, Mam. What's the harm in inviting a friend in for a cup of tea?"

She chuckled some more. "I know," she said. "I already did. Ada stayed nearly two hours, Claire. I laughed so hard I thought I was going to have a heart attack. She's a real tonic that one, and I don't care what they say—she's got a heart of gold. You know she asked if I needed any-thing done before she went, any jobs that I couldn't manage. That's more than that snooty Mavis Brant-Jefferson ever does. Anyway, that's enough of me rattling on pet. What are you and Sally up to tonight?"

"Well, Sally's out actually. With her new boyfriend."

"A boyfriend! Sally!"

"Yes." It was best to get this over with.

"Well fancy that! That's wonderful news. Why on earth didn't you tell me? Is he nice?"

"He's OK," I said. "There's no harm in him. He's quite a bit younger than she is, and he's not that swift, but he's amiable enough." *He's a good fuck is what he is,* I thought bitterly, *and brainless enough to let Sally have her own way with most things.* She still had me to talk to whenever she wanted to, so everything in her garden was just rosy.

"But what about you pet? Aren't you lonely? You and Sally were like Siamese twins. I was just telling Ada how you were two bachelor girls together. That neither of you really had room for a man in your life. She has a niece in London never married either. No one thinks anything of it these days. Eeeh Claire. I don't like to think of you sitting there on your own while she's off gallivanting."

"Actually," I said, somewhat to my own surprise, "I might go and play basketball with a friend, the new head of PE at school. She's been trying to persuade me to go for ages, and I think I might just take her up on it."

"Oh," she said. "Is that the one where they throw the ball at the basket thing? I thought that was a men's game."

"No," I said. "Women play too."

"Well, I'm glad you've got a new friend, but you be careful. Don't play if they get too rough. Your bones don't heal as quickly when you get older."

"I'm not older," I said. "I'm not even forty yet, Mam. I'm going to have fun. We can both have a bit of fun. We've earned it."

33.

I HAD IGNORED MY BODY FOR TEN YEARS, FORCED IT TO SIT CROSS-legged and idle at the pinnacle of a lonely tower. I had made it munch carrots, asked God to dissolve it, to douse my identity in a hail of white light, to render me, to boil me down into a sexless and incorporeal essence. Poor flesh! Its only sin had been to be born the way it was. Its only sin had been to be born at all really, to follow the road map of its DNA, or carry the karmic burdens of its soul's past lives, like some kind of parasite. Perhaps there was no such thing as a soul, but only the reactive mind, turning experience this way or that to make it fit. I didn't know any more. These questions were too big for me to contemplate. I gave up on certainty. In any of these cases, my body had plodded through its paces these last ascetic years, obliging but uninspired, like an elephant at the mercy of its tiny driver. It had tried to be obedient, poor thing, but its lonely flesh remembered. Deep in its cells, tightly coiled codes unraveled like springs unwinding, like the tendrils of seeds.

I had forced my torso into Jaeger suits and my legs into obnoxious stockings. I had numbed my eyes with class lists and exhausted my hands with piles of exercise books. I had tried to turn my blood to ink. But now, however much I summoned the juggernaut of my mantra to crush the world, my nose smelled the warming soil and my eyes noticed the spring flowers. Freesias undid me, and the moist centers of the daffodils unfolding for the bees. Even as I pretended to ignore Maggie when she chose to sit beside me in the staff room, as she often did, my heart registered her. My hands knew that they could touch her if I chose.

There were lesbians that night that I went to play basketball—lesbians everywhere. Their unmistakable, unquantifiable energy washed over me as we walked into the gym. They waited shoulder-to-shoulder on the benches for their turn to play, strong and clear-eyed, every one a dyke. The referee was a lesbian, the timekeeper and the scorer—secure and officious at their table, surrounded by clipboards and pens. A raucous gaggle of girlfriends loitered by a pile of jackets in the corner. One of them brandished pompoms at Maggie and me as we walked by to join Maggie's team. "Go Coasters! Go!" she screamed in a cheerleader parody, and collapsed in giggles as her friends yanked her back down. I surveyed the other women as Maggie introduced me. They gave me businesslike nods and then moved into a flurry of competent pregame jitters, stretching their quads and taping their fingers, jiggling their knees nervously up and down. What was it that betrayed them, I wondered, that spoke so hauntingly after all the years since I'd left the siren pack? It wasn't just the short hair I decided, as I watched them covertly. It was indefinable— some mastery of bearing, the easy splay of legs, the proud tilt of a head, the joy of physical being.

It was my body that revolted, pulled the stupid wax out of my ears and threw me back into the ocean. It was the squeal of sneakers turning on the wooden floor that penetrated, the summons of the whistle, the sweat forcing the bitter years out through my pores. I gasped and panted, desperate to keep up with the spirit of the moment, the swing and swoop of the game, waiting and hoping for someone to notice me, to pass me the ball, to make me part of it, part of the game, part of the team, part of the sisterhood, to cut me in on the action. Years of discipline and vegetables, the lentils of abstinence, the solemnity of satsang, the endless grind of the Holy Names fell away as someone yelled, "Cut! Cut!" and my legs remembered that they were strong and knew how to run and I dashed into the key. The ball slammed into my hands and there was someone in front of me, but I wasn't going to pull up now, not in the heat of my body's moment. I felt a softness, heard a grunt and then the shrill of the whistle. One of our team, Simone, who hadn't spoken to me yet, stuck her hand out to pull me up. "Nice play," she said. "It's one and one." I didn't know what she meant, but clearly I had done something good. Everyone was lining up along the key and looking at me expectantly. Free shots. Oh help. The ref was holding out the ball.

Maggie appeared up beside me. "Bend ze knees and look at the rim," she said, and patted me on the bum. I remembered what the men did on Channel Four, bounced the ball a couple of times and raised it above my head, squinted at the basket, prayed to God to let me do this just one time. "I've done my best," I told him. "Now I just want this. You owe me this," and willed the ball towards the hoop. It bounced and wobbled and finally went in. The second time, it sprang off the ring, but Simone snatched it out of the air and dipped her knees and put it away, ran back towards me with her hand raised. Almost too late, I realized what she wanted, and held up my hand too. High five. "Three point play," she said, then, kindly, as I turned to run back down the court, ready to kill people if I had to, "It's a time-out."

The referee strutted up to the timekeeper in her taut gray pants, ball tucked under her arm. "Three down and a minute on the clock," Maggie said, as we crouched in a circle, gasping, hands on knees. "Plenty of time. The next possession's ours. We'll run a man after that and grab the ball." The other three nodded, and I nodded with them, wisely, but I knew there wasn't plenty of time for me. The seconds were trickling down the hourglass towards my death, and I was tired of hanging on by my finger-nails, my nose pressed to the glass. I belonged here, in the company of these women, long-legged or dumpy, easy and imperfect, unapologeti-cally hungry, unreasonably optimistic. I stood shoulder-to-shoulder with them, stuck my sweaty hand in the center of our circle and felt theirs piled on top and underneath. I would have slept with any of them, with all of them if they had asked me, one by one or all at once. This was what God demanded. This was my destiny. I had sat on the bench too long. The wasted years throbbed in my veins.

As I drove Maggie home, we made polite conversation. I had played well. Thanks, but I was rusty. Yes, she could count me in for next week. "You need new boots," she told me as sternly as a mother. "Those are use-less. You need ones that come up around the ankle. You can hang onto that T-shirt I loaned you."

It was only when I stopped outside her house that she turned to look at me. "Look," she said. "I like women. You need to know that about me, if you hadn't guessed already. If you've got a problem with that, I'll understand. You can just forget I ever told you. I'll see you at the pit tomorrow and you can let me know somehow." She looked almost angry as she started to open the door.

"Hang on," I said, taking a deep breath. She sat back in her seat, glowering. "Me too," I said. "Actually, I just had a bad break-up."

She turned to look at me. "How long were you and she together?"

"Eleven years. We've been totally closeted for the last six or seven."

She whistled. "Wow. So what happened?"

"She's with a man now. Actually, we weren't, you know, fully a couple towards the end."

"But still . . ." she said.

I nodded. "No one knows. I haven't had anyone to talk to. It's been pretty shitty."

She opened her door again. "So why don't you come in?" She climbed out of the car and walked up the garden path without looking back.

We kissed as soon as she closed the front door behind us. "This is stupid," I told her. "It's really not fair on you. I'm coming off a bad break-up. You're a lot younger than I am."

She was naked before we reached the bed. There was a vase of dying crocuses on her bedside table, and I could smell the heavy pollen crusting on their stamens.

"What will happen at work?" I asked her feebly, as she started in on my clothes too.

She looked at me impatiently. "You have to have a life," she said. "Maybe I am younger than you, but I know this much. Everyone deserves a life."

34.

SALLY TURNED THE VOLUME DOWN SLIGHTLY ON THE TV AFTER SHE came in, then took off her white coat and sat in the armchair across from us to sort the day's money and checks into piles on the coffee table. Maggie sprawled along the length of the sofa, and I provided a sort of bookend to the happy idleness of her body. We'd been jogging and then had stopped at McDonald's for takeout on the way home. Crescents of almost-eaten buns and scraps of iceberg lettuce littered the coffee table. I resisted the urge to jump up and tidy away the evidence of our carnivorous indulgence.

"I'm going to make a lentil loaf," Sally said finally, "but it looks like you two won't be interested."

"We've already eaten Sally, thanks," I told her. Maggie waved her fingers just enough to be civil, her eyes glued to the screen as Martina powered a grunting volley past Chris Lloyd. We watched Chris shake her head and walk slowly back to the service line, studying the strings of her racquet. "There's no holes in it, Chrissy!" Maggie murmured. "You just got passed, is all. You just got overtaken. God! Martina's amazing. Look at those arms!" She poked my biceps. "Start weight training," she said. "I want you to have muscles like her."

My muscles still reeled from the four-mile jog, from passionate late-night sex, from basketball training once a week and a game every Tuesday. I'd never showered so often in my life. My legs had lost their frilly cellulite overlay. Maggie had insisted on some concentrated shopping. "You can't wear those," she'd say, as I pulled on an ancient pair of jeans. "No one wears straight legs any more." Right now, I wore purple Nike shorts in the new style, loose and silky, and a snappy running shirt with geometric designs.

"Are you two planning to sleep here tonight?" Sally asked.

"Why?" I asked Sally, as Chris wound up for the serve. "Is Jeff coming over?"

"How is Jeff?" Maggie asked, too innocently. "Has he decided about college yet?"

I saw Sally stiffen at Maggie's remark and at her swift, amused glance at me. Sally's high aspirations for Jeff were a source of great amusement to Maggie, and provided an irresistible opportunity for needling. I didn't know what Maggie resented most—the fact that Sally patronized her, was still possessive about me, had slept with me, or had dumped me for a man. Ironically, Jeff and Maggie got along pretty well, better than Sally and Maggie, for sure. On the rare, uneasy occasions where the four of us were together, Maggie and Jeff conversed easily and esoterically about distance running, as Sally and I listened like older relatives. In another universe, they would have made a great couple.

Just the other day Sally had said that she felt betrayed. I found this astonishing, considering the magnitude of her own betrayal of me. It was true that I had changed. I ate meat. I didn't meditate. I accumulated material possessions. I splayed my sweaty legs out on the coffee table. I drank beer after basketball games and came home singing. I pampered Maggie, indulged her whims, let her decide our agenda. I also refused to believe that Jeff was the next step in Sally's spiritual transformation—possessed of some huge spiritual insight, as she claimed, like some kind of idiot savant. As far as I was concerned, things were welcome to be just what they seemed. The weight of destiny had rolled off me, and I cared only for the moment—Maggie's hand on my thigh, where the sweat cooled into a pleasant prickle, bad dykey Martina's muscled arms pounding the ball past everybody's acceptable Wimbledon darling. I wasn't planning to make a religion out of it.

"No, Maggie, Jeff hasn't decided," Sally said repressively, "and as far as tonight is concerned, yes, Jeff's coming round later."

Maggie gave me another one of her significant looks. I didn't know if she understood just how transparent they were, and was being deliberately provocative, or if she didn't, and was just aiming for secret communication. "So you want us to make ourselves scarce?"

Sally was looking at me, too, her face somewhat grim. I tore myself reluctantly away from the compelling sight of Martina bending low for a groundstroke. "I suppose we can watch the rest of the game at the pub,"

I said, "but you might have given us some warning, Sally. It *is* my house too, and it's difficult for us. We can't spend too much time at Maggie's place because of her roommate."

"How was I meant to know you'd be here tonight?" Sally retorted. "Communication works both ways you know. And it's difficult for me and Jeff as well."

Maggie clambered to her feet and switched off the TV, her face stormy. "I'm going to take a shower, before I say something I regret," she said, and stalked out.

Sally looked at me in the sudden silence. "She's like a child."

"You don't have the right to say unkind things about Maggie."

"To hell with Maggie. What about you? I don't know you any more. You've changed so much. I mean is this it?" She gestured at the empty McDonald's wrappers and the television. "Is this all you want out of life these days?"

I got up and pushed a tape into the VCR, then hit the record button. "Look," I said. "I don't know what I'm going to want in the future, and right now I'm not thinking about it. I'm just enjoying remembering who I am. I'm enjoying being uncomplicated, having fun, being a lesbian. I'm not going to give it up to make someone else happy, or to get to some mythical heaven. This is my choice and I'm making it." I was suddenly quite angry. "You try and respect my choices, and I'll try and respect yours."

She thought about this for a while, her eyes fixed on my face. "I just can't stand to see you throwing everything away. Everything you've worked for. It's like you've thrown everything out of the window. Everything. I just don't feel she's worth it, if I'm absolutely honest. I don't."

On the TV, Chris Lloyd sat on a folding chair with a towel over her head, resting her hands on the racquet she held between her knees. Even this far along in the match, she looked like the girl next door, her depilated legs running smoothly into her bobby socks, her face classically pretty and composed. Martina drank from a paper cup of water, her eyes squinted half shut against the sun, their gaze far off, as if she saw victory out there somewhere, her face like a hunting dog, or a hawk, some frightening beast of prey.

"Well then," I said. "That's your problem, right there. Maggie's my partner right now, and I would like you not to pick at her like you do. You can think what you like and I can't stop you, but I don't want to hear it."

"Well then, tell her to leave Jeff alone."

"She gets on fine with Jeff."

"She's always putting him down on the sly. I'm not stupid and nor is he. It's quite clear what you two think."

"OK," I said. "I suppose that's fair. I'll talk to her. Look. This situation isn't easy for any of us, so I suppose that until you and I figure out what we're going to do about the house, and I can move out, we all need to stop sniping and try to get along. I do think Maggie has some right to be angry though. It is easier for you and Jeff. You do enjoy a little heterosexual privilege."

"Oh come on," she said. "Is that the kind of jargon they fill you up with at that gay support group you're going to? We're all just people, Claire. Jeff and I have problems too. His parents are really hostile because I'm older than he is."

"It's not jargon," I said wearily. "Look. What happens if you and Jeff go to the same pub night after night?"

She hesitated.

"Nothing," I told her. "You're sleeping with a patient, but no one really cares. It's a bit of gossip, but in the end they wish you luck. They accept it. These things happen. Can you imagine what would happen to me if it gets out that Maggie and I are lovers? There'd be complaints from parents. It would probably make the *Kent Chronicle,* Sally. I'd have to resign, and so would Maggie probably."

"Well you and I were together all those years and no one cared."

"We never went out. We never had any friends. We were invisible."

Sally was always fair. "We were," she said. "I never really thought about it that much."

"We never really needed to, did we?"

"Well," she said. "I'll tell you what. I'll take Jeff out tonight. We'll go for Chinese. Peace offering."

"OK. Thanks. I'm glad we talked."

"Me too," she said. "I've been missing that a bit."

"Well, let's keep doing it. Look," I said, "Martina won." She was holding up the big Wimbledon trophy to the crowd, tears streaming down her face. The crowd applauded, not as heartily as they would have for Chris, but good-naturedly enough. The camera flashed to an attractive woman in sunglasses sitting with Martina's coach, grinning from ear to ear and waving. "That must be her lover," I said.

Sally looked at me slyly. "It's sort of a coincidence that we both fell for younger people isn't it?"

"I've thought about that too."

"They're both athletes," she said.

"They are."

"At least we're getting fit," she said. "Jeff's taking me running tomorrow morning. Carl Lewis watch out!"

"I'm getting so fit I can't stand it," I said. "It's hard to keep up sometimes."

She roared with laughter. "Poor old Claire. Leading you a dance is she?"

I grinned.

"They're both studs," Sally said.

"Sally!"

"Well, what's wrong with that? I bet Maggie's really into sex. Is she?"

"We have a good time," I conceded. "But it's more than that. She's brought me back to myself somehow."

Sally looked skeptical. "Oh cut it out! You'd do anything for a big wet vagina."

"Sally!"

"Oh shut up. I know you. I'm glad. I'm glad you're happy. You'd better go and wash her back or something. She'll be feeling all jealous."

Maggie was in the bathtub when I came in. She scowled at me horribly, the effect somewhat hampered by clumps of suds that sat on top of her head like an offbeat shaving cream crown.

"Hail!" I greeted her. "Mistress of my heart."

She stuck her tongue out. "How did you stand her for all those years? She's like the bloody Ayatollah."

"Not really," I said. "You just got off to a bad start. Look. We called a truce. We're all going to stop sniping at each other. That includes you, young lady. No more significant looks whenever Jeff's name is mentioned."

She glared at me indignantly. "I didn't!"

"Yes you did." I picked up a sponge and began soaping her back.

She twisted her head around to glare at me again. "I had to miss the match because of *her.*"

"I'll make it up to you."

She looked instantly gleeful. "Ooh! How? Give me your car?"

"No."

"Buy me a house?"

"No. I will take you on a trip though, at half term."

She slid under the water to rinse off, and popped up again like a seal, her hair plastered to her head, shaking herself to clear her ears. "Where?"

"Well, I was thinking we might go up north, stay with my mother for a couple of days. It's so pretty up there, Maggie. We can hike, maybe go pony trekking up the dale. You'll get to meet my mother, and we can spoil her. She loves going out for bar meals. We can sample all the local pubs."

"Hmm," she made an interested, trying-on-for-size kind of face. "But she doesn't know you're gay, right? Can we sleep together?"

"We'll sleep upstairs in my brother's old bedroom. She doesn't come up there because of the stairs. I think it'll be fine. She doesn't *know* I'm gay, but I lived with Sally all those years, and she's somehow got used to it. It's hard to explain. She's mellowed a lot since Dad died. She's got more tolerant or something. I mean we couldn't be physical in front of her, but she'll understand that you and I are close."

"OK," she said. "Who won the game?"

"I taped it. Sally's taking Jeff out to dinner as a peace offering. There's a bottle of muscadet in the fridge."

She clambered out of the bath, flung one of Sally's extra fluffy towels around her and gave me a smile that had my silly heart capering like a dog first thing in the morning, when it wakes up to the prospect of a walk . . . and breakfast . . . and you . . . you again! "You've been a very, very clever girl," she told me, "and as a reward you get to dry me off."

I took a step towards her.

"No, no, no," she said. "It would be impossible to do a through job here. You need to dry me off everywhere. I am experiencing certain areas of moisture that may require special attention."

"Oh," I said. "I want to do a thorough job."

"You'd better."

I followed her to my bedroom.

35.

WHEN CHILDREN PLAY IN THE GRIP OF AN INCOMING TIDE, EVERY-
thing becomes more urgent. They rush to protect the sandcastle, with its
proud turrets and seaweed streamers. They have spent the happy afternoon hours rushing backwards and forwards with buckets to fill the moat,
but now, as shadows lengthen, water springs up there as if by magic, leaking up from the foundations. As the gulls wail and swoop, turning their
sharp eyes this way and that to see what the ocean has brought them,
sharp corners melt and slide. Every busy mark is covered; the rough is
made smooth, and the confused clear. From its depths, the sea throws up
weathered spars, smooth blue glass, empty shells, and old coins.

Maggie waited in the car outside Pond House, jiggling her head to a
Dire Straits tape, looking sharp in the new sunglasses I had bought her
at the service station on the way up. I sneaked down the front path and
past the rose bushes to surprise my mother. Peering in through the dusty
glass, I saw her collapsed frame, tiny against the massive armchair. The
TV flickered, and I heard an American voice yelling that someone should
stop or he would shoot, but my mother snoozed through the shouting and
the hysterical violins, her chin resting on her chest. To her right sat a
magazine rack containing *Weardale Clarion, Woman Magazine, Radio Times,
TV Mirror,* and her mail order catalogues. On the other side of her chair
was the little table I had bought her after Dad died. My mother enjoyed
demonstrating its convenient features to visitors, and was pleased to
imagine subtle signs of jealousy in their faces. She liked having something that other people wanted. On the lower flap, she kept current business—letters to be answered, the parish magazine, a pair of scissors for
cutting out articles. Weightier correspondence, such as bills, lived in a
fruit bowl in the sideboard. On the higher surface, which swung over the
chair's arm, she had arrayed her essentials: reading glasses, TV glasses, a
bag of licorice allsorts, the remote control, my dad's presentation pen, and
the telephone. At the foot of the table lay her handbag, which I knew to

contain a plastic folding rain hat, a house key, a purse, a lacy handkerchief, a diary, the leather pill box, a lucky rabbit's foot that one of Matt and Andrea's kids had given her five years ago for Christmas, a typewritten letter from the Durham County Council sympathizing with her on my fathers' death, a packet of polo mints, and a manicure set she was too arthritic to use.

A prolonged burst of gunfire roused her, and I leaned forward and tapped on the glass. In the moment that her eyes met mine, she was illuminated by joy, her face wreathed in smiles, her hands fumbling, trying all at once to wave, to find the off switch on the remote, to lever herself out of the chair. Before she was up, I had waved Maggie out of the car, and we were through the unlocked front door and back in Pond House. Maggie staggered in theatrically with our suitcase, "Bloody bricks she's packed in here, Mrs. Robson. I'm going to give myself a hernia dragging it upstairs."

"Hello pet," my mother said, fluttering around her ineffectually. "You must be Maggie that I've heard so much about from our Claire. Eeh! Be careful! Don't strain yourself now!"

Maggie set the suitcase down and flexed her biceps. "Come and feel this," she said. My mother hobbled up obligingly and set a knobby hand on Maggie's arm. "See!" Maggie told her. "Arms like steel hawsers. I could probably carry you upstairs, never mind this suitcase."

My mother chuckled. "I wish you could pet," she said, "but I'm banned from going up there. You'd be in trouble with our Claire if you did that."

Maggie looked at me. "I'm not scared of *her*," she said. "What's the worst she can do to me?" As if to prove her point, she jerked her head at the suitcase. "Come on you big lummox, give me a hand with this."

"You must be hungry after that long drive," my mother called after us. "Everything's all ready. I'll just put the kettle on." After we had set the suitcase on the bed in Matthew's room, I put my arms around Maggie and kissed her forehead. "I think my mother's fallen for you about as quickly as I did," I said.

"She's pretty gorgeous," Maggie said. "Maybe I'll make you jealous."

I held her to me, dropped my face down to the top of her head, inhaled the joy of being with someone again, being someone's lover. She was like Enid Marshall, I suddenly thought, someone who had come in to reintroduce me to the material world, to help me stand on my own two feet. Maggie had made me ready for independent living. I released her, and stepped back, smiling. "I hope you're hungry," I told her. "I hear pans rattling down there."

She made her shark face and hummed the theme tune from *Jaws*. "Give me meat," she intoned. "I must have meat."

I noticed finger marks on the fridge door as I carved the chicken and, as we ate, soup stains on my mother's blouse, but although her blue eyes were faded and there were cobwebs on the skirting boards, she was tidy in the manner of old people, searching through her memories, picking things up and looking for a place to stow them. She was telling Maggie the story of my Cousin Helen's pregnancy. "To this day I don't understand it, Maggie," she said now, shaking her head in puzzlement. "Why couldn't our Ida tell me that Helen had got herself into trouble? I shouldn't have had to hear from Mrs. Bradley in Marks and Spencer's. That's not how things should work in families." She glanced at me. "It's nice to see you enjoying a bit of chicken," she said, as if giving up a vegetarian diet was akin to giving up cigarettes. "You look healthier for it. Are you still getting up at the crack of dawn?"

Maggie grinned at me. "She's like a bloody great whale in the morning," she said. "I need a fork lift truck to get her out of bed."

"How's Sally doing with that Jeff?" my mother asked, and I registered the connection she had made.

"Well," I said cautiously, "they're still together."

"What's the big attraction then?"

"I don't really know," I told her, hoping she'd change the subject soon. "They fight a lot. She must have broken up with him a dozen times."

"Sally was a very argumentative person," my mother said. "Your dad didn't like her much."

I was amazed. "He was always very nice to her. I thought you both liked Sally."

"Well, there's no point parents getting all agitated when they're not that keen on their children's friends," my mother said, handing a piece of bread and butter to Maggie, who took it obediently. "She was a nice enough lass. Her heart was in the right place, but you always seemed a bit overshadowed by her somehow." She glanced at Maggie. "She did all the talking, if you know what I mean, Maggie. She had very definite views on everything."

Maggie laughed delightedly, gave me a told-you-so look and hurried to swallow. "She still does. Poor Jeff doesn't know if he's coming or going. He can't keep up."

"So what *does* Sally see in him then?" she persisted. "What do you think, Maggie?"

"Oh that's easy. He's GIB."

My mother looked puzzled.

"Good In Bed," Maggie explained.

My mother stared at her, entranced. "G—I—B," she said slowly. "Good in bed. Well I never heard that one before!" She cackled and put her hand over Maggie's. "What is it again?" Solemnly, Maggie took out her Cross pen and wrote the letters down on a paper napkin. "Oh yes! GIB. Good in bed. Wait till I tell Ada Wilkie!" She stowed the napkin carefully in her cardigan pocket and leaned forward, her eyes alight at the prospect of good gossip. "So you really think that that's what it is then Maggie?"

"Oh, absolutely," Maggie said, winking at me. "Trust me on that one."

Some time later that evening, I left Maggie watching basketball on Channel Four and went to help my mother take a bath. As I helped her to struggle out of her clothes, I marveled that her wreck of a body was functional. Her neck and upper back were twisted by arthritis, the vertebrae standing out in an unhappy curve. Her hands looked like old tree roots—gnarled and knotted, the joints swollen, and the skin stretched over them red and shiny, as if polished. Her feet were covered with chilblains and calluses; her toes curled together. Tired flesh sagged over its clotheshorse of thin brittle bones. As I seized her firmly by one arm and lowered her fragile body into the hot suds, I felt my fingers sink into her flesh, and underneath, the grinding of arthritic joints.

She sank into the steamy water with a happy sigh. "This is heaven," she said. "I do miss my bath at night. It's not the same just once a week and in the daytime. The district nurse is very nice, but I can tell that she just wants me to hurry up so she can get on to scrubbing the next silly old biddy."

"Look," I said, soaping up the flannel. "You're not a silly old biddy. I don't like it when you say that."

"What am I then? I'm hardly a spring chicken with my gammy leg and my false teeth."

"Well. I'm not saying that you're not old. You are."

"Oh, charming!"

"Well you are old. But you're not silly, and I bet you're not a biddy. I'm not even sure what a biddy is."

She leaned forward so that I could soap her back. "Nor am I, but it doesn't sound very nice does it?"

"No."

She lifted up her head to squint at me. "If I'm not a silly old biddy, what would you say I was then?"

I thought for a moment. "A powerful woman," I said.

"So powerful I have to ask people to open my tins for me," she said with a snort.

"I don't mean that," I said, "and you know it. I mean that you're a strong person. You've been ill and in pain most of your life but you never gave up. You kept going. You made Sunday dinners and birthday cakes and ironed our clothes for us. Look at how you've coped since Dad died. You've been amazing."

She peered up at me through her sudsy hair, pleased as Punch. "Really? I thought everybody thought I was an old fusspot. So you think I'm powerful? My mother used to say I was as stubborn as the roads."

I laughed. "That's what *my* mother says about me."

"It's true about you," she said, quick as a flash. She lay back and wriggled her toes. "Maybe you got something from me after all. You got your brains from your dad, you know, but maybe you got your stickability from me. You've always gone your own way. Do you remember those Emma Peel trousers I bought you?" She chuckled. "You used to throw your legs and arms about doing the karate chops. Remember the time you had all the boys lined up and you threw them down one by one with your hip throws? You never did like feminine things, and it used to be a regret for me, you know. I was that happy when you were born. I thought I could dress you up. I thought we could cook together and talk about clothes and maybe you'd get married and live somewhere local and I'd help you with your house and your children, but it's our Matthew that's done that, really. I knew you were different from the start. You would never play with dolls, you know, even when you were little. I just didn't want to see it. I had to come to terms with it."

"Well, you did buy me those trousers."

She looked shocked at the memory. "Forty pounds they were," I saved up for weeks, but you wore them till they fell apart in the washing machine." She sighed. "The thing I feel terrible about is that you went and married that Luke just to make me happy."

"Oh, come on Mam," I said. "I chose to get involved with Luke. It wasn't your fault."

She shook her head in real distress, and a couple of tears rolled down her face. "Yes, but maybe you would have realized that he wasn't the one if I hadn't been so old-fashioned. I worry that I ruined your life. Our Matthew's so happy with his family, and you've never settled down. Maybe you would have found love if I hadn't been so straight-laced."

"I've found love," I told her, suddenly realizing that it was true. "It's just different from the kind you and Dad had."

"Really?" she said.

"Yes," I told her. "I seem to need to keep moving, to keep trying different things. I'm not sure that one person can be everything to me. But I am loved, or I'm starting to be loved. I'm starting to see that I can be loved. I'm happy with my life, Mam. Just don't hold your breath waiting for me to settle down. I don't think I'm cut out for it."

She brightened up. "You're not the marrying kind," she pronounced, and there was some kind of peace in that for her in the finality of that diagnosis, as if it were an avocation. "Well my mother always said that you can't change anyone's nature. She used to say that you can make someone unhappy with who they are but you can't change them. Well,

I'm glad you're happy, and I'll stop worrying about you." She grinned up at me. "And now you'd better haul this powerful woman out of the bath so she can get dry and toddle down the hall to put her milk money out. Maggie'll be thinking we've both drowned."

36.

As I drove north six months later, the old A1 was in its foulest
mood. Everything frightened me: the rain, which rode the wind to smash
itself on the windscreen; the wipers, which had one of those gremlins the
garage men never understood or managed to fix; the lorries in the outside
lane, which made me clench my eyes, my chest, my hands on the wheel
as I passed them in a shower of spray. On the back seat lay a sensible selection of essentials I had flung together. "What about a dark suit?" Sally
had asked, still maternally concerned, but I had refused to plan for a
funeral. The windscreen wipers seemed like heartbeats, tiny footsteps on
a vast journey. They ticked life away. I had never listened to them so
closely till there came the chance that something inexplicable and random could stop them dead.

I stopped once, at a roadside café—the place where I had bought
Maggie the sunglasses six months earlier. I wondered if she had forgiven
me yet, if she'd understood my flat refusal to be tugged or pulled any
more, my refusal to fit. I was too deliberately bloody-minded to work on
any relationship right now. I smiled though, to think that I knew exactly
what Maggie would have ordered from the formulaic menu and exactly
how much Sally would have despised it. I was free at last, but lonely.
When the waitress arrived, I hated the charade of my self-control and
wished my anxiety were stamped across my forehead. I wanted the waitress to ask where I was off to, to ask if I was OK, to call me "luvvy" or
"ducks" in her matey Midlands voice. I would have told her that my
mother was dying and I was driving up to see her, that I had played the
same Eurhythmics tape at full volume over and over again for six hours
to numb my brain—*thorn in my side, that's all you ever were.* That I wanted
to be there now, and that I wanted never to get there, that maybe she was
dead already, but for some reason I wouldn't call to find out, was caught
up in an ostrich limbo of uncertainty, hiding my head under the covers
and pretending that none of this was happening.

. . .

She lay collapsed, her mouth undone. A drip ran into her right arm, and a tube full of greenish, brownish fluid drained patchily, sluggishly downwards from under the crisp, almost preternaturally white sheet. An unopened bottle of Lucozade sat on her locker, its magical restorative powers untested. The inevitable black rubbish bag hung useless and empty, taped to the locker. The life that had animated Norah May Robson for sixty-eight years had settled to a weak pulse. For a moment, I let myself imagine that she was merely regrouping, ready for the next incredible comeback.

"They'd given me up for dead you know! They had to take all my intestines out because they'd gone bad. When I opened my eyes, the nurses all said, 'Eeh Mrs. Robson! You've a tough streak somewhere!'"

She seemed focused on breathing—exhaling with a groaning sigh, then pausing, uphill every time, before she labored to pull life in again. Everything was in balance, finely poised. She drew the bleak little room and its cheap sterility into her quiet exploration of the knife-edge that had cut away too much, just too much to allow her to carry on, and left her just enough to breathe, on the knife-edge. Under the antiseptic lay the smell of corruption.

"Does she know we're here?" Matthew whispered to the nurse.

"I don't think she's aware of much," said the sister. "It's a deep coma, the doctor said. She hasn't suffered."

"You're certain we can't do anything?"

"There's nothing," she said. "It could be hours or days. We just can't tell."

"I'm off to work," Matthew said, looking at me, his face miserable. "I can't just sit here, watching. I'll go nuts."

"I'm just going to stay for five minutes," I said, "if that's all right, Sister?"

"Of course it is. You take as long as you want. I'll be in to check on her now and again, but don't let that worry you."

Left alone, it felt natural to sit down beside her, instead of staring across the room, and then to stroke the hair back from her forehead. As I touched her, the walls, the floor, the rushing traffic faded and ceased to matter. I felt the feeble tick of pulse, heard her letting go of breath with gratitude, and then pause, as if deciding whether or not to try again. In the same way, she must have lain in bed morning after morning, waiting for the sun to rise and for life to struggle back into her numbed, resisting joints, stumbling to get the kettle on, warmth flowing with the first sips of PG Tips.

As I watched her, I began to understand that what had seemed a helpless struggle was actually resolution, an ordered movement towards a conscious end. Watching her face, I noticed that a point was reached in every cycle where it gathered in pain, her breathing paused and the weight of life seemed to settle in her features. Everything hung in the balance: the things that hurt her and those she lived and fought for settled on her chest, till, reluctantly, she breathed again. Her dying ceased to appear as a random re-ordering of cells to be typed up on a death certificate. It became the culmination of a life, a solemn examination by those who watch at the gate. I had become one with a fundamental process. All I feared now was her fierce resistance, her blind tenacious grip on life.

Every hour or so, I slipped out to walk, smoke, or buy coffee from the vending machine. On these occasions, I watched the rest of the world with amazement, as if through a glass wall, or the inside of a bell jar. One or two people spoke to me, to ask for change, or a light. I treasured these exchanges, and treated my enquirers tenderly, careful not to betray their fragility. Simple transactions, like buying a box of matches, became poems, rituals; the long blank corridor from the ward to the world became a lifetime. I watched everything avidly: a porter pushing a wheelchair containing an old lady who smiled and clutched a box of Kleenex to her chest, two naughty children making a noise. The resounding smack they received from their mother reverberated through my body. *I'm changed*, I thought. *I'm irreversibly changed.*

The nurse's entry was a violation, and it was with reluctance that I left the room to take my brother's phone call. "I thought you might still be there," Matthew said. "I called to check. Look, you've been there nearly six hours. I think you should get some fresh air. How about I come and take you for something to eat?"

"I'm not going to leave," I said. "It'll be very soon." I felt calm, and was surprised to hear my voice refuse to obey me.

His voice went quiet. "Has the doctor been in then?"

"It's not that. I can't tell you how I know. I just do." I'd taken the call in the nurses' office, and was suddenly aware of their averted sympathy, their quiet respect for feelings they had seen time and time again. I choked on tears, angry that this was not what I felt at all.

"You don't sound too good."

"That's not the point. You should just come down here." I hung up the phone and went back to my mother. Before long, Matthew arrived to take his place on the other side of the bed. The rhythm, so familiar to me now, became more insistent. I was proud of her, pleased that Matthew was here to see how well she was doing. It was a joyous and fitting event that was to take place, like birth. I smiled encouragingly at him, and felt the contractions quicken.

Her pulse flooded and faded before she stopped breathing. I felt it in her hand, recognized it instantly, and shared it with her, murmuring, "That's it. That's it."

Her next intake of life faltered, drew in, and then exhaled slowly, totally emptying her. Her brows furrowed as if in doubt, as if she were about to reprimand someone for meddling with a process which had gone on for so many years, but the breath continued to flow out of her. Her lips worked together, as though relishing the last drops of something precious. She looked like a baby, surprised at a new taste.

At last, quiet.

I sat back in satisfaction at something well finished. Matthew and I looked at each other in wonder, and slowly realized that we were still alive, and that there were things to be done. He left briefly, to return with a well-drilled squad of nurses, who ripped into the peace of the room, and began to bustle and tidy. Tremendous sobs began to rise in my chest, as though pulled up by suction, born of emptiness. The ward sister gave me a professional glance, and bundled me off. I remember being pleased that there were Kleenex before I opened my mouth and the grief poured out, seeming, in a strange way, to have little connection with me.

Epilogue

Claire Pet,

This is from Beyond the Grave and I want you to know it's Very Nice up here and we're all in the Best of Spirits. Everyone I love is here—your Granda that you never met, and your Mam and Dad of course, and your Auntie Ida and a lot of the old neighbours from Station Road. You may have heard your Mam talk of Amy Richardson, the butler's wife in my second situation passed on to me everything I know—like using the blue bag to draw out bee stings and how to make that Spring medicine you liked so much and how to manage your husband. We talk over all the old times and eeh Claire—you should hear us laugh! Sometimes I think I'm going to die and then I remember—we already have.

You will know that your poor Auntie Phyllis joined us recently. It was a Blessed Release for her in the end, Claire, because she had become very lonely and thought the Martians were putting wires in her head. But all our cares and worries and aches and pains have gone, even your Mam's rheumatoid arthritis. So don't feel sad when you think of us. We lack for nothing.

Anyway Claire, the thing is, and this is what I'm writing to tell you is that it's all right that you're a Lesbian. You're probably shocked rigid to hear me use that word but we can see things a bit better from up here. Life's Far Too Short to live for other people. Your Mam agrees and says she's sorry.

God Works in Mysterious Ways His Wonders to Perform and it's been hard for you I know but I like the way you've turned out.

Well that's pretty much it, pet. I'll not be writing again. You have your own life to lead now and you won't want me nagging on about this and that putting my three-penny-worth in and we're not really allowed anyway. You'll do fine on your own.

I like to keep in touch, so there's a place I visit in the old Pennines. Look for me in a vein of granite near Belhope Tarn those rocks are tough pet like you and me and you can't change their nature. That's what I'm telling you. Go up to the old picnic spot and choose yourself a piece of that rock. Any piece—the shape doesn't matter. Keep it on your desk when you write. It'll help you stay honest.

Love from,
Your Granny Hodgson

Kate Donahue

CLAIRE ROBSON is a British-born writer who taught high school English for sixteen years and spent seven years as an assistant principal. She relocated to the United States in 1989 to complete *Love in Good Time,* financing her creative endeavors by working as a storefront window cleaner. Claire's fiction and poetry have been published in numerous journals and literary reviews, and she has featured at bookstores, cafes, and literary events throughout New England. New Voices, the series Claire founded in 1990 and still hosts, is one of Boston's best spoken-word venues. Claire teaches writing in Boston and in New Hampshire, where she lives with her partner. In addition to running her own workshops and writing retreats, Claire works with young writers in schools and libraries and teaches workshops at the invitation of Plymouth State College and the Northern New England Arts Alliance. She facilitates two ongoing groups for established writers, in which she focuses closely on the critique process, since she believes that it is in the work of re-vision that magic happens. In her spare time, Claire is a church deacon, a court appointed advocate for abused and neglected children, and an avid gardener of anything edible.